TURN THE PULPIT LOOSE

TURN THE PULPIT LOOSE

TWO CENTURIES OF AMERICAN WOMEN EVANGELISTS

Priscilla Pope-Levison

First published in 2004 by
PALGRAVE MACMILLAN™
175 Fifth Avenue, New York, N.Y. 10010 and
Houndmills, Basingstoke, Hampshire, England RG21 6XS
Companies and representatives throughout the world.

PALGRAVE MACMILLAN is the global academic imprint of the Palgrave Macmillan division of St. Martin's Press, LLC and of Palgrave Macmillan Ltd. Macmillan® is a registered trademark in the United States, United Kingdom and other countries. Palgrave is a registered trademark in the European Union and other countries.

ISBN 0–3122–4022–8
ISBN 1–4039–6529–3

Library of Congress Cataloging-in-Publication Data

Pope-Levison, Priscilla, 1958–
    Turn the pulpit loose : two centuries of American women evangelists / Priscilla Pope-Levison.
        p. cm.
    Includes bibliographical references and index.
    ISBN 0–3122–4022–8—ISBN 1–4039–6529–3 (pbk)
        1. Women evangelists – United States – Biography. I. Title.

BV3780P67 2004
251'.0092'273—dc22   2004040098

A catalogue record for this book is available from the British Library.

Design by Newgen Imaging Systems (P) Ltd., Chennai, India.

First edition: November 2004

10 9 8 7 6 5 4 3 2 1

Printed in the United States of America.

For Jack
my huckleberry friend

[God] absolutely broke every fetter . . . It was the first time in her life that she could turn the pulpit loose—she ran from one end of the large platform to the other and shouted and praised God, and preached with the Holy Ghost sent down from above. . . . It was a permanent loosing from that day, and she has never been bound again. Although of a shrinking, backward disposition, she has never seen a crowd since that day large enough to make her knees tremble, and she has preached to thousands.

Mary Lee Cagle

CONTENTS

Acknowledgments

I recall the successive autobiographies—seven in all—of Maria Woodworth-Etter in which she increasingly excised references to those who had supported her endeavors—her husband, female coworkers, and various ministerial mentors. I puzzled over her habit of rewriting these people out of her past because the completion of a book provides a grand opportunity for recognizing those who have invested in the project and, by doing so, invested in the author. In the course of writing this book, I have accumulated quite a list of individuals and institutions to acknowledge, and I relish now the opportunity to recall them to mind.

Several institutions—the Association of Theological Schools and the American Academy of Religion—have generously provided grants for me to accomplish the necessary archival research, from the eastern tip of Nova Scotia to the Iowa heartlands. I was afforded ample hours and days to concentrate on research and writing thanks to a Lilly Research Grant from the Association of Theological Schools and a Summer Stipend from the Louisville Institute. Two Faculty Research Grants from Seattle Pacific University provided funding to hire Shannon Smythe, bless her, who spent one summer searching meticulously and patiently for the book's photographs and securing the necessary copyright permissions and another summer compiling the indices. In addition, I am grateful for these capable student assistants at Duke Divinity School and Seattle Pacific University, who provided hours of willing grunt work on research details: Alicia Akins, Lori Filban, Kevin Holder, Sarah Johnson, Ned Martin, Kortnee Osborne, and Erica Shutes.

One of the truly delightful aspects of working on this book was getting to know enthusiastic and knowledgeable archivists and librarians, who selflessly offered their time and services as well as wonderful conversations. I am grateful to Elder Minerva Bell of the Mount Sinai Holy Church of America (Teaneck, New Jersey), Rodney Birch at Vennard College (University Park, Iowa), Kate Currie at the Beaton Institute (Cape Breton, Nova Scotia), Stan Ingersol at the Nazarene Archives (Kansas City, Missouri), Bill Kostlevy at Asbury Theological Seminary (Wilmore, Kentucky), Susan Mitchem at the Salvation Army Archives (Alexandria, Virginia), Ron Patkus and John Atteberry at the John J. Burns Library (Boston College), Roberta Schaafsma at the Duke Divinity School library (Durham, North Carolina), Robert Shuster at the Billy Graham Center (Wheaton, Illinois), and Wayne Warner at the Flower Pentecostal Heritage Center (Springfield, Missouri). Even as I list their names, I do them a disservice. The kindnesses of each one—"thrown" rolls at a restaurant in Springfield, Missouri, a barbeque lunch in Kansas City, a copier put to heavy use in Minerva Bell's basement in Teaneck, New Jersey, and lunch at Solomon's Porch in Wilmore, Kentucky—rise to greet me as I peruse the list.

Then there is a remarkable coterie of scholars who have read and commented upon chapters in their area of expertise: Minerva Bell; Catherine Brekus; Joanne Carlson Brown; Rob Cruver; Kathryn Kobes Dumez; Michael Hamilton; Stan Ingersol; Bill Kostlevy; Randy Maddox; Ed McKinley; Susie Stanley; Matt Sutton; and Wayne Warner. Nancy Hewitt offered encouragement as this project first began to take shape. Catherine Brekus and Grant Wacker consulted about the parameters of the project. Michael Hamilton lent his insight to the framing of the introduction. Randy Maddox has consistently provided bibliographical references, theological insights, and editorial wisdom. Those of you who know these people will not be surprised by their generosity and interest; they are exceptional people.

The sustained interest I have enjoyed over the course of several years from another arena—my family—continues to amaze me. My sister, Deborah Pope, herself a poet, literary scholar, and English professor, served up cups of tea and consulted with me about the contours of the project, while her sons played with my children. It was she who first envisioned the interdisciplinary implications of the primary source materials in the book and then cast her keen editorial eye over the book's introduction sentence by sentence. My children, Chloe and Jeremy, kept me wonderfully rooted in a daily life not measured by the number of pages written but by the ordinary events of walking to school, baking brownies, watching videos on Friday nights in front of a fire, talking about the day's events at the dinner table, watching them play softball, baseball, and soccer, and listening to their music from a clarinet and a plastic guitar and amplifier from Sears. Their pride in this project and their love for me is most humbling.

My husband, Jack, is my life's love and closest companion. His imprint is on every word of every page of this book, including its title. We had peppered each other *ad nauseum* with possible titles, even while hiking around beautiful Lake Moran on Orcas Island, where we celebrated our twentieth wedding anniversary. Finally, one Saturday morning, with the title deadline fast approaching, he spied Mary Lee Cagle's phrase, "turn the pulpit loose," and immediately knew that it was the right title. This exemplifies his enthusiastic and enduring commitment to the book, which at times exceeded mine and kept me going when the difficulties seemed insurmountable. I joyfully and lovingly dedicate this book to Jack, my huckleberry friend.

INTRODUCTION

Stretching out before me into an indefinite ocean of faces, sit fourteen thousand people. They are strangers to me, and have seemed to come from nowhere into here. Outside the rain is beating down upon this great metropolis in torrents and the streets in some places seem almost rivers. Yet here, in the new Madison Square Garden, people are singing songs of praise and the choir of hundreds of voices rises behind me like some huge mountain, it seems to me. And oh, how they do sing! . . .

It is all so much of a miracle to me: these fourteen thousand faces, these exultant voices of praise, these "Amens" I hear. A miracle because I realize it is all the working of my Saviour whose love fills my heart with melody today.[1]

This was the scene unfolding before fourteen-year-old evangelist, Uldine Utley, as she stood poised on the mammoth stage of Madison Square Garden before a vast sea of strangers on this Halloween evening in 1926. This night was Uldine's final service of a four-week, two-sermons-a-day evangelistic campaign in New York City, where the crowds had responded enthusiastically to the diminutive, blue-eyed, fair-haired evangelist, outfitted in her customary white robe, hose, and shoes, with a bulky, leather-bound Bible held high in her petite hand. No venue could be more appropriate for the climactic conclusion of her evangelistic campaign. Madison Square Garden, dubbed the "palace of pleasure," had a long tradition of staging the unusual since its 1874 incarnation as P.T. Barnum's Monster Classical and Geological Hippodrome, when it hosted a circus of elephants, Japanese acrobats, tattooed fire eaters, and female chariot drivers. Now, five decades later, scheduled between prize fights, six-day bicycle races, beauty contests, and horse shows, another curiosity was drawing crowds by the thousands to this legendary venue, "Dedicated to Athletics, Amusements and the Industrial Arts."[2]

For this final service, Uldine departed from her typical fare of preaching from a biblical passage, delivering instead an extended autobiographical narration of her conversion to Jesus Christ and her subsequent calling to be an evangelist. Her story was replete with homey touches and simple pleasures, depicting life on a raisin-ranch near Fresno, California, which was rich in happiness despite meager means. She recalled that there was "plenty of play, plenty of grapes and figs, plenty of laughter" on the ranch where her father worked as a handyman. Living in the shadow of

Hollywood, the young Uldine dreamed of becoming an actress who would entertain audiences with her singing and dancing. Even on the day of her conversion, this dream motivated her. She recounted that she and her grandfather drove to the local drama studio to pick up a script for the play in which she had the lead, only to find the studio door locked. What transpired next would alter her life irrevocably. Despite Uldine's protests, her grandfather took her to the town auditorium where evangelist Aimee Semple McPherson was holding services. During the service, Uldine was converted.

In the glowing aftermath of that life-changing moment, she began giving her testimony rather than acting in plays. On the dirt playground where she used to entertain her friends with song and dance routines, she now read aloud from the New Testament, labored to win souls, and organized a Bible study for her fifth-grade classmates. Weekends now became workdays as she traveled to preach in nearby towns, dressed in her patched gingham "next-to-best dress" and wearing black shoes mended with white thread by her grandmother. The local folks expressed their appreciation by buying her a new Bible from the Montgomery Ward catalog which was so oversized that she had to hold it with both hands. A local seamstress made a white pulpit gown for her tiny frame, which became her standard preaching uniform. These small town folks quickly became crowds of thousands in Oakland, San Francisco, Kansas City, and other American cities. Now in Madison Square Garden, Uldine rose to the zenith of her evangelistic career less than five years after she began.

While Uldine's age made her unique, she was not exceptional as a female evangelist in New York City or anywhere else around the country. Even as Uldine was capturing the city's newspaper headlines, Evangeline Booth was also in New York City presiding over the American branch of The Salvation Army and doubling its membership in its effort "to win souls and make Soldiers."[3] The following summer, Aimee Semple McPherson would preach two Friday morning services for several thousand people who gathered inside the sanctuary and overflowed on the sidewalk outside of the city's oldest Pentecostal congregation only a few blocks from Times Square. Thirty miles away in Zarephath, New Jersey, Bishop Alma White was overseeing the self-contained Christian community begun fourteen years earlier for her converts. This community, with its extensive farm lands, printing press, and post office, also maintained schools for every age—an elementary school, Alma Preparatory School, a Bible Seminary, and Alma White College, state certified to offer degrees in arts and sciences. Indeed, Bishop White's work spanned the nation, so that by 1926 she had opened Christian schools in Cincinnati, Baltimore, Los Angeles, Jacksonville, and several in the state of Colorado. Also nearby New York City, Bishop Ida Robinson had recently established headquarters in Philadelphia for her new denomination, The Mount Sinai Holy Church of America. In a caravan of black limousines, she and other black-robed female elders traveled the Atlantic coast, from northern New Jersey to Florida, holding evangelistic services and planting new churches.

Women evangelists were traversing every other part of the country as well. Mary Lee Cagle and her husband were busy in evangelism from Tennessee to Wyoming. In the midwest, Iva Durham Vennard was in her sixteenth year as Principal of Chicago Evangelistic Institute, a training school for men and women preparing to be evangelists, pastors, or missionaries. Kathryn Kuhlman was in the Pacific Northwest region assisting her older sister and brother-in-law in their itinerant evangelistic ministry. Within a year, she and pianist Helen Gulliford would form an evangelistic team known as "God's Girls" and spend five years preaching across Idaho in towns like Twin Falls, Emmett, and Payette. Yet, 1926 was no more remarkable than any other in terms of the presence of women evangelists. Year after year, women stepped deep into muddy streets or up onto elevated pulpits; they traveled by foot, by horse and buggy, by stagecoach, canal boat, railroad, and automobile, traversing America in their work as evangelists, spurred on by their relentless passion to be messengers of the good news of Jesus Christ.

Their enormous impact in shaping American religious life from the nation's infancy to the present is evident in a plethora of arenas. In terms of *numbers*, audiences gathering to hear them often numbered in the thousands. On May 27, 1832, Harriet Livermore preached in Congress, during Andrew Jackson's presidency, to a crowd of one thousand people.[4] During her 1889 Oakland revival, Maria Woodworth-Etter repeatedly packed to capacity her 8,000-seat tent. Aimee Semple McPherson's church in Los Angeles, Angelus Temple, had a 5,300-seat auditorium which filled up three times on a Sunday for services. Uldine Utley preached in Madison Square Garden to a crowd of 14,000, and Kathryn Kuhlman's 1974 meeting in Providence, Rhode Island, filled to capacity the 14,000-seat Civic Center, while 10,000 people gathered outside. Numbers are impossible to gauge for Aimee Semple McPherson's radio program on KFSG (Kall Four Square Gospel), or Kathryn Kuhlman's radio program, "Heart-to-Heart," which was regularly broadcast for over forty years, or her long-running television program on CBS.

In terms of *institutions*, the women in this volume provided for the education and nurture of converts as well as for future generations. These included founding four denominations, more than thirty educational institutions for students ranging in age from grade schoolers through college undergraduates, a host of churches in American towns and cities from New York to California, and a town named Zarephath in New Jersey. Many of these institutions continue the evangelistic legacy of their founders to this day.

In terms of *literature*, they wrote extensively. Fifteen of the women included in this volume published at least one book. Many were bestsellers, requiring multiple printings. Such was the case with the first thousand copies of Jarena Lee's autobiography, Phoebe Palmer's *Way of Holiness*, which went through "three editions in its first year of print and was still being issued—by then in its fifty-second edition—some twelve years after Palmer's death,"[5] and Kathryn Kuhlman's *I Believe in Miracles*, which sold over a million copies. In addition, five evangelists founded or edited monthly religious periodicals.

In terms of *social impact*, they often incorporated a component of social outreach with their evangelistic work. Sojourner Truth solicited aid for freed slaves living in squalid camps in the nation's capital city. Phoebe Palmer began Five Points Mission, one of America's first urban mission centers, in a New York City slum. Amanda Berry Smith and Ida Robinson began schools for the education of African American children. Within two months after Aimee Semple McPherson's Angelus Temple Free Dining Hall opened in 1931, its workers had already fed more than 80,000 hungry people,[6] and the Angelus Temple Commissary, opened in 1927, was crucial to the survival of many in Los Angeles during the Depression. Evangeline Booth maintained The Salvation Army's outreach to the poor, unemployed, addicted, and friendless through social programs, such as homes and hospitals for unwed mothers, parole programs for released convicts, and Evangeline Residences—safe and affordable housing for young working women in urban areas. In terms of race relations, women evangelists wielded influence by holding integrated meetings, beginning with Jarena Lee, whose audiences in the 1820s included "white and colored," "slaves and the holders," and "Indians." This practice continued into the twentieth century with Aimee Semple McPherson's and Kathryn Kuhlman's racially integrated services.

In terms of *political impact*, women evangelists directed their energies toward influencing the nation's leaders as well as the populace. Harriet Livermore preached in Congress several times about the predicament of Native Americans. Sojourner Truth generated a petition and presented it to President Ulysses S. Grant requesting that a colony for freed slaves be established in the western United States. Most women evangelists in the late nineteenth century lobbied for temperance, like Jennie Fowler Willing, whose speech on women and temperance in 1874 prompted many who heard it to consider forming a national temperance organization. She then chaired for a year the meetings which eventually gave rise to the politically powerful, national temperance organization, the Woman's Christian Temperance Union.[7] Through her periodical, *Woman's Chains*, Alma White supported the platform of the National Woman's Party, including the Equal Rights Amendment. In the 1934 California gubernatorial campaign, Aimee Semple McPherson catalyzed her followers to help defeat the Democratic candidate, Upton Sinclair, whom she believed supported atheism and communism.[8] Though their emphasis lay purportedly in the salvation of souls, their impact ranged more widely to the provision of food and employment as well as to legislation for women's equal rights.

Women Evangelists: A Forgotten History

Although hundreds of American women left home, often as prodigal daughters, wives, and mothers to join this great company of evangelists, theirs is a forgotten history. Their significant contribution to American religious life, past and present, has yet to be seriously considered. They are notably absent from the history of American evangelism which conventionally moves in a single-gender trajectory through successive generations of male evangelists from Jonathan Edwards (1703–1758) to Charles Finney (1792–1875) to Dwight Moody (1837–1899) to Billy Sunday (1862–1935), to Billy Graham (1918–).[9] As I consulted available material for an introductory lecture on the history of American evangelism, I was inundated by information on these men. With my simple question—were there any women evangelists in America?—the first stirrings toward this anthology began.

Women evangelists have succumbed to no less egregious neglect in women's history, where they are repeatedly eclipsed by social reformers whose lives and organizations have been mined aggressively and routinely by scholars. Take, for example, the settlement house movement whose beginnings are traced to Hull House in Chicago. Numerous studies analyze the movement itself, as well as its connection with other reform movements and early twentieth-century women reformers like Jane Addams.[10] Yet, Iva Durham Vennard, who incorporated settlement work in her evangelistic training institute in St. Louis in 1901, receives no attention. A decade later, Iva continued in settlement work in Chicago, not far from Hull House, which she visited soon after moving to the windy city. However, unlike Jane Addams, who is inevitably included among the luminaries of women's history, Iva Durham Vennard and her accomplishments are left in complete darkness. It is perhaps the religious cast to Iva's settlement work that causes her to be excluded by historians who focus on the secular social reform of Jane Addams and others like her.

The result of this preference for social reformers is an incomplete and potentially misleading historiography because they were actually in a minority of women who were well educated, from families of substantial means, and often more than critical of the Christian tradition. In contrast, many ordinary women, like women evangelists, remained rooted to their churches and to evangelical Christianity. In her study of the earliest women evangelists in America, Catherine Brekus emphasizes precisely this point, "Even though female preachers were exceptional women, most were relatively poor and uneducated, and they shared many of the same values as the countless numbers of anonymous women who sat in the church pews every Sunday."[11] At the same time, women evangelists were also extraordinary in terms of their public activities, institution building, travels, literary output, political impact, and vocation outside of the domestic sphere. It is this unusual combination of popular religion and extraordinary public activity that underscores the importance of these women, as Brekus notes, ". . . it is precisely because these women were neither entirely radical nor entirely traditional that they offer such a revealing glimpse of early American history."[12]

Scholars have recently begun to notice women evangelists, an interest prompted in part by two significant books. William L. Andrews' volume, *Sisters of the Spirit: Three Black Women's Autobiographies of the Nineteenth Century*, featuring the autobiographies of Jarena Lee, Julia Foote, and Zilpha Elaw, precipitated interest in these evangelists. These autobiographies continue to be analyzed alongside additional writings by women evangelists in two recent monographs: *Some Wild Visions: Autobiographies by Female Itinerant Evangelists in 19th-Century America* (Elizabeth Elkin Grammer) and *Holy Boldness: Women Preachers' Autobiographies and the Sanctified Self* (Susie Stanley).

Along with Andrews' work, Catherine Brekus' *Strangers & Pilgrims: Female Preaching in America, 1740–1845*, which examines the lives and ministries of more than one hundred female preachers, represents the most thoroughgoing analysis to date. Brekus establishes, once and for all, the widespread activity of women evangelists from the mid-eighteenth century. Equally important, she identifies themes that persist through generations of women evangelists, such as a proclivity toward social conservatism, a need to market themselves, a grasp of the middle ground between the public and private spheres, and a courageous resolve in the face of rampant opposition.

The present anthology extends these initial studies in significant ways. First, it covers a 200-year period, more than any other study to date. Second, it cuts across a wide swath of Christian traditions, from Roman Catholicism to African American Pentecostalism, with intermediate stops in such fascinating ecclesial locales as The Pillar of Fire denomination, which constructed its own self-supporting town, and The New Testament Church of Christ, a denomination which grew largely from the efforts of women evangelists. Third, it explores the various vocational hats these women evangelists wore as preachers, teachers, healers, church leaders, and writers. Fourth, and perhaps most significant, it allows these women to speak *in their own voices*. Many, in fact, have been silenced for a century or more, consigned to distant archives, and they are given public voice here for the first time since their death. Although any figure of history is vulnerable to the bias of his or her interpreters, I have chosen excerpts with extreme care and regard each as a fair representation of the evangelist. This anthology takes, therefore, a major step toward rewriting evangelists into women's history and the history of evangelism.

Women Evangelists: Who They Were

Clearly no single paradigm fits each woman, and even nuanced generalizations will admit exceptions. Still, some salient points of personal and denominational issues emerge, including similar backgrounds, education, denominational affiliation, and family life.

Background and Education

These women were very ordinary in their lineage and educational achievements; most were raised in rural areas where their family subsisted on farming or manual labor. Economic straits often compelled them to forfeit a formal education, an element of their childhood they lamented. The early years of Maria Woodworth-Etter exemplify this scenario. When her father died leaving her mother with eight children to feed and clothe, Maria and her older sisters were forced to end their formal education and provide for their family. This deeply disappointed her: "I wanted to go to school where I could learn, for I longed for an education; and I often cried myself to sleep over this matter. I would have my books in the kitchen, where I could read a verse and commit it to memory, then read another, and so on, thus improving every opportunity while at my work."[13]

They also encountered a suspicion in their churches about too much education. Such a bias prevented Iva Durham Vennard, who accomplished the most among these women in terms of a formal education, from completing the final year of a university degree. Vennard was graduated from Illinois State Normal University with a teacher's degree, and, after teaching for several years, she completed an academic year at Wellesley College, where she met Dr. Charles DeGarmo, newly appointed president of Swarthmore College. DeGarmo offered her a scholarship to Swarthmore for her senior year, as well as an extended stay in Europe with his family. Before embarking in this direction, Iva became reacquainted with the Reverend Joseph Smith, who had been instrumental at significant moments in her spiritual growth. Smith expressed disappointment with her educational plans. "When I knew you a few years ago, I thought you were one young woman who was going to be spiritual; and more than that—a spiritual leader. But I see you seem to have gone mostly 'to top.' "[14] His remarks awoke a restlessness and dissatisfaction in Iva. After praying through the night, she resolved to decline the scholarship. Later in life, however, as Principal of an educational institution, she seemed to regret that night's decision, recognizing that a university degree would have improved her institution's stature.

For the African American women in this volume, access to a formal education was restricted as well by racial prejudice. Amanda Berry Smith's education was fragmentary since it took place around the edges of the time allotted to white children. "There were a great many farmers' daughters, large girls, and boys, in the winter time, so that the school would be full, so that after coming two and a half miles, many a day I would get but one lesson, and that would be while the other scholars were taking down their dinner kettles and putting their wraps on. All the white children had to have their full lessons, and if time was left the colored children had a chance. I received in all about three months' schooling."[15] Since Sojourner Truth and Ida Robinson were illiterate, their need to rely on an amanuensis to transcribe their words added one more element of another's imprint.

For this reason, Sojourner Truth's autobiography exists as a compilation of her words intertwined with the opinions of her amanuensis.

Among these eighteen women, three exceptions to this common scenario were Harriet Livermore, Phoebe Palmer, and Helen Sunday, each born into prosperous families. The Livermores were an elite New England family with an impressive political and military lineage who sent Harriet to prestigious New England boarding schools. Her superior education and familial connections helped propel her nascent evangelistic work to national attention, including multiple invitations to preach in Congress. Phoebe's and Helen's fathers owned successful businesses, Phoebe's in New York City and Helen's in Chicago, and their families were leading members in prominent, urban churches. These backgrounds served them well in their later dealings with civic and religious leaders. Under Phoebe's leadership, the Tuesday Meeting for the Promotion of Holiness evolved into a powerful gathering of bishops, ministers, and influential laymen and women which met in her home. Helen's business savvy, garnered from her father, served her well when, as business manager for her husband, she negotiated with leading businessmen in every city which hosted a Billy Sunday evangelistic campaign.

Denominational Affiliation[16]

With one exception, all of these evangelists were Protestant, and within it, they gravitated toward denominations that exhibited such evangelical characteristics as the centrality of preaching, a strong belief in biblical authority, an emphasis on the heart over the head, evidence of conversion, and the witness of the Holy Spirit. In such an atmosphere, gender roles were more flexible, innovations were encouraged, and a lack of education could be considered an asset. The denominations most represented in this volume are connected to two movements in American religious life: the holiness movement in the nineteenth century and Pentecostalism in the twentieth century. The holiness movement, initially associated with Methodism, coalesced in the mid-nineteenth century, creating informal networks and some new denominations. The movement was united by a shared emphasis on a "second work of grace" in believers' lives, an experience of the Holy Spirit's sanctifying power subsequent to one's conversion. According to John Wesley, sanctification removed the bent toward sinning which all humanity inherits from Adam and Eve, thus enabling a person to embody perfect love toward God and neighbor. This led to an emphasis in the movement on the holy life—with a particular insistence on abstaining from cards, alcohol, dances, jewelry and fancy clothes, cigarettes, and membership in secret societies—as the evidence of the Spirit's work. Oftentimes the experience of sanctification also imparted to women a "holy boldness" for giving public testimony concerning God's work in their life.[17] Venues for these testimonies—prayer meetings, camp meetings, and worship services—were held specifically to promote the experience of sanctification. Almost without exception, the nineteenth-century evangelists presented here found a platform within the holiness movement.

Several decades later, beginning in the early twentieth century, a movement arose that gave priority to a different life-transforming event following conversion known as Holy Ghost baptism.[18] This event was confirmed by the phenomenon of speaking in tongues, or glossalalia, as happened when tongues of fire rested on those gathered in Jerusalem, enabling them to speak in other languages. According to Acts 2, this event took place on the Day of Pentecost, hence the name, Pentecostals. As with the holiness movement, Pentecostals recognized the power of the Holy Spirit as validating and authorizing men and women to preach.[19] Twentieth-century evangelists in this volume embracing Pentecostalism, include Maria Woodworth-Etter, Aimee Semple McPherson, Ida Robinson, and Kathryn Kuhlman.

Despite the fact that all but Harriet Livermore, Sojourner Truth, and Kathryn Kuhlman claimed denominational affiliations, the connection between evangelist and denomination was often tangential. This distance was usually occasioned by opposition to their evangelistic work from denominational leaders and clergymen. Denominational disapprobation was so common that women evangelists cast their ministry wider. Long before the ecumenical movement came to the fore in the early twentieth century, their audiences were a potpourri of denominations. They spoke to whomever would listen, no matter what their religious background or pre-sent affiliation. Jarena Lee took particular note of her audience, and the list was surprisingly diverse: Methodists, Baptists, Quakers, Wesleyan Methodists, and Presbyterians. In one of the few diatribes in her autobiography, Jarena expressed disdain for denominational barriers, "Oh, how I long to see the day when Christians will meet on one common platform — Jesus of Nazareth — and cease their bickerings and contentions about non-essentials — when 'our Church' shall be less debated, but 'our Jesus' shall be all in all."[20] In the twentieth century, Kathryn Kuhlman recounted a similar ecumenicity of those who attended her services. "They come — Roman Catholic, Greek Orthodox, Lutheran, every denomination, people from around the world — gathering in the sanctuary of the First Presbyterian Church. Everybody forgets their denominational ties. We worship together on the common ground of Calvary."[21]

A more radical option pursued by several twentieth-century evangelists in the face of strong opposition, was to begin a denomination with policies and doctrines more amenable to women. Alma White took this route in 1901 when she left Methodism behind and with fifty charter members founded a new church that would eventually become The Pillar of Fire denomination. She faced opposition from Methodist leaders in Colorado critical of women preaching, as well as from Methodist holiness leaders who snubbed her preaching and mission work. Rather than suffer with the Methodists, she launched out on her own. Similarly Ida Robinson perceived restrictions on women's ministry when clergymen in The United Holy Church were debating women's ordination and pastoral authority. After ten days in prayer and fasting, she believed God called her to "Come out on Mount Sinai" in order to "loose the women," so she founded The Mount Sinai Holy Church in America.[22]

Licensing and Ordination

The benefit of a looser denominational connection was autonomy for evangelists to labor anywhere they were welcome without restrictions. From all indications, they preferred to be evangelists, rather than ministers, whose primary tasks were to preach and celebrate the sacraments for the same congregation week after week. As evangelists, their calling was to bring the good news of Jesus Christ in order to save souls; once they had fulfilled that role, they moved on to the next venue, leaving behind the saved and unsaved for local ministers to nurture and educate. In this respect, the women in this volume differed from women seeking ordination as ministers, such as Anna Oliver in The Methodist Episcopal Church and Sarah Ann Hughes in The African Methodist Episcopal Church, both of whom unsuccessfully petitioned their denominations for ordination in the 1880s.[23]

In his article on Sarah Ann Hughes' ordination controversy, Stephen Ward Angell asserts that women evangelists chose a less-complicated route in comparison with ordination.

> Possibly this story would have ended differently if these women [Hughes and Margaret Wilson who both sought ordination], like Jarena Lee, Zilpha Elaw, Amanda Berry Smith, and the women of Mr. Wesley's Methodism had not felt impelled by the Holy Spirit to seek placement in a pastorate or formal ordination, but had remained free-lance evangelists. As long as preaching women stayed outside of the male power structure, nineteenth-century male preachers were less likely to see them as a threat. Hughes, however, sought the benefits and recognition that status equality with her ministerial brethren could bring.[24]

Most likely Angell is correct in his conclusion.[25] However he overstates the ease with which women evangelists superceded "the male power structure." Every woman evangelist in this volume without exception was opposed by male clergy, male denominational leaders, by males in their audience, or males in their family. For instance, Jarena Lee, cited by Angell as someone who "stayed outside of the male power structure," could not escape relentless criticism by clergymen, even after she secured permission to preach from the bishop. Similarly, Amanda Berry Smith could not travel far enough from opposition, for even in Africa she faced criticism from American missionaries concerning her preaching. Being a "free-lance evangelist" did not guarantee an obstacle-free ministry.

In addition, Angell's term, "free-lance," also needs qualification because in truth, most evangelists in this volume did have an official permission of some sort. These "permission forms" can be grouped into three types: (1) A letter of recommendation or license from a denominational leader; (2) A license to preach from a denomination; and (3) Ordination by a local church or a denomination. The earliest evangelists, Jarena Lee and Harriet Livermore, had the first type of official permission. Jarena Lee claimed the authority of a license from the bishop with his signature and marked with the United States seal. Harriet Livermore carried with her a letter of recommendation from Elder Jones of the Christian Connection, ". . . desiring them to treat me kindly, assisting in whatsoever business I had need."[26] These "permission forms" were the most informal because they were granted simply by an individual leader without necessarily the larger approval of the denomination.

The second type of official permission, a license to preach, developed several decades later. In 1873, Jennie Fowler Willing was granted such a document by the Methodist conference in which her husband was the presiding official; however, despite denominational approval, it was not secure. Seven years later by General Conference vote, all local preacher licenses issued to women were revoked. The policy changed once more in 1920 when local preacher licenses were granted to women again. That same year, Iva Durham Vennard was given a license by her minister before embarking on a year-long mission tour.

Maria Woodworth-Etter also had a license that was rescinded. When the 39th Indiana Eldership of The Church of God (Winebrenner) granted her a license to preach in 1884, she was considered a minister in the denomination, though she continued as an itinerant evangelist. Fifteen years later, after her wide-ranging itinerancy kept colliding with denominational polity, her license was revoked.[27] Her response was that she would preach wherever God led her, church polity notwithstanding, and she left the denomination. Thus, even though licenses granted by a denomination would appear to be more official, they were easily canceled.

The third type of permission was outright ordination, and a few evangelists in this anthology were so entitled, thus accorded the full rights and privileges of their brother ministers. In the 1870s, Hulda Rees was recorded as a minister by the Quaker meeting in which she was raised. She and her husband, Seth, established a routine of copastoring churches for nine months during the fall, winter, and spring and then itinerating as evangelists during the summer. Ida Robinson, ordained in 1919 by The United Holy Church of America, was appointed as minister of one of the denomination's small mission churches, making her one of the few women in this anthology to pastor a church on her own.

The two most prominent women evangelists in the twentieth century, Kathryn Kuhlman and Aimee Semple McPherson, were officially ordained, but their ordinations carried certain distinctions. Kathryn was ordained by a nondenominational organization, The Evangelical Church

Alliance, which specifically provides ordination for those working outside of established denominational lines. Aimee Semple McPherson had arguably the most checkered ordination history. Before forming her own denomination, she had three separate types of "permission forms," each from different denominations. She simultaneously held "Assemblies of God ministerial credentials, a Methodist exhorter's license, and a Baptist preaching license."[28]

Two women were ordained by denominations they helped create. Mary Lee Cagle's first husband founded The New Testament Church of Christ on his deathbed, which Mary and a handful of female evangelists subsequently expanded through evangelism and church planting. Mary was then ordained as a minister by the denomination she had been instrumental in building. Then, when her denomination merged with The Church of the Nazarene, Mary continued as one of their ordained ministers. Similarly, in 1902, Alma White was ordained in the denomination she founded, The Pillar of Fire, and then on September 1, 1918, she became the first woman bishop in America.

Evangeline Booth's situation does not fall neatly into any of the three categories. When she was rising in the ranks, The Salvation Army did not ordain its officers. However, she had the Army's official sanction, having been appointed to an Army post of her own by her late teens. In 1917, when she was Commander of the American branch of The Salvation Army, the United States Government recognized The Salvation Army as an official denomination, and since that time, the Army's commissioning ceremony has been legally recognized as ordination.[29]

Finally, three evangelists in this volume sought neither approval nor license from a denomination. The earliest was Sojourner Truth who never confined herself to one organization for long. During her lifetime, she participated in religious and secular communities that included the Methodist Church, Matthias' Kingdom, Northampton Association for Education and Industry, and a Spiritualist community, but she always moved on after a while. Phoebe Palmer and Amanda Berry Smith, though lifelong Methodists, considered any sort of official permission unnecessary having received their ordination from God. Phoebe drew her understanding from a biblical passage that set ordination in God's hands, "And now, my dear sister, do not be startled, when I tell you that you have been *ordained* for a great work. Not by the imposition of mortal hands, or a call from man. No, Christ, the great Head of the church, hath chosen you, 'and ordained you, that ye should go and bring forth fruit.' "[30] Amanda quoted the same passage as her rationale for not pressing women's ordination at the 1872 General Conference of The African Methodist Episcopal Church, even though her detractors expected her to support the proposal. She recorded her inward response to their jibes in her autobiography.

"What does she want to go for?"
"Woman preacher; they want to be ordained," was the reply.

"I mean to fight that thing," said the other. "Yes, indeed, so will I," said another. Then a slight look to see if I took it in. I did; but in spite of it all I believed God would have me go. He knew that the thought of ordination had never once entered my mind, for I had received my ordination from Him, Who said, "Ye have not chosen Me, but I have chosen you, and ordained you, that you might go and bring forth fruit, and that your fruit might remain."[31]

Thus, while most evangelists had various sorts of "permission forms"; a few had none at all. Nevertheless, human recommendations were secondary to God's orders. Each one fervently believed that her calling to evangelism was from God, and this assurance superceded any affirmation or document from human hands.

An Exception

While these broad strokes encapsulate the Protestants in this anthology, one evangelist was markedly different in every respect. Martha Moore Avery was Roman Catholic. She could not be ordained, but as a Roman Catholic laywoman, she addressed public audiences and itinerated from town to town with the official sanction of the Archbishop of Boston. She is also unique in this volume for being the oldest convert to Christianity. By the age of fifty-three, her circuitous search for truth had propelled her through Unitarianism, Pantheism, Spiritualism, and Socialism, until it came to fruition when she joined The Roman Catholic Church and became its ardent evangelist. The manner of her conversion also diverged from the others in that it did not occur in an evangelistic service, but rather under the intellectual tutelage of a Jesuit priest on the faculty of Boston College. Her conversion involved a lengthy decision process governed by head more than heart. Emotion was negligible. Reason was the operative word for Martha, her constant guide and measuring rod. Because of this, her public presentations also deviated widely from Protestant evangelists who preached on biblical texts and closed their meetings with emotional appeals designed to catalyze conversions. Instead, Martha employed reasoned arguments in a lecture format to instruct her hearers about Catholic doctrine and practices.

Family Life

In their domestic life, these women were initially quite ordinary. All but two were married; twelve birthed at least one child, and two adopted children. Only Harriet Livermore remained single and childless. Otherwise, these women experienced what women commonly do — marriage, keeping a home, pregnancy, childbirth, infant and child morality, and childrearing. Then suddenly, a divine call as they interpreted it, broke into their home and incited them to leave and begin evangelizing. At this juncture, the mundane yet monumental question arose: how? What had to happen at home in order that the wife, the mother, the daughter, could leave? Because women were expected, particularly in the nineteenth and early twentieth centuries, to find their full-time occupation and satisfaction at home, this pivotal conundrum affected every woman in this volume. Therefore, to leave home, to forsake their domestic duty, was to face the accusation of being a prodigal. No matter that they were completely unlike the infamous prodigal son of Jesus' parable;[32] no matter that they went forth empty-handed, without familial inheritance or even blessing. There remained an illicit element to their decision to venture forth as evangelists.

As wives, they had to anticipate and handle their husband's reaction, which ran the full range from completely supportive to adamantly opposed. Anchoring one end of the spectrum was Thomas Vennard who willingly sacrificed his career as an architect and mason contractor for Iva's evangelistic work. Even wedding plans were put on hold at Iva's insistence until her evangelistic training school was on secure footing. Thomas' response was simply, "I am willing to be your background of support." True to his word, when Iva's school required extensive renovation work but no funds were available, Thomas relinquished his position with an architectural firm in Chicago's Loop and personally completed the necessary remodeling with student help.

Not all spouses were as accommodating. Both Amanda Berry Smith and Maria Woodworth-Etter initially hoped to marry men alongside whom they could be active in ministry, but instead they faced antagonism at home. Amanda married her second husband, James Smith, in large part because he expressed, falsely so in order to win her affections, a desire to become an ordained minister. Her hope to be industrious as a minister's wife went unfulfilled as perpetual conflicts kept them separated throughout most of their married life. Not until her husband's resentment ended with his death did Amanda become a full-time evangelist in her own right. Similarly Maria aspired to marry an "earnest Christian," but her first husband, Philo Woodworth, proved to be otherwise. As her self-proclaimed business manager, he threatened to damage his wife's reputation by his mercenary enterprises during her meetings. "Sunday morning he was dispensing cigars and plugging watermelons for the million, and the nickels, dimes and quarters flowed into his till in a steady stream, while the wife was laboring with care-burdened sinners."[33] Their marriage only ended, however, when Maria sued for divorce on the grounds of repeated adultery.

Where some couples did attempt evangelistic partnerships, the results varied. Phoebe Palmer was an evangelist for twenty years on her own while Walter kept up his medical practice and managed their household. Later they joined forces for an extended, four-year evangelistic tour of Great Britain. In contrast, Alma and Kent White's short-lived partnership ended in rampant rivalry and bitter accusations. Even though Alma preached her first sermon in Kent's pulpit and they shared the preaching for several years, their rapport disintegrated as she became the more successful preacher. Eventually they separated and were never reconciled.

Husbands of course were not the only consideration; many evangelists were also mothers for whom child-care concerns were paramount. While situations varied depending on the number and age of the children and the willingness of relatives, friends, and husbands to cooperate, mothers agonized over leaving their children for their evangelistic work. When Alma White left her two-year-old son, who was recovering from a serious illness, in the care of her own mother, she was still plagued with worry. "To leave him in care of others was almost like taking a mother's heart from her body, but the Lord had spoken and it would have been perilous to disobey. It was no more than He required of others, and why should I have any controversy."[34]

A perplexing phenomenon occurred in some instances when mothers who had felt a call to evangelism, then experienced the deaths of several children and, by virtue of these deaths, saw their child-care anxieties removed. In the midst of grief, they interpreted these tragic events as evidence of God's insistence that they leave home to be evangelists. In other words, they believed that God had purposefully removed the children who stood in the way of their mothers being obedient to the divine call. Maria Woodworth-Etter was one who promoted such an interpretation. At first she fretted over leaving her young children, but when five of the six died, she believed that God had thus freed her from domestic responsibilities. Similarly, Amanda Berry Smith lost four of her five children. When Amanda finally became an evangelist, after hesitating for many years due to family constraints, her only surviving child was an adolescent, enabling her to travel without child-care worries.

Without a doubt, women were affected by their domestic obligations more profoundly than their male colleagues, who were neither encumbered with child care, nor required to seek spousal permission. Male evangelists simply followed the call and expected their dependents to accommodate them. Billy Sunday leaned heavily on Helen to alleviate his loneliness while he was away from home for weeks at a time. Helen had to bear multiple burdens of being a single-parent for four children and lending administrative help to Billy's evangelistic campaigns, all the while offering personal encouragement to her husband. Not until she nearly collapsed from exhaustion did she simplify her life. Subsequently, the children were left in a nanny's care, and she joined Billy as his campaign manager.

Because most women evangelists had to devote their early adult years to their family, there was a gap of at least ten years between the time of their call to evangelism and their departure from home. Most were in their mid- to late thirties before beginning their evangelistic career. This decade gap differs significantly for male evangelists who were able to launch their evangelistic work in their twenties without domestic considerations or cultural expectations. The implications of this gap can only be inferred, but it is reasonable to speculate that an earlier start for the women, when they were younger and prior to multiple childbirths and deaths, might well have diminished the fatigue and illness that many suffered. As it was, significant portions of their lives, sometimes for months on end, were spent resting and recuperating. For instance, nearly every year in her autobiography, Jarena Lee referred to periods of ill-health. In 1831 she wrote, "I stopped a few weeks with my sister and Dr. Burton; boarded with her, and he seeing my debilitation of body, rendered medical assistance, which helped me much; but I was unable to labor and preach for some months."[35] The next year included this reference, "Having gained my health, I returned in peace to Philadelphia . . . "; while the year, 1836, concluded with this comment, "After I arrived my health was much impaired, and I had a severe spell of sickness. So ended 1836."[36] On that occasion, she rested at least three months, not traveling again until March. While these women lived a relatively long time, an average of seventy-four years, their careers were more sporadic due to disjointed time periods between evangelizing and convalescing.

Format of the Volume

By its very nature, any anthology is a selective representation of a larger phenomenon; its aim is to offer examples that embody the broader picture. In this anthology, eighteen evangelists stand in for hundreds of American women who also actively pursued the art of soulwinning. These were chosen in large part for their significant primary sources. Substantial excerpts from sermons, books, journal and magazine articles, diaries, letters, newsletters, speeches, and autobiographies, saturate each chapter. A number of these sources are published for the first time in this anthology after lying fallow in American and Canadian archives. These include letters recounting evangelistic meetings written by Hulda Rees to her sister; a handwritten autobiography by Martha Moore Avery; recently cataloged speeches by Evangeline Booth; and a complete volume of *Inasmuch*, the journal of Epworth Evangelistic Institute (1901–1910), edited by Iva Durham Vennard. Even with this volume in place, however, a sizeable amount of material on women evangelists remains to be analyzed and incorporated into the trajectory of American history.[37]

For the purposes of this volume, each woman is presented chronologically by birthdate, ranging from Jarena Lee's in 1783 to Uldine Utley's in 1912. First names are utilized because it was the name that remained constant, whereas their surname changed with marriage and sometimes again with a second marriage. Each chapter is organized in a similar format, first establishing the context of her birth, family situation, and early life preceding her conversion, then providing an account of her conversion, which occurred for most by their late teens or early twenties.[38] The conversion excerpts resemble each other in their movement from sin to salvation, from despair to delight. They describe how conviction, the experience of becoming acutely aware of sin, settled on her heart and mind. When under conviction, many experienced a time of extended distress, which effected their moods, actions, ability to sleep, even their ability to eat due to a sudden distaste for food. The conversion excerpt continues with acknowledgment of sin and the forgiveness that resulted. Then when all was well, when conversion was their condition, they exulted in their victory in Jesus. Vivid images—light following darkness, joy replacing judgment, the air sparkling "with diamonds"—poured forth. Amanda Berry Smith felt so filled with the likeness of a new being that she ran from the basement to the dining room in her employer's house to consult the mirror for any alteration in her skin color.

After these excerpts, the life narrative resumes and describes the period during which most married, birthed children, and attended to their domestic situation. At this point in life, some shattering crisis typically occurred. As they emerged from the crisis, these women frequently received what they interpreted as a divine green light to leave home and begin a new life as an evangelist. For those who recorded details of this experience, they are included in the chapter.

In their evangelism, they utilized a combination of methods. The most common was preaching. They stood before a gathered audience, delivered commentary on a biblical text, and then beseeched hearers to repent from their sin and follow Jesus Christ. In order to preach regularly to new audiences, most were itinerant evangelists, traveling from a church, to a camp meeting, to a town hall, or wherever a crowd gathered. In addition, these women were also teachers, principals, denominational leaders, business managers, and writers. Excerpts specifically reflect this wide variety of evangelistic methods, offering detailed accounts of the ways in which evangelism has been practiced through nearly two centuries of American history.

The narrative section that follows the excerpt on evangelistic method details the progression of their evangelistic careers. Then, the final section in each chapter, a combination of narrative and excerpt, is simply titled, "On Women." The material here stems from the indisputable fact that women evangelists were considered a curiosity. As such, they were constantly required to explain themselves, and they uniformly obliged with some statement or rationale. Most often, they presented a biblical excursus authorizing women's right to preach, populating their defense with Deborah the judge, Huldah the prophet, Mary Magdalene the announcer of the risen Christ, and other prominent women in the Bible. They also appealed to other scriptures about women, particularly the dominant text that inspired them: "This is what was spoken through the prophet Joel: 'In the last days it will be, God declares, that I will pour out my Spirit upon all flesh, and your sons and your daughters shall prophesy . . . ' " (Acts 2:16). Moving from scriptural appeal to personal experience, particularly their call from God, the women reminded their readers that this "job," as Kathryn Kuhlman put it, was not one for which they applied, but for which God hired them. Similarly, Uldine Utley, while acknowledging that a girl preaching instead of "great big men" might be construed as foolishness, reminded her readers that it was God's foolishness, not her own.

Readers will notice that these women accepted and utilized traditional notions about women as talkative, sensitive, stronger in heart than head, and instinctively nurturing. Mary Lee Cagle found a constructive use for women's verbal penchant when she declared, "Why did God give women such a talent to talk, if not to be used for Him? If God did not intend for women to use their tongues for Him He certainly did give the devil a great advantage in the beginning, for women can talk. The men are generally our superiors; but there are some things that we can excel them in. And one of them is talking . . . "39 Jennie Fowler Willing claimed that women's sensitivity to others makes them "designed and fitted for evangelism." She reasoned that, "A true woman never attempts to force a way for the truth with which she is entrusted. As dumb things know when the weather will change, she knows when it will do to crowd a plan, and when she must wait. She enters into the sorrows and joys of others, and so gains power over them."40 With but a few exceptions, they believed that women and men were designed for separate spheres, women in the domestic sphere and men in the public sphere. Martha Moore Avery was the most outspoken on this matter, declaring that men and women had different yet complementary, God-given roles. "Women build in the hearts of the little ones, in the hearts of men, in the world of emotion and intuition. Masculine building, on the other hand, is exterior: men organize governments and build up the intellectual and moral codes that show the designs of Almighty God."41 But Martha was not alone. Aimee Semple McPherson, for example, followed suit, claiming that women rocked the cradle, men blazed new trails.

Sometimes we wish we were men, that we might go out into the byways and blaze new trails. How wonderful it would be to get out into the far reaches of the world? Nevertheless, God has a work for the women of today with their sweet voices, their shining faces, their tender hands, and their loving spirit. Just as there is room for a father and a mother in family life, so there is room for both the servant and the handmaiden in the Lord's work. Each have their place. The father surely is needed with his ruggedness, his ability to provide bread for the larder, and his advice and counsel. But who would say we do not need the mother in the home to rock the little ones and teach them the tender things of life? Besides the mother often can reach the heart of a child when the father has failed.42

Aimee's penchant for separate spheres was particularly ironic because she did not embody this sweet, maternal portrait. Rarely was she home long enough to rock a cradle; rather she was blazing new trails "into the far reaches of the world." There was, consequently, a radical disjuncture between evangelists' lives and the assumptions they held out to their admirers, many of whom were women. The question remains what spoke more clearly, their words or their example.

An exception to this trend was Sojourner Truth who spoke out on behalf of women's rights and whose infamous "Ain't I A Woman" speech has served as a rallying cry for subsequent generations of feminists. Similarly, Alma White actively championed the Equal Rights Amendment. Her belief in women's equality was centered in the biblical creation story in Genesis, where "God gave men and women copartnership and control of all that He had created. But His order has been reversed and woman has become man's servant or slave, and as a result the social fabric is going to pieces and the world is well-nigh wrecked."[43] Thus, this final section, "On Women," highlights varieties in approaches to women's issues that were adopted by these evangelists.

Not to be overlooked are each chapter's extensive endnotes, providing essential information on religious terms and movements, references to biblical passages, and brief discussions of secondary source material. Because these women habitually interspersed biblical phrases, terms, and figures in their writings, the reader will gain a deeper understanding of their materials by noting such references. Two final glossaries provide information on biblical figures and churches and denominations cited throughout the book.

Notes

1. Uldine Utley, *Why I Am a Preacher: A Plain Answer to an Oft-Repeated Question* (New York: Fleming H. Revell, 1931), 13.
2. Joseph Durso, *Madison Square Garden: 100 Years of History* (New York: Simon and Schuster, 1979), 138.
3. Edward H. McKinley, *Marching to Glory: The History of The Salvation Army in the United States of America, 1880–1992*, 2nd edn. (Grand Rapids: Eerdmans, 1995), 186–87.
4. Cynthia A. Jürisson, "Federalist, Feminist, Revivalist: Harriet Livermore (1788–1868) and the Limits of Democratization in the Early Republic," Ph.D. Dissertation (Princeton Theological Seminary, 1994), 228.
5. Harold E. Raser, *Phoebe Palmer: Her Life and Thought*, Studies in Women and Religion, vol. 22 (Lewiston, NY: Edwin Mellen, 1987), 58.
6. Edith Blumhofer, *Aimee Semple McPherson: Everybody's Sister*, Library of Religious Biography (Grand Rapids: Eerdmans, 1993), 347.
7. Joanne Carlson Brown, "Shared Fire: The Flame Ignited by Jennie Fowler Willing," in *Spirituality and Social Responsibility: Vocational Vision of*

Women in The United Methodist Tradition, ed. Rosemary Skinner Keller (Nashville, TN: Abingdon, 1993), 101.

8. Matthew Sutton, "Clutching to 'Christian' America: The Origins of Pentecostal Political Activism," unpublished paper.

9. Heretofore, major books on evangelism failed utterly to discuss women evangelists and the significant role they have played in spreading the Christian faith. Among them can be counted Paulus Scharpff's comprehensive classic, *History of Evangelism* (Eerdmans, 1964) which spans 300 years and several continents yet mentions but a single woman (Countess Huntingdon) and a group of women serving at the Women's Training Centers in Germany. Women in evangelism on American soil are notably absent. Equally illustrative—and far less excusable in a more recent work—is the complete absence of women evangelists in John Mark Terry's *Evangelism: A Concise History* (Broadman, 1994).

10. This is a partial list of articles, books, and dissertations on the settlement house movement: *Women and the Settlement Movement* (Katherine Bentley Beauman); "Reflections in a Mirror: The Progressive Women and the Settlement Experience" (Elizabeth Palmer Hutcheson Carrell); "Maternal Government: The Social Settlement Houses and the Politicization of Women's Sphere, 1889–1920" (Maureen Fastenau); "Visions of a Christian City: The Politics of Religion and Gender in Chicago's City Missions and Protestant Settlement Houses, 1886–1929" (Mary Mapes); "A Puzzle With Missing Pieces: Catholic Women and the Social Settlement Movement, 1897–1915" (Margaret M. McGuinness); "Hull House in the 1890s: A Community of Women Reformers" (Kathryn Kish Sklar); "Catholic Ladies Bountiful: Chicago's Catholic Settlement Houses and Day Nurseries, 1892–1930" (Deborah Ann Skok). Jane Addams has been the subject of scores of studies, including these books published within the past five years: *The Education of Jane Addams* (Victoria Brown); *The Selected Papers of Jane Addams* (Mary Lynn McCree Bryan, Barbara Bais, and others); *American Heroine: The Life and Legend of Jane Addams*, revised edn. (Allen Freeman Davis); *A Useful Woman: The Early Life of Jane Addams* (Gioia Diliberto); *Jane Addams and the Dream of American Democracy: A Life* and *The Jane Addams Reader* (Jean Bethke Elshtain); *On Addams* (Marilyn Fischer); *With One Bold Act: The Story of Jane Addams* (Barbara Garland Polikoff).

11. Catherine Brekus, *Strangers & Pilgrims: Female Preaching in America, 1740–1845* (Chapel Hill: University of North Carolina, 1998), 7.

12. Brekus, *Strangers & Pilgrims*, 7.

13. Maria B. Woodworth, *The Life and Experience of Maria B. Woodworth* (Dayton: United Brethren Publishing House, 1885), 16–17.

14. Mary Ella Bowie, *Alabaster and Spikenard: The Life of Iva Durham Vennard, D.D., Founder of Chicago Evangelistic Institute* (Chicago: Chicago Evangelistic Institute, 1947), 46.

15. Amanda Smith, *An Autobiography: The Story of the Lord's Dealings with Mrs. Amanda Smith, The Colored Evangelist* (Chicago: Christian Witness Co., 1921), 27.

16. Denomination comes from the Latin word, *denominare*, which means "to name." It refers to a group of churches sharing the same beliefs about

Christianity and a similar organizational format, who have banded together into one larger institution. "Denominations help to provide some type of religious identity amid the pluralism of belief. They also provide needed resources for local communities of faith, such as facilities for training ministers, for publishing curriculum resources, and for overseeing certification procedures." [Craig D. Atwood, "Religion in America," in *Handbook of Denominations in the United States*, 11th edn., eds. Frank S. Mead, Samuel S. Hill, and Craig D. Atwood (Nashville, TN: Abingdon, 2001), 23.] Denominations are integral to the development of Protestantism in America. Those cited in the book can be found in the Glossary of Churches and Denominations.

17. Susie Stanley, *Holy Boldness: Women Preachers' Autobiographies and the Sanctified Self* (Knoxville: University of Tennessee, 2002).

18. Prior to Pentecostals adopting the phrase, Holy Ghost baptism, it had been used by other movements to refer to a dramatic, post-conversion, spiritual experience. For instance, the holiness movement used the phrase, baptism of the Holy Spirit, to refer to the experience of sanctification. See Donald Dayton, *Theological Roots of Pentecostalism* (Grand Rapids: Zondervan, 1987), 78–80.

19. For an overview of women in Pentecostalism, see Grant Wacker, *Heaven Below: Early Pentecostals and American Culture* (Cambridge, MA: Harvard University, 2002), 158–76.

20. Jarena Lee, *Religious Experience and Journal of Mrs. Jarena Lee, Giving An Account of Her Call to Preach the Gospel* (Philadelphia: printed and published by Jarena Lee, 1849), 26.

21. Kathryn Kuhlman with Jamie Buckingham, *A Glimpse Into Glory* (Plainfield, NJ: Logos International, 1976), 22.

22. "Brief History of Mount Sinai," Pamphlet prepared for the Sixty-Fifth anniversary, 3; given to the author by Elder Minerva Bell, Historian, Mount Sinai Holy Church of America.

23. Anna Oliver, for one, believed it important to clarify that she was not asking for "licensing for evangelist work, but for ordination to the pastorate." Kenneth E. Rowe, "The Ordination of Women: Round One; Anna Oliver and the General Conference of 1880," in *Perspectives on American Methodism: Interpretive Essays*, eds. Russell E. Richey, Kenneth E. Rowe, and Jean Miller Schmidt (Nashville, TN: Abingdon, 1993), 303.

24. Stephen Ward Angell, "The Controversy over Women's Ministry in the African Methodist Episcopal Church During the 1880s: The Case of Sarah Ann Hughes," in *This Far By Faith: Readings in African-American Women's Autobiography*, eds. Judith Weisenfeld and Richard Newman (New York: Routledge, 1996), 94.

25. There is some difficulty with Angell's suggestion that Jarena Lee's situation in the 1830s is parallel to Hughes' in the 1880s. According to Mark Chavez's study on women's ordination, both decades were significant in terms of "intense activity connected to the women's movement;" however, the rationale for supporting women's ordination, as well as the very meaning of ordination, was drastically different for each of those decades. [Mark Chavez, *Ordaining Women: Culture and Conflict in Religious Organizations* (Cambridge, MA: Harvard University, 1997), 63.] Chaves explains that the

quest for gender equality in the 1880s significantly changed the nature and import of the debate over women's ordination from that which took place in the 1830s. That being said, Angell's comparison of two such different time periods, nearly half a century apart, is questionable.

26. Harriet Livermore, *Narration of Religious Experience, In Twelve Letters* (Concord, NH: Jacob Moore, 1836), 156.

27. According to church polity, Maria overstepped boundaries when she, an elder in Southern Indiana, held evangelistic services in Pennsylvania without first securing the permission of the entire Pennsylvania eldership. After the first incident, Maria issued an apology and retained her license. For the second violation, she was asked to relinquish her license.

28. Blumhofer, *Aimee Semple McPherson*, 16. In addition, she had been ordained by two different independent Pentecostal congregations. Edith Blumhofer clarifies the meaning of these ordinations. "Her ordination illustrates again how differently ordination was viewed in the networks in which Aimee moved. When a recognized worker embarked on a new project, it was not unusual for that worker to be ordained again. In this context, ordination was commissioning for a new task." Blumhofer, *Aimee Semple McPherson*, 121.

29. I am grateful to Ed McKinley for his insight and information on this matter.

30. John 15:16. Phoebe Palmer, *Faith and Its Effects: or, Fragments from My Portfolio* (New York: Published for the Author, Joseph Longking, Printer, 1852), 290; cited in Nancy A. Hardesty, *Your Daughters Shall Prophesy: Revivalism and Feminism in the Age of Finney* (Brooklyn, NY: Carlson, 1991), 103.

31. John 15:16. Smith, *An Autobiography*, 199–200.

32. Luke 11:15–32.

33. *Weekly Courier* (Wabash, Indiana) August 21, 1885; cited in Wayne Warner, *The Woman Evangelist: The Life and Times of Charismatic Evangelist Maria B. Woodworth-Etter*, Studies in Evangelicalism No. 8, eds. Kenneth E. Rowe and Donald W. Dayton (Metuchen, NJ: Scarecrow, 1986), 133–34.

34. Alma White, *Truth Stranger Than Fiction: God's Lightning Bolts* (Zarephath, NJ: Pentecostal Union, 1913), 48.

35. Lee, *Religious Experience and Journal*, 61.

36. Lee, *Religious Experience and Journal*, 63, 79.

37. For those wishing to research figures regrettably omitted here, the following partial list offers suggestions for evangelists whose materials are more accessible: D. Willia Caffray, Zilpha Elaw, Julia Foote, Laura Haviland, Lura Mains, Lela McConnell, Emma Ray, Hannah Reeves, Lydia Sexton, Hannah Whitall Smith, Jennie Smith, Nancy Towle, and Maggie Newton Van Cott.

38. This is consistent with Virginia Brereton's findings in her study on women's conversion narratives. "Few converts had gone beyond their twenties before 'giving their hearts to God' . . ." Virginia Lieson Brereton, *From Sin to Salvation: Stories of Women's Conversions, 1800 to the Present* (Bloomington: Indiana University, 1991), 4.

39. Mary Lee Cagle, *The Life and Work of Mary Lee Cagle: An Autobiography* (Kansas City, MO: Nazarene Publishing House, 1928), 171.

40. Jennie Fowler Willing, "Every Woman a Missionary," *The Guide to Holiness* (November 1896): 178.
41. Martha Moore Avery, "Spread of Social Disorder," *America* (October 9, 1915): 78.
42. Aimee Semple McPherson, "To the Servants and the Handmaidens; Baccalaureate Sermon," *Bridal Call* 13 (February 1930), 5, International Church of the Foursquare Gospel Archives, Los Angeles, California.
43. Alma White, *Woman's Chains* (Zarephath, NJ: Pillar of Fire, 1943), 41.

MRS JARENA LEE.

Preacher of the A. M. E. Church.

Aged 60 years on the 11th day of the 2nd month 1844.

Philad.a 1844.

African Methodist Episcopal evangelist, author of the first narrative published in America by an African American woman, *The Life and Religious Experience of Jarena Lee, A Coloured Lady*

Courtesy of the American Antiquarian Society.

Chapter 1

Jarena Lee (1783–?)

[handwritten marginalia: convicted / small meetings / Let God move her]

J arena was born in 1783 in Cape May, New Jersey. At the age of seven, she was hired by a family sixty miles away to work as a servant maid; she would not see her mother again until she was nearly forty years old. In her autobiography, Jarena related little about her early life, except that she had scarcely three months of schooling and that her parents were not religious, being "wholly ignorant of the knowledge of God."[1] At the age of twenty-one, after a several-month process of increasing conviction, Jarena was converted.

On Her Conversion

The manner of this great accomplishment was as follows: In the year 1804, it so happened that I went with others to hear a missionary of the Presbyterian order preach. It was an afternoon meeting, but few were there, the place was a school room; but the preacher was solemn, and in his countenance the earnestness of his master's business appeared equally strong, as though he were about to speak to a multitude.

At the reading of the Psalms, a ray of renewed conviction darted into my soul. These were the words, composing the first verse of the Psalms for the service:

> Lord, I am vile, conceived in sin,
> Born unholy and unclean.
> Sprung from man, whose guilty fall
> Corrupts the race, and taints us all.[2]

This description of my condition struck me to the heart, and made me to feel in some measure, the weight of my sins, and sinful nature. But not knowing how to run immediately to the Lord for help, I was driven of Satan, in the course of a few days, and tempted to destroy myself.

There was a brook about a quarter of a mile from the house, in which there was a deep hole, where the water whirled about among the rocks; to this place it was suggested, I must go and drown myself.

At the time I had a book in my hand; it was on a Sabbath morning, about ten o'clock; to this place I resorted, where on coming to the water I sat down on the bank, and on my looking into it; it was suggested, that drowning would be an easy death. It seemed as if some one was speaking to me, saying put your head under, it will not distress you. But by some means, of which I can give no account, my thoughts were taken entirely from this purpose, when I went from the place to the house again. It was the unseen arm of God which saved me from self murder.

But notwithstanding this escape from death, my mind was not at rest—but so great was the labour of my spirit and the fearful oppressions of a judgment to come, that I was reduced as one extremely ill. On which account a physician was called to attend me, from which illness I recovered in about three months.

But as yet I had not found him of whom Moses and the prophets did write, being extremely ignorant: there being no one to instruct me in the way of life and salvation as yet. . . .

Soon after this I again went to the city of Philadelphia; and commenced going to the English Church, the pastor of which was an Englishman, by the name of Pilmore, one of the number, who at first preached Methodism in America, in the city of New York.[3]

But while sitting under the ministrations of this man, which was about three months, and at the last time, it appeared that there was a wall between me and a communion with that people, which was higher than I could possibly see over, and seemed to make this impression upon my mind, *this is not the people for you*.[4]

But on returning home at noon I inquired of the head cook of the house respecting the rules of the Methodists, as I knew she belonged to that society, who told me what they were; on which account I replied, that I should not be able to abide by such strict rules not even one year;—however, I told her that I would go with her and hear what they had to say.

The man who was to speak in the afternoon of that day, was the Rev. Richard Allen,[5] since bishop of the African Episcopal Methodists in America. During the labors of this man that afternoon, I had come to the conclusion, that this is the people to which my heart unites, and it so happened, that as soon as the service closed he invited such as felt a desire to flee the wrath to come,[6] to unite on trial with them—I embraced the opportunity. Three weeks from that day, my soul was gloriously converted to God, under preaching, at the very outset of the sermon. The text was barely pronounced, which was: 'I perceive thy heart is not right in the sight of God,'[7] when there appeared to *my* view, in the centre of the heart *one* sin; and this was *malice*, against one particular individual, who had strove deeply to injure me, which I resented. At this discovery I said, *Lord I forgive every* creature. That instant, it appeared to me, as if a garment, which had entirely enveloped my whole person, even to my fingers ends, split at the crown of my head, and was stripped away from me, passing like a shadow, from my sight—when the glory of God seemed to cover me in its stead.

That moment, though hundreds were present, I did leap to my feet, and declare that God, for Christ's sake, had pardoned the sins of my soul. Great was the ecstasy of my mind, for I felt that not only the sin of *malice* was pardoned, but all other sins were swept away together. That day was the first when my heart had believed, and my tongue had made confession unto salvation—the first words uttered, a part of that song, which shall fill eternity with its sound, was *glory to God*. For a few moments I had power to exhort sinners,[8] and to tell of the wonders and of the goodness of him who had clothed me with *his* salvation.[9] During this, the minister was silent, until my soul felt its duty had been performed, when he declared another witness of the power of Christ to forgive sins on earth, was manifest in my conversion.[10]

She continued to wrestle for several years with an internal agitation for which she blamed Satan. As before her conversion, she again felt the urge to commit suicide by drowning or hanging herself, an impulse that she had to resist three times between the years 1804 and 1808. Then she was introduced to the doctrine of sanctification. For three months, she sought the blessing of sanctification, and then one day, she heard a voice commanding her, "Ask for sanctification." She obeyed. "That very instant, as if lightning had darted through me, I sprang to my feet, and cried, 'The Lord has sanctified my soul!' There was none to hear this but the angels who stood around to witness my joy—and Satan, whose malice raged the more. . . . I now ran into the house and told them what had happened to me, when, as it were, a new rush of the same ecstasy came upon me, and caused me to feel as if I were in an ocean of light and bliss."[11] Jarena was the first African American woman to tell about her experience of sanctification.[12] About five years after her sanctification, she heard a call from God to preach the gospel.

On Her Call to Preach

Between four and five years after my sanctification, on a certain time, an impressive silence fell upon me, and I stood as if some one was about to speak to me, yet I had no such thought in my heart. But to my utter surprise there seemed to sound a voice which I thought I distinctly heard, and most certainly understood, which said to me, "Go preach the Gospel!" I immediately replied aloud, "No one will believe me." Again I listened, and again the same voice seemed to say—"Preach the Gospel; I will put words in your mouth,[13] and will turn your enemies to become your friends."

At first I supposed that Satan had spoken to me, for I had read that he could transform himself into an angel of light,[14] for the purpose of deception. Immediately I went into a secret place, and called upon the Lord to know if he had called me to preach, and whether I was deceived or not; when there appeared to my view the form and figure of a pulpit, with a Bible lying thereon, the back of which was presented to me as plainly as if it had been a literal fact.

In consequence of this, my mind became so exercised, that during the night following, I took a text, and preached in my sleep. I thought there stood before me a great multitude, while I expounded to them the things of religion. So violent were my exertions, and so loud were my exclamations, that I awoke from the sound of my own voice, which also awoke the family of the house where I resided. Two days after, I went to see the preacher in charge of the African Society, who was the Rev. Richard Allen, the same before named in these pages, to tell him that I felt it my duty to preach the gospel. But as I drew near the street in which his house was, which was in the city of Philadelphia, my courage began to fail me; so terrible did the cross appear, it seemed that I should not be able to bear it. Previous to my setting out to go to see him, so agitated was my mind, that my appetite for my daily food failed me entirely. Several times on my way there, I turned back again; but as often I felt my strength again renewed, and I soon found that the nearer I approached to the house of the minister, the less was my fear. Accordingly, as soon as I came to the door, my fears subsided, the cross was removed, all things appeared pleasant—I was tranquil.

I now told him, that the Lord had revealed it to me, that I must preach the gospel. He replied, by asking, in what sphere I wished to move in? I said, among the Methodists. He then replied, that a Mrs. Cook, a Methodist lady, had also some time before requested the same privilege; who it was believed, had done much good in the way of exhortation, and holding prayer meetings; and who had been permitted to do so by the verbal license of the preacher in charge at the time. But as to women preaching, he said that our Discipline[15] knew nothing at all about it—that it did not call for women preachers. This I was glad to hear, because it removed the fear of the cross— but not no sooner did this feeling cross my mind, than I found that a love of souls had in a measure departed from me; that holy energy which burned within me, as a fire, began to be smothered. This I soon perceived.[16]

In 1811, she married Mr. Joseph Lee, and they moved six miles away from Philadelphia to the community of Snow Hill, where her husband pastored a church. Jarena's discontent in Snow Hill was palpable. She was lonely for her friends in Philadelphia, and she was frustrated without any prospects to preach the gospel. In her great despondency, she became quite ill and was unable even to sit up. Her greatest fear while she was ill was that she would never be able to preach. Although she eventually did regain her health, her suffering persisted. In the course of six years at Snow Hill, she experienced multiple deaths in her family, including her husband's. When she returned to Philadelphia, she was a widow with two young children—a two-year old and a six-month old.

Once again, she visited Richard Allen, now Bishop of The African Methodist Episcopal Church (AME), this time to request his permission to hold a prayer meeting in her home and to exhort as seemed appropriate. To this request, he assented. Soon, however, Bishop Allen was forced to decide a second time whether or not he would sanction Jarena's preaching. During a church service, when she felt that the preacher had "lost the spirit," she stood up "by an altogether supernatural impulse" and proceeded to preach from the text that had been read from the book of

Jonah, comparing herself to Jonah who had fled from God's call to preach. In her autobiography, she recalled, "During the exhortation, God made manifest his power in a manner sufficient to show the world that I was called to labour according to my ability, and the grace given unto me, in the vineyard of the good husbandman."[17] Bishop Allen, who was in the congregation that day, was convinced of her call, and gave her official church approval to preach eight years after her first request.[18] The next Sunday her itinerant evangelistic ministry began.

On Her Evangelistic Method: Evangelistic Meetings

The next Sabbath day, while sitting under the word of the gospel, I felt moved to attempt to speak to the people in a public manner, but I could not bring my mind to attempt it in the church. I said, Lord, anywhere but here. Accordingly, there was a house not far off which was pointed out to me, to this I went. It was the house of a sister belonging to the same society with myself. Her name was Anderson. I told her I had come to hold a meeting in her house, if she would call in her neighbours. With this request she immediately complied. My congregation consisted of but five persons. I commenced by reading and singing a hymn, when I dropped to my knees by the side of a table to pray. When I arose I found my hand resting on the Bible, which I had not noticed till that moment. It now occurred to me to take a text. I opened the Scripture, as it happened, at the 141st Psalm, fixing my eye on the 3d verse, which reads: 'Set a watch, O Lord, before my mouth, keep the door of my lips.' My sermon, such as it was, I applied wholly to myself, and added an exhortation. Two of my congregation wept much, as the fruit of my labour this time. In closing, I said to the few, that if any one would open a door, I would hold a meeting the next sixth-day evening; when one answered that her house was at my service. Accordingly I went, and God made manifest his power among the people. Some wept, while others shouted for joy. One whole seat of females, by the power of God, as the rushing of a wind,[19] were all bowed to the floor at once, and screamed out. Also a sick man and woman in one house, the Lord convicted them both; one lived, and the other died. God wrought a judgment—some were well at night, and died in the morning. At this place I continued to hold meetings about six months. During that time I kept house with my little son, who was very sickly. About this time I had a call to preach at a place about thirty miles distant, among the Methodists, with whom I remained one week, and during the whole time, not a thought of my little son came into my mind; it was hid from me, lest I should have been diverted from the work I had to do, to look after my son. Here by the instrumentality of a poor coloured woman, the Lord poured forth his spirit among the people. Though, as I was told, there were lawyers, doctors, and magistrates present, to hear me speak, yet there was mourning and crying among sinners, for the Lord scattered fire among them of his own kindling. The Lord gave his handmaiden[20] power to speak for his great name, for he arrested the hearts of the people, and caused a shaking amongst the multitude, for God was in the midst.

I now returned home, found all well; no harm had come to my child, although I left it very sick. Friends had taken care of it which was of the Lord. I now began to think seriously of breaking up housekeeping, and forsaking all to preach the everlasting Gospel. I felt a strong desire to return to the place of my nativity, at Cape May, after an absence of about fourteen years. To this place, where the heaviest cross was to be met with, the Lord sent me, as Saul of Tarsus was sent to Jerusalem,[21] to preach the same gospel which he had neglected and despised before his conversion. I went by water, and on my passage was much distressed by sea sickness, so much so that I expected to have died, but such was not the will of the Lord respecting me. After I had disembarked, I proceeded on as opportunities offered, toward where my mother lived. When within ten miles of that place, I appointed an evening meeting. There were a goodly number came out to hear. The Lord was pleased to give me light and liberty among the people. After meeting, there came an elderly lady to me and said, she believed the Lord had sent me among them; she then appointed me another meeting there two weeks from that night. The next day I hastened forward to the place of my mother, who was happy to see me, and the happiness was mutual between us. With her I left my poor sickly boy, while I departed to do my Master's will. In this neighborhood I had an uncle, who was a Methodist, and who gladly threw open his door for meetings to be held there. At the first meeting which I held at my uncle's house, there was, with others who had come from curiosity to hear the coloured woman preacher, an old man, who was a deist,[22] and who said he did not believe the coloured people had any souls—he was sure they had none. He took a seat very near where I was standing, and boldly tried to look me out of countenance. But as I laboured on in the best manner I was able, looking to God all the while, though it seemed to me I had but little liberty, yet there went an arrow from the bent bow of the gospel, and fastened in his till then obdurate heart. After I had done speaking, he went out, and called the people around him, said that my preaching might seem a small thing, yet he believed I had the worth of souls at heart. This language was different from what it was a little time before, as he now seemed to admit that coloured people had souls, as it was to these I was chiefly speaking; and unless they had souls, whose good I had in view, his remark must have been without meaning. He now came into the house, and in the most friendly manner shook hands with me, saying, he hoped God had spared him to some good purpose. This man was a great slave holder, and had been very cruel; thinking nothing of knocking down a slave with a fence stake, or whatever might come to hand. From this time it was said of him that he became greatly altered in his ways for the better. At that time he was about seventy years old, his head as white as snow; but whether he became a converted man or not, I never heard.[23]

From her home base of Philadelphia, she itinerated throughout New England, north into Canada, and west into Ohio, traveling by foot, stagecoach, and boat to preach wherever a location was available—in churches, schools, camp meetings, barns, and homes. In the second edition of her autobiography, she paused at several points to catalog her ministry in terms of the number of miles traveled and sermons preached. "That year I traveled two thousand three hundred and twenty-five miles, and preached one hundred and seventy-eight sermons. Praise God for health and strength, O my soul, and magnify his name for protection through various scenes of life."[24] Across the miles, she also crossed denominational boundaries, preaching to Methodists, Baptists, Quakers, Wesleyan Methodists, and Presbyterians, sometimes one denomination at a time, sometimes several denominations together. In one of the few brief diatribes she allowed herself, she expressed disapproval of denominationalism. "Oh, how I long to see the day when Christians will meet on one common platform—Jesus of Nazareth—and cease their bickerings and contentions about non-essentials—when 'our Church' shall be less debated, but 'our Jesus' shall be all in all."[25]

Jarena habitually recounted her audience's racial composition as well. She categorized audiences as "white," "colored," "Indian," "white and colored," or "slaves and the holders." A particularly inclusive audience, both denominationally and racially, heard her preach at Wilkesbarre: "I spoke at Wilkesbarre to both White and Colored, Baptists and Methodists, and had an invitation to preach in the afternoon, had good congregations, and tears of contrition were visible in many places."[26] However, even though she frequently held meetings where "white and colored" attended together, she experienced the hostility of racism, like the encounter with a "white man who came and set at the end of the table twice while I was laboring, thinking I would say something to implicate myself and wanted me arrested so badly . . ."[27] As with denominationalism, she made a few brief comments in her autobiography denouncing racism. When she was preaching to a "little settlement of Colored people" known as Hole in the Wall, Jarena recalled that she was particularly helped by a man over one hundred years old. In her reflections about him, she included this critique against slavery: "I had no help but an old man, one hundred and odd years of age; he prayed, and his prayers made us feel awful, he died in the year 1825, and has gone to reap the reward of his labor; freed from the toils and cares of life, *no more to labor under a hard task master, but to rest where the slave is freed from his master*."[28] Her awareness of racial relations was also heightened by her attendance at several American Anti-Slavery Conventions. ". . . I heard some very eloquent speeches which pleased me very much, and my heart responded with this instruction: 'Do unto all men as you would they should do unto you;' and as we are all children of one parent, no one is justified in holding slaves. I felt that the spirit of God was in the work, and also felt it my duty to unite with this Society. Doubtless the cause is good, and I pray God to forward on the work of abolition until it fills the world, and then the gospel will have free course to every nation, and in every clime."[29]

Jarena's autobiography was the first "prose narrative" to be published in America by an African American woman, and it precedes by more than two decades the publication of African American women's slave narratives.[30] In 1833, she paid an editor $5 to correct the manuscript. Two years later, she financed the printing of 1,000 copies of her autobiography and sold them at various meetings and on the streets. Within three years, successful sales prompted a second printing of 1,000 copies.

However, in 1844, the AME's publishing committee responded negatively to her request to finance the printing of a second, longer edition of her autobiography. The committee's rationale cited that the manuscript "has been written in such a manner as it is impossible to decipher much of the meaning contained in it. We shall have to apply to Sister Lee to favor us with an explanation of such portions of the manuscript as are not understood by us."[31] Whether the committee followed through or not on their "application" to Jarena is not known. Nevertheless, Jarena proceeded to publish, again at her own expense, a second and substantially longer edition of her autobiography in 1849.[32]

Between the years 1849 and 1857, there is no recorded history about Jarena. The last known event in her life was a visit she made to the home of Rebecca Cox Jackson[33] in Philadelphia on New Year's Day in 1857, an occasion noted in Rebecca's diary. Jarena and Rebecca had both been itinerant evangelists with the AME in the early to mid-1830s. For some reason, they became estranged from one another. Rebecca referred to Jarena in her diary as "one of my most bitter persecutors."[34] Jarena's visit was presumably intended to mend their discord.

After this occasion, at the age of seventy-three, Jarena slipped from the annals of recorded history; nothing else is known about her life, including how, when, or where she died.

On Women

Jarena was constantly besieged by opponents of women preachers. Nearly every page of her autobiography's second edition recalled an antagonistic incident, which prompted her at one point to pen a sarcastic blessing on her detractors, "May the Lord pardon their errors, and *make them be careful how they handle edged tools.*"[35] Her own denomination capitulated over recognizing her preaching ability; sometimes they supported her, other times not, as was true for Bishop Allen, who initially rebuked her request to preach, then later changed his mind after hearing her preach. Allen subsequently asked her to preach at AME churches and official denominational gatherings. He also aided Jarena in a very personal way by caring for her son, who lived with the Allen's and was educated by them. Other ministers in the denomination, however, did not always welcome her. In one instance, someone she called "an antagonist, who was ready to destroy my character," sent a letter, presumably to a denominational official, requesting that she stop preaching. She appealed to Bishop Allen, asking him to bring the matter before the denominational conference. "I wrote a letter to Bishop Allen to let him know of my grievances, as I was innocent of any crime. I felt under no obligation to bear the reproaches of progressing preachers; and I wanted it settled at Conference. But it was looked upon with little effect by the preachers and leaders."[36]

Before turning to her one extended comment on women's right to preach, it is significant to note that references to women preaching served as bookends for her autobiography's second edition. The first bookend appeared on the top of the first page, with the citation of Joel 2:28: "And it shall come to pass . . . that I will pour out my Spirit upon all flesh; and your sons, and your *daughters* shall prophecy." The last line of the book served as the second bookend: "Thus ends the Narrative of Jarena Lee, the first female preacher of the First African Methodist Episcopal Church."[37]

Her statement on women's right to preach immediately followed the narrative about Bishop Allen's initial censure of her request to preach.

O how careful ought we to be, lest through our by-laws of church government and discipline, we bring into disrepute even the word of life. For as unseemly as it may appear now-a-days for a woman to preach, it should be remembered that nothing is impossible with God. And why should it be thought impossible, heterodox, or improper, for a woman to preach? seeing the Saviour died for the woman as well as the man.

If the man may preach, because the Saviour died for him, why not the woman? seeing he died for her also. Is he not a whole Saviour, instead of a half one? as those who hold it wrong for a woman to preach, would seem to make it appear.

Did not Mary *first* preach the risen Saviour,[38] and is not the doctrine of the resurrection the very climax of Christianity—hangs not all our hope on this, as argued by St. Paul?[39] Then did not Mary, a woman, preach the gospel? for she preached the resurrection of the crucified Son of God.

But some will say, that Mary did not expound the Scripture, therefore, she did not preach, in the proper sense of the term. To this I reply, it may be that the term *preach*, in those primitive times, did not mean exactly what it is now *made* to mean; perhaps it was a great deal more simple then, than it is now:— if it were not, the unlearned fishermen[40] could not have preached the gospel at all, as they had no learning.

To this it may be replied, by those who are determined not to believe that it is right for a woman to preach, that the disciples, though they were fishermen, and ignorant of letters too, were inspired so to do. To which I would reply, that though they were inspired, yet that inspiration did not save them from showing their ignorance of letters, and of man's wisdom; this the multitudes soon found out, by listening to the remarks of the envious Jewish priests. If then, to preach the gospel, by the gift of heaven, comes by inspiration solely, is God straitened; must he take the man exclusively? May he not, did he not, and can he not inspire a female to preach the simple story of the birth, life, death, and resurrection of our Lord, and accompany it too, with power to the sinner's heart. As for me, I am fully persuaded that the Lord called me to labour according to what I have received, in his vineyard.[41] If he has not, how could he consistently bear testimony in favour of my poor labours, in awakening and converting sinners?

In my wanderings up and down among men, preaching according to my ability, I have frequently found families who told me that they had not for several years been to a meeting, and yet, while listening to hear what God would say by his poor coloured female instrument, have believed with trembling—tears rolling down their cheeks, the signs of contrition and repentance towards God. I firmly believe that I have sown seed, in the name of the Lord, which shall appear with its increase at the great day of accounts, when Christ shall come to make up his jewels.[42]

Notes

1. Jarena Lee, *The Life and Religious Experience of Jarena Lee, A Coloured Lady, Giving an Account of Her Call to Preach the Gospel* (Philadelphia: printed and published by Jarena Lee, 1836), 3.

2. This quotation appears to be a combination of words and ideas from Psalm 51:1–5 and Jarena herself. Her addition of the word, "race," in the last verse prompted the suggestion that she consciously manipulated the text to include a "carefully embedded subtext" about racism. See Phebe Davidson, *Religious Impulse in Selected Autobiographies of American Women* (ca. 1630–1983): *Uses of the Spirit* (Lewiston, NY: Mellen, 1993), 173; cited in Richard J. Douglass-Chin, *Preacher Woman Sings the Blues: The Autobiographies of Nineteenth-Century African American Evangelists* (Columbia: University of Missouri, 2001), 45; see also Katherine Clay Bassard, *Spiritual Interrogations: Culture, Gender, and Community in Early African American Women's Writing* (Princeton, NJ: Princeton University, 1999), 96–97.

3. Joseph Pilmore (1739–1825) was an English Methodist minister who came to America to preach. Many African Americans came to hear him until they began to form their own places of worship.

4. Commentators on her autobiography find a "veiled criticism of the racism existing there [in the white church]," where Jarena sensed a wall between herself and the people (see Douglass-Chin, *Preacher Woman*, 36–37). That same afternoon she went to an African American service where the Rev. Richard Allen, an African American clergyman, preached. Three weeks later, among "the people to which my heart unites," Jarena was converted. The contrast between the white and black church community was clear yet understated in her autobiography. "It is through such brief, implicit references only that she examines issues of race and racism." Douglass-Chin, *Preacher Woman*, 37.

5. Richard Allen (1760–1831), a former slave and Methodist minister, was one of the founders of The African Methodist Episcopal Church. In 1816, when the denomination was formed, he was consecrated as a bishop.

6. Matthew 3:7; Luke 3:7. This phrase was also used as the single requirement for membership in a Methodist class meeting (see n. 2, chapter 6).

7. Acts 8:21.

8. An exhortation was an emotional talk, generally following the sermon, that called sinners to salvation. Often the exhortation was the catalyst that affected a person most, so exhorters had to be effective communicators. Exhorting differed from preaching. Whereas the preacher explained a biblical text in the context of a more formal sermon, often delivered from a pulpit, the exhorter spoke more personally, spontaneously, and informally from the pew once the sermon was finished. However in this case, Jarena's exhortation occurred "at the very outset of the sermon"; the biblical text had been "barely pronounced." Exhorting provided a way for women, even

children, to speak in public, though it had its drawbacks. "Exhorters occupied the lowest position in the church's preaching hierarchy and had to have permission before addressing individual congregations. They could lead Sunday School classes and prayer meetings, but in formal church services they usually spoke at the sufferance of the presiding minister and only in response to the biblical text that he had selected for the day. As exhorters women remained dependent on the male leadership of the church for access to the ears of a congregation and to the Bible itself." William L. Andrews, *Sisters of the Spirit: Three Black Women's Autobiographies of the Nineteenth Century* (Bloomington: Indiana University, 1986), 14.

9. 2 Chronicles 6:41; Isaiah 61:10.
10. Lee, *The Life and Religious Experience*, 3–6.
11. Lee, *The Life and Religious Experience*, 11–12.
12. Gloria Davis Goode, "Preachers of the word and singers of the Gospel: The ministry of women among nineteenth century African-Americans," Ph.D. Dissertation (University of Pennsylvania, 1990), 240. Sanctification was a second, marked experience that followed at some point after conversion. According to John Wesley, sanctification removed inbred sin, which all humanity inherited from Adam and Eve. Another outcome of sanctification was perfect love of God and neighbor as described in Luke 10:27: "You shall love the Lord your God with all your heart, and with all your soul, and with all your strength, and with all your mind; and your neighbor as yourself." For more on sanctification in general and its impact on women evangelists in particular, see Susie Stanley, *Holy Boldness: Women Preachers' Autobiographies and the Sanctified Self* (Knoxville: University of Tennessee, 2002), 1–5, 13–17, 68–99.
13. Jeremiah 1:9.
14. 2 Corinthians 11:14.
15. The Methodist Discipline contains the rules and regulations of the denomination.
16. Lee, *The Life and Religious Experience*, 12–13.
17. John 15:11, King James Version. Lee, *The Life and Religious Experience*, 21.
18. Her "official church approval" was a license to preach issued by Bishop Allen. On one occasion when opposition raged against her, she rejoined that she had a "License from the bishop, with his own signature." [Jarena Lee, *Religious Experience and Journal of Mrs. Jarena Lee, Giving An Account of Her Call to Preach the Gospel* (Philadelphia: printed and published by Jarena Lee, 1849), 55.] On another occasion, a group of nearly a dozen disgruntled white men came to the house where Jarena was staying in order to "see the preacher." Their opposition to her was not settled until the local magistrate examined her credentials, complete with the United States seal on them. Lee, *Religious Experience and Journal*, 36.
19. Acts 2:2.
20. Luke 1:48, King James Version.
21. Romans 15:25, 30–32; Acts 21:27–36.
22. Deists believed in the primacy of human reason and intelligence, which mitigated the need for divine revelation. Because they denied that God interfered with the laws of the universe, they were able "to cleanse Christianity of its vulgar supernaturalist superstitions." Mark A. Noll, *America's God: From Jonathan Edwards to Abraham Lincoln* (New York: Oxford University, 2002), 144. Thomas Paine, Benjamin Franklin, and Thomas Jefferson were leading deists in early America.

23. Lee, *The Life and Religious Experience*, 21–23.

24. Lee, *Religious Experience and Journal*, 51.

25. Lee, *Religious Experience and Journal*, 26. She used the same phrase, "non-essentials," in reference to antagonism against women preachers. Her hope was that people would concentrate on the essentials of the gospel, rather than "non-essentials," such as denominational divisions and criticisms of women preachers: "The Bishop was pleased to give me an appointment at Bethel Church, but a spirit of opposition arose among the people against the propriety of female preaching. My faith was tried—yet I felt my call to labor for souls none the less. . . . Shall I cease from sounding the alarm to an ungodly world, when the vengeance of offended heaven is about to be poured out, because my way is sometimes beset with scoffers, *or those who lose sight of the great Object, and stop on the road to glory to contend about non-essentials?*" Lee, *Religious Experience and Journal*, 32. Italics added.

26. Lee, *Religious Experience and Journal*, 59.

27. Lee, *Religious Experience and Journal*, 37.

28. Lee, *Religious Experience and Journal*, 37. Italics added.

29. Lee, *Religious Experience and Journal*, 90.

30. Bassard, *Spiritual Interrogations*, 87.

31. Daniel Alexander Payne, *History of the African Methodist Episcopal Church* (Nashville: Publishing House of the A.M.E. Sunday-school Union, 1891), 190. Whether there were other factors at work in the committee's refusal is a matter of conjecture. It is perhaps noteworthy that the committee's five members were male, since Jarena often received a hostile reception from her denomination's clergymen. It also might be significant that the AME's Book Concern was perpetually in serious financial trouble. Immediately preceding the reference to Jarena's request, the committee's report stated that there were not sufficient resources to publish two biographies of the denomination's early leaders. "There are several publications much wanted among us, which we have hitherto mentioned, but *for the want of means* we have in a great measure been prevented from attending to them." The report then mentioned the names of Bishop Allen and Joseph M. Corr. Payne, *History of the African Methodist Episcopal Church*, 190.

32. The second edition (*Religious Experience and Journal of Mrs. Jarena Lee*) comprised primarily a travelog of her preaching itinerary from the years, 1821–1842. According to Elizabeth Elkin Grammer, this travelog style was adopted by Lee and other female evangelists at the time. Grammer's description of Nancy Towle's autobiography, another female itinerant evangelist, also applies to Lee's style. "Here, on page 19 of her almost-300-page narrative, she begins the account—or, rather accounting—of her evangelical labors . . . And from this point on the narrative assumes the paratactic plot I noted earlier: 'I went. . . . I proceeded. . . . I visited. . . . I then went.' She composes her spiritual narrative as one might compose a list. To be sure, there are places in the autobiography that seem activated by narrative energy, where she interrupts this breakneck pace of reporting her engagements to tell a story and to reflect upon its meaning or significance." [Elizabeth Elkin Grammer, *Some Wild Visions: Autobiographies by Female Itinerant Evangelists in Nineteenth-Century America* (New York: Oxford University, 2003), 114.] For an interpretation of Jarena's traveling as "prophetic journeying," see Chanta Haywood, *Prophesying Daughters: Black*

Women Preachers and the Word, 1823–1913 (Columbia: University of Missouri, 2003), 51–71. The recent upsurge of interest in Jarena can be credited largely to William Andrews, who published the first edition of her autobiography in his volume, *Sisters of the Spirit*. His rationale for not including the longer edition is based upon its more "tedious" travelog style. "This journal [the 2 edn.], however, reads very much like a log of distances traveled, scriptural texts expounded, places visited, and numbers of people converted. Contemporary readers unused to the formulaic character of nineteenth-century ministerial journals and autobiographies are likely to find the added pages of the 1849 edition often tedious reading and rarely if ever revelatory of the inner character of the woman who wrote them. Because the added length of the 1849 edition does not offer us an appreciably expanded self-portrait of Jarena Lee, this volume reprints the first edition of Lee's autobiography." [Andrews, *Sisters of the Spirit*, 23.] Kathryn Bassard, writing more than a decade later, questions Andrew's decision, which, in her opinion, relegated the longer, second edition to obscurity. She suggests, rather, that the first edition is actually an "excerpt" from the second edition. "When we reconstruct *Life* [1 edn.] as a 'portion' of a larger writing, at the time of its publication (rather than as a complete work to which Lee penned a 'sequel,' as Andrews's 'Textual Note' implies), the relationship between the two 'editions' becomes more complicated. Lee's intertextual reference, which embeds *Life* within *Journal*, not only produces a 'text within a text' effect but figures the writing and publication of the earlier narrative as an *event* within the narrative line of the second text." [Bassard, *Spiritual Interrogations*, 90.] In addition to Bassard's observations, it is important to note that Jarena paused the travelog in the second edition to exert her own voice against denominationalism, racism, and sexism, as has been noted in this chapter.

33. Rebecca Cox Jackson (1795–1891) was an evangelist associated for a while with The African Methodist Episcopal Church until she joined the Shakers in the 1840s. In 1851, she founded a Black Shaker community in Philadelphia. She had frequent visions of Mother Ann Lee, whom Shakers considered the "female Christ," "the Mother-nature of God." Rosemary Skinner Keller and Rosemary Radford Ruether, eds., *In Our Own Voices: Four Centuries of American Women's Religious Writing* (Louisville, KY: Westminster John Knox, 1995), 348. For more on Rebecca Cox Jackson, see Jean McMahon Humez, ed., *Gifts of Power: The Writings of Rebecca Jackson, Black Visionary, Shaker Eldress* (Amherst: University of Massachusetts, 1981).

34. Humez, *Gifts of Power*, 262. For a discussion of their differences, see Bassard, *Spiritual Interrogations*, 108–116 and Humez, *Gifts of Power*, 262.

35. Lee, *Religious Experience and Journal*, 77. Italics added.

36. Lee, *Religious Experience and Journal*, 55.

37. Lee, *Religious Experience and Journal*, 97.

38. John 20:11–18.

39. 1 Corinthians 15:17–19.

40. This is a reference to the four disciples of Jesus who were fishermen: James, John, Simon, and Andrew.

41. Matthew 20:1–16.

42. Malachi 3:17, King James Version. Lee, *The Life and Religious Experience*, 14–15.

HARRIET LIVERMORE.

Engraved by J.B. Longacre from a Painting by Waldo and Jewett

1827

Itinerant evangelist, preached before Congress, author of many books, including *A Narration of Religious Experience, Scriptural Evidence in Favour of Female Testimony,* and a novel, *A Wreath from Jessamine Lawn*

Courtesy of the National Portrait Gallery, Smithsonian Institution.

CHAPTER 2

HARRIET LIVERMORE (1788–1868)

Rich
Decided on religion
Millenialist

Harriet Livermore is an exception in this anthology for she was born into wealth, comfort, and ancestral connections. For seven generations in New England, the Livermores had amassed an impressive political and military lineage. Harriet's own father was a U.S. District Attorney appointed by George Washington, a justice on the New Hampshire Supreme Court, and a member of the U.S. Congress for three terms. When Harriet was five, her mother died. From the age of eight until her late teen years, Harriet attended boarding schools in New England. While her father was in Congress, Harriet enjoyed for several years the "Washington social circuit as an attractive, well dressed, and eligible daughter of one of New England's elite families."[1] Suddenly in 1811 at the age of twenty-three, Harriet resolved to discard her life of ease and pleasure and "to commence a religious life." In that year, she experienced her conversion.

On Her Conversion

It was in September, A.D. 1811, that tired of the vain, thoughtless life I had led, sick of the world, disappointed in all my hopes of sublunary bliss, I drew up a resolution in my mind to commence a religious life—to become a religious person. . . . Neither fears of hell, nor desire for Heaven influenced the motion. I fled to the name and form of religion, as a present sanctuary from the sorrows of life. I was honestly determined to discard all kinds of vanity, and be very sober and strict in every particular. It is very probable, had my lot been cast in some part of Europe, instead of America, I should have immured myself within the walls of a cloister. . . .

I was engaged, and ardently too, in outer court work about a fortnight, before I felt any convictions of my lost and perishing condition by nature. My devotions, as I viewed them, were regular, constant, and *lengthy*. I read much in the Scriptures, and repeated over long prayers; . . . I read daily in religious books, and was particularly interested in memoirs of pious women, abridged from Gibbons by Dr. Dana.[2] In perusing his sketches of the life of Mary, Queen to the Prince of Orange, the Countess of Suffolk, etc., I fell in love with ideal piety. As yet, I knew nothing of the substance of religion, which is brought to the soul, through great travail and tribulation, by a new creation in Christ Jesus.[3] I resolved to try, by imitation, the effect of a life like theirs, as far as I could go; and I think to this moment that my endeavours pleased God . . . .

Present attention to religious duties could not make amends for past neglect. Where were the hours I had sacrificed to the God of this world, in dancing, card playing, novel reading, and foolish talking? They had entered their report in the ears of my judge, and the recording angel enrolled the list of my follies among the archives of divine justice. My sins were set in order before me; every imprudent action, every falsehood, and profanation of the Sabbath, were marshalled before me. My food became tasteless. I scarce took enough to prevent starvation. Sleep fled from my eyes "to light on lids unsullied with a tear." In the lapse of a few days, "my flesh declin'd, my spirits fell, and I drew near the dead." I was convinced that all my own efforts to become good, were useless. . . .

My object now, was to obtain a pardon. My whole life required divine forgiveness. I was convinced that Jesus Christ was my only refuge; yet I durst not apply to him. I saw, in his character, the Majesty of Infinite holiness. How could I, my dear sister, think of approaching so Holy a Being? . . .

In that state of condemnation, I can recollect no object that wore the least placidity, or gave me the smallest degree of pleasure. Creation was shrouded in the deepest gloom. The splendid Orb which rules the day, and rides his circuit through the skies,[4] in obedience to the Great Architect of Heaven and earth, seemed to reproach my rebellion—a comet that appeared by night, to my mind was ominous of general destruction. I gazed upon the brilliant meteor, as the signal of war and ruin, recollecting the account of the blazing star, resembling a drawn sword, which appeared over Jerusalem a year previous to its overthrow, by the Roman army; and my melancholy soul presaged like fate to my country, while I dreaded yet more the sword of divine justice unsheathed over my defenseless head. . . .

Indeed, all the Creation of God, seemed with one consent to mark me for a rebel against him. I was secluded most of my time, keeping the light from my chamber, brooding over a mind and state where mental darkness reigned. . . .

A darker morning perhaps never opened upon a mortal, in a spiritual sense, since Eve partook of the forbidden fruit,[5] and fell from the grace of God. I rose early, and walked out. Finding a place to kneel down, beside a cart-body which was placed upon the ground, I bowed myself there before God, and attempted to pray. I remember pleading for a new heart. I obtained no relief—no comfort. I was almost overpowered. My heart was hard and cold. This was the morning of the first day of the week, my dear sister, which celebrates the resurrection of the Son of God; but there was no risen Jesus appeared to me then;[6] but at "evening time it came to pass that there was light." . . .

After meeting in the afternoon, I retired to my chamber and locked my door. No eye then, but those flames of fire which fill all Heaven with light, was upon me. I sat in the corner of the room, trying to meditate upon my situation, when a sudden impulse moved me to give myself away to Jesus. I dropped quick on the floor, crying, "Jesus, thou Son of David, have mercy upon me."[7] I can recollect no more, till I stood upon my feet; and walked the room, where all about me seemed wrapt in mystery. I believe that cry was heard, and granted. . . .

Finding a solemn stillness in my mind, as I walked the room, I could not account for the alteration, as it had so recently resembled the surging waves in a violent gale. The noise of an accusing conscience was suddenly hushed— the rattling chariots, and prancing horses, that pursued me from Egypt, were gone down to the bottom of the sea[8]—I saw them no more; for they sank like a stone in the flood. The first thought that I recollect passing through my mind, breathed perfect purity; it was this—O, I hope I shall never sin again. . . .

The evening I mentioned, when I gave myself away to Jesus, crying for mercy, was peaceful and pleasant. My sleep was quiet and refreshing—"tir'd Nature's sweet Restorer," again waved his downy pinions over my pillow. The next morning I opened my eyes, to behold, as it were, a new world. "The heavens declared the glory of God,"[9] and the earth to my view was covered with his Royal Robe of glory. I saw the brightness of that ineffable Majesty who came from Tenan, and the Holy One who descended on Mount Paran,[10] whose glory covered the Heavens, and the earth was full of his praise. I burst forth in a morning song—for it was the morn of my spiritual day. . . . It is impossible for me to describe the ecstacy that filled my soul. Better felt than can be expressed, are the raptures of a pardoned sinner. I believe the angelic host participated in my joys at that season, for they saw a prodigal return;[11] and Jesus spoke of their gladness at such a sight. Oh! how charming was the name of Jesus to my ear, my eye, my heart.[12]

For several years after her conversion, she attended various churches— Episcopalian, Presbyterian, Quaker, Methodist, and Congregational—but each one fell short of her expectations. In 1821, Harriet encountered a small denomination, The Freewill Baptists, whose emphasis on the spontaneity of the Holy Spirit empowered women to speak publicly. Harriet spoke in public with men present for the first time at Freewill Baptist meetings that summer; once in prayer she spoke aloud, and once after a sermon, she spoke for about five minutes. When friends heard what she had done, their severe criticism prompted her to stop attending the meetings. Eventually, she defied these critics and concluded that she must be baptized by immersion, which the Baptists practiced. On January 2, 1823, a hole was cut in the ice during a winter storm, and Harriet was plunged into the frigid waters.

On Her Evangelistic Method: Itinerant Visitation and Exhortation[13]

Coincident with her baptism was her decision to dedicate "the whole of my time" to God. She inquired of God, " 'Lord, what wouldst thou have me to do?' It came into my mind with much sweetness to go and visit the christian churches, exhorting the children of God to stand fast in the liberty wherewith Christ hath made them free . . ."[14] Harriet then embarked on a ministry of itinerant visitation and exhortation, particularly to members of another small denomination, The Christian Connection, who also encouraged women's leadership in the church. She took with her a letter of recommendation from an elder in The Christian Connection, which requested that churches treat her well and assist her with her work. For over a year between 1823 and 1824, she undertook an arduous regime of visitation and exhortation throughout New England. In the span of one three-month period, she traveled to twenty-three different locations, visiting in homes and exhorting at meetings, as she recounted in this excerpt.

I left Assonet, early in October, and went to Wrentham in Massachusetts. I had received from Elder Jones, directions where to land, that is what house to go to, in every town where the Christian brethren resided who belong to the Mass. Conference. My lodgings in W. were at the mansion of Jacob Mann, Esq. since deceased. I attended a church meeting, and afterward a number of public meetings. On the sabbath evening following my entrance there, I felt a remarkable impression that God would work in the meeting. While a mother in Israel sung, "The angels are hov'ring round," &c. I felt an assurance that the meeting would be blest; and I kneeled down to pray. My heart was dissolved, my eyes poured forth a flood; when I rose, I observed a number of youth in tears, and suddenly a girl, twelve years of age, came to me almost throwing herself into my arms, with these words, "Miss Livermore, pray for my poor soul."—I kneeled down with her, and prayed as long as I felt any liberty. When I ceased, I said to her, you must pray for yourself. She broke forth in language like this, Lord Jesus forgive my sins, and give me religion.—O do give me religion. I am young in years, but a great sinner. After pleading thus a few minutes, she said, "Lord put a new song in my mouth," and very soon she sprung from her knees, exclaiming with apparent ecstacy, "I am converted; Jesus has heard my cries, he has converted my soul." She took my hand, saying, "how I love you; O, I praise the Lord for sending you here." . . .

I left W. in about one week after; and went to Boston, Salem, Haverhill, and Hawke, took my winter clothes, resolving to face the south and west, until I could see the N.Y. churches. This was my mind; but God ordered otherwise. I returned to Wrentham, went to Cumberland, R. I. There I was received kindly by the christian brethren; visited Attleborough and Mansfield, in Mass.; from thence I went to Patuckset, in Cranston, R. I., to search for a few scattered children, who were baptized by Elder Farnham. You may judge, if you can, of my disappointment, as well as surprise, on discovering there was no christian church there. The children were all scattered, backslidden[15] or dead. In November, toward night on Saturday, I found myself among strangers indeed; but I felt calm, and believed God would appear for my help. I exhibited my recommendations to the man I was directed to apply to, who went out and brought in a Deacon,[16] in the Calvin Baptist church. After conversing with me a short time, the Deacon went to the minister, and society, or church committee, with my letters of commendation, who agreed that I should have liberty to improve in their meeting house, half the following day, (Sabbath.) I went into the Deacon's seat, and spoke from these words, "In my Father's house are many mansions, if it were not so, I would have told you. I go to prepare a place for you," &c.[17] Elder Shurtliff spoke his approbation of my testimony, and closed the meeting with thanksgiving and prayer. As soon as the Congregation was dismissed, he came to me and expressed a desire that I should address the people in the afternoon. I did so—and after meeting Gen. R. sent his son with a chaise, to convey me to his house. There I was hospitably entertained. On Monday the Gen. carried me to Warwick, where I attended one meeting. From thence I went to Coventry, R. I. Next to Sterling, Connecticut; attending meeting with the brethren thanksgiving day, and eleven meetings afterwards; visited the brethren at Foster. Went to Hampton, from thence to Goshen-parish, and then to Windham.[18]

Within several years, she was traveling farther distances, staying longer in one place, including five weeks in Philadelphia, and she was preaching more than visiting and exhorting. She preached to Congress on January 8, 1827, with President John Quincy Adams in attendance. A letter written at the time recalled particulars of the event. ". . . the Hall, lobby, and Gallery were all filled to capacity, more so than ever before, and that even more people were outside on the avenue, unable to get in. . . . She was judged to be an extremely eloquent speaker, as well as an extraordinarily fine singer, whose singing greatly augmented her message."[19] Harriet spoke to Congress three more times between the years 1832 and 1843.[20]

On Women

Despite these impressive opportunities, Harriet referred often to the difficulties of her life as a female preacher. She testified to being "viewed as a lunatick."[21] She wrote further, "A female preacher is a spectacle and sufferer—a female autobiographer is a victim,"[22] and she was both. Added to these obstacles were the inconveniences and dangers of itinerant travel, which in her day were only exacerbated for women due to the vagaries associated with their gender. There was the constant threat of sexual assault, increased vulnerability to robbery, and quite uniquely, arrival at a destination only to face the hostility of crowds that were opposed to women preachers.

Early on in her evangelistic work, Harriet wrote a book advocating the right of women to speak in public on biblical grounds. *Scriptural Evidence in Favour of Female Testimony in Meetings for Christian Worship* was a series of letters to Julia, an acquaintance whom Harriet had met while she was recuperating from an illness. Julia had asked Harriet "to select and transcribe for her those passages or portions of Scripture, which favor the subject of female preaching."[23] Most of the book cataloged a host of female biblical characters and their participation in God's work. This excerpt from the book's last chapter provides insight into Harriet's understanding of men's and women's roles in the church.

You may possibly wish me to subjoin to my defence of female preaching, a statement of my views concerning their latitude in the use or improvement of gospel gifts.

Respecting the rise, progress and extent of the privileges and usefulness of women in the Church of Christ, should my opinion here be given, it is advanced as individually that is, for myself only, not to bind the conscience or determine the mind of another.—On this principle, I will discover my belief on this critical and very delicate subject.

The scriptures are silent respecting the ordination of females. I conclude it belongs only to the male sex. The title of evangelist, or minister, I do not find in the department of Anna, Priscilla, Phebe, or any other christian women, left in bible record. The administration of gospel ordinances, Baptism and the Lord's supper, uniting persons in marriage, I believe are confined to the male sex; and to me it exhibits an anti-christian spirit for a female to wish or believe them resting on her. I do not believe the spirit of truth will influence a woman to ask for ordination, and the connected duties, &c. &c.

The gift of illustrating scripture in public religious assemblies, may be conferred upon devoted female saints; this gift I cannot boast of; I never conceived it so profitable as exhortation in a female testimony. Men, who possess this power to an eminent degree, are in danger of making shipwreck on the quicksands of spiritual pride; women are in greater danger, on account of the general depression of their sex; few women wear the laurel of glory; rarity possesses a wonderful charm over the human mind; such a key held in a female hand, while it bursts the lock on divine mysteries, is in danger of opening a door to self-importance and self-applause. Those women who possess this power, have cause to pray unceasingly to God for preservation from a spirit of exaltation through the abundance of revelations given them; and very constantly guard every avenue to their hearts, lest spiritual pride should exert its destructive power, and prove their overthrow.

Praying, exhorting, and singing in meetings, for the public worship of God, I believe belong to either sex, upon whom the Holy Ghost descends while waiting upon God, with his quickening and commanding influences under the banner of Emmanuel's[24] cross; visiting and praying with the sick, I believe are duties very closely binding on the mothers in Israel;[25] exhorting and praying at burials may occasionally devolve upon female labourers in the Lord's vineyard;[26] and praying at the family altar, giving thanks for temporal food at the usual meal times, exhorting children, and offering prayer in schools, all are, I believe demanded of the daughters of Zion,[27] in proportion to their faithfulness, and devotion to the cause of God.

I am not myself very much in favour of females taking the pulpit in this day of reigning prejudice against female preaching; let those small inclosures, generally esteemed so sacred, be occupied by men only, is my judgement; but I will not insist on this point either way—let every one be fully persuaded in her own mind!

Journeying to visit churches, appoint meetings, and in them (no matter how public) if the providence of God permit, and his divine spirit assist, to extol the stem of Jesse's rod,[28] I really in my very heart do believe, belongs to the daughters of Zion, as well as to the ministers of the gospel; and woe to them who refuse or neglect going when God calls. True this class of laborers are suffering characters, they are "hated by the world despised by fools" and laughed at by those whose eternal welfare lays near their hearts, for whom they mourn, weep and pray. The sons and daughters of worldly prosperity cross the ocean, to serve themselves—either health, science or pleasure may tempt them to venture across the deep. "Gentlemen and Ladies" as they call themselves and one another, can travel from Maine to Ohio, for recreation, or lucrative purposes, and never incur a censure; females in large cities frequently resort to the theatre, where their sex are prime actors in diabolical scenes, whose foundation must be in hell. This is no dishonour, although the midnight hour overtake them, while sitting there. Survey the ball room—a throng of people, jumping about one another, panting for breath in the vain exercise of dancing—the mother there, whose tender babe requires her presence in the nursery—the matron, over whose head, perhaps forty summers have rolled in rapid succession; and even the venerable signal of old age, the "almond blossom,"[29] might if sought for, beneath the borrowed tresses, or costly turban, reveal the solemn truth that "the winds of sixty winters have wistled [sic] through those branches;" but this—all this is polite—decent, innocent amusements—respectable recreations. Ah! let a female, who loves the cause of Zion,[30] and the souls of her fellow creatures, travel to visit churches, and speak in meetings for the worship of God; and what a commotion is raised! She is a disgrace to her sex, her relations and the name of religion! But I forbear—it is sufficient that God knoweth all things, to whom just judgement doth alone belong.[31]

As she grew older, her beliefs became stridently millennialist, that is, she fervently expected that Jesus was coming again soon. To that end, she developed a particular concern for Native Americans because she believed they were descendants of the lost tribes of Israel. The necessity of their conversion became linked in her mind with her millennial hopes; if these "lost tribes" were converted, then Jesus would return. This belief prompted her in 1832 to travel to Kansas to preach to and comfort Native Americans, but she was turned back by the Commissioner of Indian Affairs at Fort Leavenworth. Thwarted in this effort, Harriet then turned her focus to the Jews and particularly to Jerusalem as the epicenter of Jesus' return. Between 1836 and 1858, she made at least four trips to Jerusalem; the last trip was at the age of seventy. Her purpose was to "bear witness to and hopefully be witness to the literal return of the Lord, or to die there, whichever came first."[32]

Harriet did not die in Jerusalem; she died alone in a Philadelphia almshouse and was buried, as she requested, in an unmarked grave. Despite her affluent background, she spent her last years in poverty. Her popularity and resources dwindled particularly in the 1840s when her millennial beliefs intensified, and the generosity of friends, family, and churches became more parsimonious. Eventually she was completely dependent upon freewill offerings and the income from her books, neither of which was plentiful. At one critical juncture, Harriet pawned silver spoons to underwrite her itinerancy. "Since I have traveled and appointed meetings in the name of the Lord I have often carried an empty purse. And by this means twice I have been obliged to travel on foot till my feet were badly festered, and my whole frame entirely exhausted. I have, or rather once had, three large silver spoons and six small ones, formerly the property of my deceased mother. . . . These spoons have been of service to me, since I have been exposed to the open world, a selfish unfeeling theater of gain, in affording me present relief in any sudden exigency, by pawning them to some wealthy, trusty Christian for the money I needed."[33] Harriet lived and died true to her self-description—a stranger and pilgrim on earth.[34] She was immortalized, though not in a flattering way, as a character in John Greenleaf Whittier's poem, "Snow-Bound."

> A woman tropical, intense
> In thought and act, in soul and sense,
> She blended in a like degree
> The vixen and the devotee,
> Revealing with each freak or feint
> The temper of Petruchio's Kate,
> The raptures of Siena's saint.
> Her tapering hand and rounded wrist
> Had facile power to form a fist;
> The warm, dark languish of her eyes
> Was never safe from wrath's surprise. . . .[35]

Notes

1. Cynthia A. Jürisson, "Federalist, Feminist, Revivalist: Harriet Livermore (1788–1868) and the Limits of Democratization in the Early Republic," Ph.D. Dissertation (Princeton Theological Seminary, 1994), 35.
2. Daniel Dana, *Memoirs of eminently pious women: who were ornaments to their sex, blessing to their families, and edifying examples to the church and world, abridged from the large work of Dr. Gibbons* (Newburyport, MA: Angier March, 1803).
3. 2 Corinthians 5:17; Galatians 6:15.
4. Psalm 19:5–6.
5. Genesis 3:1–7.
6. Matthew 28:9–10; Mark 16:9; John 20:14–18, 19–23, 26–29; 21:1–14; Acts 1:1–12.
7. This phrase occurs in the gospels as people cry out to Jesus for healing: Matthew 9:27, 12:32, 15:22, 17:15, 20:30; Mark 10:47; Luke 18:38.
8. Exodus 14:1–15:21.
9. Psalm 19:1.

10. References to Paran in Deuteronomy 33:2 and Habakkuk 3:2 describe in poetic terms a mountain on which divine demonstration happened.
11. Luke 15:11–32.
12. Harriet Livermore, *Narration of Religious Experience, In Twelve Letters* (Concord, NH: Jacob Moore, 1836), 30–33, 36–40, 46–50, 53–55.
13. See n. 8, chapter 1.
14. Livermore, *Narration of Religious Experience*, 144.
15. Backslidden refers to someone who once professed to believe in Jesus Christ but has since drifted away from a fervent, active faith.
16. A deacon is a leader in the church; see 1 Timothy 3:8–13.
17. John 14:2–3.
18. Livermore, *Narration of Religious Experience*, 167–69, 172–74.
19. Jürisson, "Federalist, Feminist, Revivalist," 227.
20. Jürisson, "Federalist, Feminist, Revivalist," 228–30.
21. Livermore, *Narration of Religious Experience*, 9.
22. Livermore, *Narration of Religious Experience*, 13, 15.
23. Livermore, *Narration of Religious Experience*, 198.
24. Isaiah 7:14; Matthew 1:23. In Hebrew, Emmanuel (Immanuel) means "God is with us."
25. Judges 5:7; 2 Samuel 20:19.
26. Matthew 20:1–16.
27. This phrase personifies the city of Jerusalem as a young woman. It occurs numerous times in prophetic books of the Hebrew Bible (e.g. Isaiah, Jeremiah, Micah, and Zechariah, as well as in the Book of Lamentations).
28. Isaiah 11:1.
29. Ecclesiastes 12:5.
30. Zion generally refers to the city of Jerusalem (2 Samuel 5:6–10), or more specifically to the Temple Mount area of Jerusalem (Psalm 2:6, 46:4, 78:68–69).
31. Harriet Livermore, *Scriptural Evidence in Favour of Female Testimony, In Meetings for Christian Worship, In Letters to a Friend* (Portsmouth, NH: R. Foster, 1824), 120–24.
32. Jürisson, "Federalist, Feminist, Revivalist," 293; cited in Harriet Livermore, *A Letter to John Ross, the Principal Chief of the Cherokee Nation* (Philadelphia: Harriet Livermore, 1838), 24.
33. Samuel Livermore, *Harriet Livermore, The Pilgrim Stranger* (Hartford: Case, Lockwood, and Brainard Company, 1884), 63–64.
34. On the title page of a book she authored, this phrase appears below her name. See Harriet Livermore, *The Glory of the Lord in the Land of the Living, By Redemption of the Purchased Possession*, 2nd edn. (Philadelphia: L. R. Bailey, 1848), title page.
35. John Greenleaf Whittier, *Snow-Bound: A Winter's Idyll* (Boston, MA, 1867), 39–40; cited in Catherine Brekus, "Harriet Livermore, the Pilgrim Stranger: Female Preaching and Biblical Feminism in Early-Nineteenth-Century America," *Church History* 65 (September 1996): 403. For more on Greenleaf's poem and Harriet's life, see Elizabeth F. Hoxie, "Harriet Livermore: 'Vixen and Devotee' " *The New England Quarterly* 18 (March 1945): 39–50.

I Sell the Shadow to Support the Substance.

SOJOURNER TRUTH.

Itinerant evangelist, abolitionist, women's rights activist, emancipated slave, an author by amaneunsis of *The Narrative of Sojourner Truth*

Courtesy of the National Portrait Gallery, Smithsonian Institution.

CHAPTER 3

SOJOURNER TRUTH (ca. 1797–1883)

S ojourner's birth name was Isabella. Her family was owned by a wealthy Dutch farmer in Ulster County, New York, and they spoke the language of their owners. When she was a young child, Isabella was sold along with a flock of sheep to an English-speaking family. She marked this cataclysmic event in her young life with these poignant words, ". . . her trials in life may be dated from this period. She says, with emphasis, *Now the war begun.*"[1] When she did not understand her owner's orders, spoken in English, they whipped her with a ferocity that left permanent scars. She was sold to another owner and then sold again to the Dumont family. During the sixteen years with them, she married a slave named Thomas, and they had five children.

Meanwhile, the New York State Legislature decreed that all slaves born before 1799 would be free on July 4, 1827. Despite the law regarding her freedom, Mr. Dumont would not comply, claiming Isabella still owed him work. She had sustained a hand injury the previous year, which prevented her from working for a time. Isabella resolved to leave anyway after she had spun all the Dumonts wool, about one hundred pounds worth. One morning before dawn, Isabella, with baby Sophia in her arms, walked away from the Dumonts. She took refuge with the Van Wagenens, an abolitionist family who lived five miles away. When Mr. Dumont came to retrieve Isabella and Sophia, the Van Wagenens paid him $25 for the two, and Isabella stayed on to work for them. During this time, she experienced her conversion and was active in the nearby Methodist Church.

On Her Conversion

When Isabella had been at Mr. Van Wagener's[2] a few months, she saw in prospect one of the festivals approaching. She knows it by none but the Dutch name, Pingster—as she calls it—but I think it must have been Whitsuntide, in English.[3] She says she "looked back into Egypt,"[4] and everything looked "so pleasant there," as she saw retrospectively all her former companions enjoying their freedom for at least a little space, as well as their wonted conviviali-ties, and in her heart she longed to be with them. With this picture before her mind's eye, she contrasted the quiet, peaceful life she was living with the excellent people of Wahkendall, and it seemed so dull and void of incident, that the very contrast served but to heighten her desire to return, that, at least, she might enjoy with them, once more, the coming festivities. These feelings had occupied a secret corner of her breast for some time, when, one morning, she told Mrs. Van Wagener that her old master Dumont would come that day, and that she should go home with him on his return. They expressed some surprise, and asked her where she obtained her information. She replied, that no one had told her, but she felt that he would come.

It seemed to have been one of those "events that cast their shadows before;" for, before night, Mr. Dumont made his appearance. She informed him of her intention to accompany him home. He answered, with a smile, "I shall not take you back again; you ran away from me." Thinking his manner contradicted his words, she did not feel repulsed, but made herself and child ready; and when her former master had seated himself in the open dearborn, she walked towards it, intending to place herself and child in the rear, and go with him. But, ere she reached the vehicle, she says that God revealed himself to her, with all the suddenness of a flash of lightning, showing her, "in the twinkling of an eye,[5] that he was *all over*"—that he pervaded the universe—"and that there was no place where God was not."[6] She became instantly conscious of her great sin in forgetting her almighty Friend and "ever-present help in time of trouble."[7] All her unfulfilled promises arose before her, like a vexed sea whose waves run mountains high; and her soul, which seemed but one mass of lies, shrunk back aghast from the "awful look" of Him whom she had formerly talked to, as if he had been a being like herself; and she would now fain have hid herself in the bowels of the earth, to have escaped his dread presence. But she plainly saw there was no place, not even in hell, where he was not: and where could she flee?[8] Another such "a look," as she expressed it, and she felt that she must be extinguished forever, even as one, with the breath of his mouth, "blows out a lamp," so that no spark remains.

A dire dread of annihilation now seized her, and she waited to see if, by "another look," she was to be stricken from existence, —swallowed up, even as the fire licketh up the oil with which it comes in contact.

When at last the second look came not, and her attention was once more called to outward things, she observed her master had left, and exclaiming aloud, "Oh God, I did not know you were so big," walked into the house, and made an effort to resume her work. But the workings of the inward man were too absorbing to admit of much attention to her avocations. She desired to talk to God, but her vileness utterly forbade it, and she was not able to prefer a petition. "What!" said she, "shall I lie again to God? I have told him nothing but lies; and shall I speak again, and tell another lie to God?" She could not; and now she began to wish for some one to speak to God for her. Then a space seemed opening between her and God, and she felt that if some one, who was worthy in the sight of heaven, would but plead *for* her in their own name, and not let God know it came from *her*, who was so unworthy, God might grant it. At length a friend appeared to stand between herself and an insulted Deity; and she felt as sensibly refreshed as when, on a hot day, an umbrella had been interposed between her scorching head and a burning sun. But who was this friend? became the next inquiry. Was it Deencia, who had so often befriended her? She looked at her with her new power of sight—and, lo! she, too, seemed all "bruises and putrifying sores,"[9] like herself. No, it was some one very different from Deencia.

"Who *are* you?" she exclaimed, as the vision brightened into a form distinct, beaming with the beauty of holiness, and radiant with love. She then said, audibly addressing the mysterious visitant—"I *know* you, and I *don't* know you." Meaning, "You seem perfectly familiar; I feel that you not only love me, but that you always *have* loved me—yet I know you not—I cannot call you by name." When she said, "I know you," the subject of the vision remained distinct and quiet. When she said, "I don't know you," it moved restlessly about, like agitated waters. So while she repeated, without intermission, "I know you, I know you," that the vision might remain—"Who are you?" was the cry of her heart, and her whole soul was in one deep prayer that this heavenly personage might be revealed to her, and remain with her. At length, after bending both soul and body with the intensity of this desire, till breath and strength seemed failing, and she could maintain her position no longer, an answer came to her, saying distinctly, "It is Jesus." "Yes," she responded, "it is *Jesus*."

Previous to these exercises of mind, she heard Jesus mentioned in reading or speaking, but had received from what she heard no impression that he was any other than an eminent man, like a Washington[10] or a Lafayette.[11] Now he appeared to her delighted mental vision as so mild, so good, and so every way lovely, and he loved her so much! And, how strange that he had always loved her, and she had never known it! And how great a blessing he conferred, in that he should stand between her and God! And God was no longer a terror and a dread to her.

She stopped not to argue the point, even in her own mind, whether he had reconciled her to God, or God to herself, (though she thinks the former now,) being but too happy that God was no longer to her as a consuming fire,[12] and Jesus was "altogether lovely."[13] Her heart was now full of joy and gladness, as it had been of terror, and at one time of despair. In the light of her great happiness, the world was clad in new beauty, the very air sparkled as with diamonds, and was redolent of heaven. She contemplated the unapproachable barriers that existed between herself and the great of the world, as the world calls greatness, and made surprising comparisons between them, and the union existing between herself and Jesus, —Jesus, the transcendently lovely as well as great and powerful; for so he appeared to her, though he seemed but human; and she watched for his bodily appearance, feeling that she should know him, if she saw him; and when he came, she should go and dwell with him, as with a dear friend.[14]

Isabella was legally freed by the state of New York on July 4, 1827, but her son, Peter, had been sold illegally into slavery in Alabama at the age of six. She went to court to reclaim him, and her litigation was successful. In the fall of 1828, when she was about thirty-two years old, Isabella and Peter moved to New York City. She worked as a live-in domestic for several years and became friends with a close circle of wealthy whites who practiced an ascetic form of Christianity with regard to money, food, and sexual relations. This group, including Isabella, came to believe that God's representative on earth was an itinerant preacher, Robert Matthews, who literally arrived at the door one day claiming to be the prophet, Matthias. They formed a community known as the Kingdom with Matthias as the leader, and they all relocated to a farm outside the city. Isabella's life in the Kingdom replicated her experience as a slave; she was assigned the heaviest workload and was beaten by Matthias. When one of the Kingdom's members died unexpectedly, Matthias was charged with murder, and Isabella was charged as a co-conspirator. Both were acquitted. Isabella then returned to the city and to domestic service.

On June 1, 1843, Isabella turned her back on New York City and sojourned to the east with a few provisions in a pillowcase. She marked this turning point in her life by taking a new name—Sojourner.[15] In her *Narrative*, she recounted the conversation with her employer about her intentions. ". . . about an hour before she left, she informed Mrs. Whiting, the woman of the house, where she was stopping, that her name was no longer Isabella, but SOJOURNER; and that she was going east. And to her inquiry, "What are you going east for?" her answer was, "The Spirit calls me there, and I must go."[16] Several lines later, she further clarified her purpose. "Her mission was not merely to travel east, but to 'lecture,' as she designated it; 'testifying of the hope that was in her'—exhorting[17] the people to embrace Jesus, and refrain from sin . . ."[18]

On Her Evangelistic Method: Camp Meetings[19]

A recent biographer divides Sojourner's life into "three great chapters"—slavery, evangelism, and antislavery feminism.[20] During her life's "second chapter," Sojourner was most active as an evangelist, though she never stopped "testifying of the hope that was in her." This excerpt described a camp meeting where she, alone, was able to subdue a rowdy crowd through her singing and preaching.

Another Camp-Meeting

When Sojourner had been at Northampton a few months, she attended another camp-meeting, at which she performed a very important part.

A party of wild young men, with no motive but that of entertaining themselves by annoying and injuring the feelings of others, had assembled at the meeting, hooting and yelling, and in various ways interrupting the services, and causing much disturbance. Those who had the charge of the meeting, having tried their persuasive powers in vain, grew impatient and tried threatening.

The young men, considering themselves insulted, collected their friends, to the number of a hundred or more, dispersed themselves through the grounds, making the most frightful noises, and threatening to fire the tents. It was said the authorities of the meeting sat in grave consultation, decided to have the ring-leaders arrested, and sent for the constable, to the great displeasure of some of the company, who were opposed to such an appeal to force and arms. Be that as it may, Sojourner, seeing great consternation depicted in every countenance, caught the contagion, and, ere she was aware, found herself quaking with fear.

Under the impulse of this sudden emotion, she fled to the most retired corner of a tent, and secreted herself behind a trunk, saying to herself, "I am the only colored person here, and on me, probably, their wicked mischief will fall first, and perhaps fatally." But feeling how great was her insecurity even there, as the very tent began to shake from its foundations, she began to soliloquize as follows:—

"Shall I run away and hide from the Devil? Me, a servant of the living God?[21] Have I not faith enough to go out and quell that mob, when I know it is written—'One shall chase a thousand, and two put ten thousand to flight'?[22] I know there are not a thousand here; and I know I am a servant of the living God. I'll go to the rescue, and the Lord shall go with and protect me."

"Oh," said she, "I felt as if I had *three hearts!* and that they were so large, my body could hardly hold them!"

She now came forth from her hiding-place, and invited several to go with her and see what they could do to still the raging of the moral elements. They declined, and considered her wild to think of it.

The meeting was in the open fields—the full moon shed its saddened light over all—and the woman who was that evening to address them was trembling on the preachers' stand. The noise and confusion were now terrific. Sojourner left the tent alone and unaided, and walking some thirty rods to the top of a small rise of ground, commenced to sing, in her most fervid manner, with all the strength of her most powerful voice, the hymn on the resurrection of Christ—

'It was early in the morning—it was early in the morning,
    Just at the break of day—
When he rose—when he rose—when he rose,
    And went to heaven on a cloud.'[23]

All who have ever heard her sing this hymn will probably remember it as long as they remember her. The hymn, the tune, the style, are each too closely associated with to be easily separated from herself, and when sung in one of her most animated moods, in the open air, with the utmost strength of her most powerful voice, must have been truly thrilling.

As she commenced to sing, the young men made a rush towards her, and she was immediately encircled by a dense body of the rioters, many of them armed with sticks or clubs as their weapons of defence, if not of attack. As the circle narrowed around her, she ceased singing, and after a short pause, inquired, in a gentle but firm tone, "Why do you come about me with clubs and sticks? I am not doing harm to any one." "We ar'n't a going to hurt you, old woman; we came to hear you sing," cried many voices, simultaneously. "Sing to us, old woman," cries one. "Talk to us, old woman," says another. "Pray, old woman," says a third. "Tell us your experience," says a fourth. "You stand and smoke so near me, I cannot sing or talk," she answered.

"Stand back," said several authoritative voices, with not the most gentle or courteous accompaniments, raising their rude weapons in the air. The crowd suddenly gave back, the circle became larger, as many voices again called for singing, talking, or praying, backed by assurances that no one should be allowed to hurt her—the speakers declaring with an oath, that they would "*knock down*" any person who should offer her the least indignity.

She looked about her, and with her usual discrimination, said inwardly— "Here must be many young men in all this assemblage, bearing within them hearts susceptible of good impressions. I will speak to them." She did speak; they silently heard, and civilly asked her many questions. It seemed to her to be given her at the time to answer them with truth and wisdom beyond herself. Her speech had operated on the roused passions of the mob like oil on agitated waters; they were, as a whole, entirely subdued, and only clamored when she ceased to speak or sing. Those who stood in the background, after the circle was enlarged, cried out, "Sing aloud, old woman, we can't hear." Those who held the sceptre of power among them requested that she should make a pulpit of a neighboring wagon. She said, "If I do, they'll over-throw it." "No, they sha'n't—he who dares hurt you, we'll knock him down instantly, d—n him," cried the chiefs. "No we won't, no we won't, nobody shall hurt you," answered the many voices of the mob. They kindly assisted her to mount the wagon, from which she spoke and sung to them about an hour. Of all she said to them on the occasion, she remembers only the following:—

"Well, there are two congregations on this ground. It is written that there shall be a separation, and the sheep shall be separated from the goats.[24] The other preachers have the sheep, *I* have the goats. And I have a few sheep among my goats, but they are *very* ragged." This exordium produced great laughter. When she became wearied with talking, she began to cast about her to contrive some way to induce them to disperse. While she paused, they loudly clamored for "more," "more,"— "sing," "sing more." She motioned them to be quiet, and called out to them: "Children, I have talked and sung to you, as you asked me; and now I have a request to make of you: will you grant it?" "Yes, yes, yes," resounded from every quarter. "Well, it is this," she answered: "if I will sing one more hymn for you, will you then go away, and leave us this night in peace?" "Yes, yes," came faintly, feebly from a few. "I repeat it," says Sojourner, "and I want an answer from you all, as of one accord. If I will sing you one more, you will go away, and leave us this night in peace?" "Yes, yes, yes," shouted many voices, with hearty emphasis. "I repeat my request once more," said she, "and I want you *all* to answer." And she reiterated the words again. This time a long, loud "Yes—yes—yes," came up, as from the multitudinous mouth of the entire mob. "AMEN! it is SEALED," repeated Sojourner, in the deepest and most solemn tones of her powerful and sonorous voice. Its effect ran through the multitude, like an electric shock; and the most of them considered themselves bound by their promise, as they might have failed to do under less imposing circumstances. Some of them began instantly to leave; others said, "Are we not to have one more hymn?" "Yes," answered their entertainer, and she commenced to sing:

> I bless the Lord I've got my seal—to-day and to-day—
> To slay Goliath in the field—to-day and to-day;
> The good old way is a righteous way,
> I mean to take the kingdom in the good old way.

While singing, she heard some enforcing obedience to their promise, while a few seemed refusing to abide by it. But before she had quite concluded, she saw them turn from her, and in the course of a few minutes, they were running as fast as they well could in a solid body; and she says she can compare them to nothing but a swarm of bees, so dense was their phalanx, so straight their course, so hurried their march. As they passed with a rush very near the stand of the other preachers, the hearts of the people were smitten with fear, thinking that their entertainer had failed to enchain them longer with her spell, and that they were coming upon them with redoubled and remorseless fury. But they found they were mistaken, and that their fears were groundless; for, before they could well recover from their surprise, every rioter was gone, and not one was left on the grounds, or seen there again during the meeting. Sojourner was informed that as her audience reached the main road, some distance from the tents, a few of the rebellious spirits refused to go on, and proposed returning; but their leaders said, "No—we have promised to leave—all promised, and we must go, all go, and you shall none of you return again."[25]

Several months after she went east, as the weather turned colder, Sojourner settled into a utopian community, the Northampton Association for Education and Industry, whose purpose was to transcend class, race, and gender distinctions. The community lasted less than five years because the manufacture of silk, its sole economic base, was not profitable. Nevertheless, many reform-minded, influential people visited Northampton, such as abolitionist leaders, Frederick Douglass and William Lloyd Garrison, and through these connections, Sojourner began speaking on the antislavery lecture circuit.

On Women

Sojourner also met women's rights activists at Northampton, and in 1851, she attended the Ohio Woman's Rights Convention in Akron, where she gave her infamous "Ain't I A Woman" speech. The speech has survived in several versions, the most popular and well known of which was written twelve years after the event by Frances Dana Gage, chair of the Akron Convention. Gage undoubtedly embellished and exaggerated the speech, but it is her version

that has survived for posterity.[26] Recent historians convincingly argue that
the most reliable account was written immediately after the event by Marius
Robinson, who was the secretary of the convention and a friend of
Sojourner's. Sojourner frequently stayed with Robinson and his wife for several weeks at a time, and Robinson knew well her manner of talking. This
excerpt was Robinson's account of Sojourner's speech.

One of the most unique and interesting speeches of the Convention was
made by Sojourner Truth, an emancipated slave. It is impossible to transfer it
to paper, or convey any adequate idea of the effect it produced upon the
audience. Those only can appreciate it who saw her powerful form, her
whole-souled, earnest gestures, and listened to her strong and truthful tones.
She came forward to the platform and addressing the President said with
great simplicity:
　　May I say a few words? Receiving an affirmative answer, she proceeded; I
want to say a few words about this matter. I am a woman's rights. I have as
much muscle as any man, and can do as much work as any man. I have plowed
and reaped and husked and chopped and mowed, and can any man do more
than that? I have heard much about the sexes being equal; I can carry as much
as any man, and can eat as much too, if I can get it. I am as strong as any man
that is now. As for intellect, all I can say is, if a woman have a pint and man a
quart—why cant she have her little pint full? You need not be afraid to give
us our rights for fear we will take too much,—for we cant take more than
our pint'll hold. The poor men seem to be all in confusion, and don't know
what to do. Why children, if you have woman's rights give it to her and you
will feel better. You will have your own rights, and they wont be so much
trouble. I can't read, but I can hear. I have heard the bible and have learned
that Eve caused man to sin.[27] Well if woman upset the world, do give her a
chance to set it right side up again. The lady has spoken about Jesus, how he
never spurned woman from him, and she was right. When Lazarus died, Mary
and Martha came to him with faith and love and besought him to raise their
brother. And Jesus wept—and Lazarus came forth.[28] And how came Jesus
into the world? Through God who created him and woman who bore him.[29]
Man, where is your part? But the women are coming up blessed by God and
a few of the men are coming up with them. But man is in a tight place, the
poor slave is on him, woman is coming on him, and he is surely between a
hawk and a buzzard.[30]

　　By 1857, Sojourner had bought a house with the help of white friends in
Harmonia, a small Spiritualist[31] community near Battle Creek, Michigan.
She supported herself through speaking engagements and selling photographs of herself[32] as well as her book, *Narrative of Sojourner Truth*, written by amaneunsis, since Sojourner was illiterate.[33]
　　When the Civil War began, she threw her energy into soliciting food
and clothing for the volunteer regiments of black soldiers. She then turned
her attention to the plight of freed slaves, many of whom were living in

refugee camps in the nation's capital. Her close encounter with this desperate situation prompted her fervent belief that government hand outs to African Americans were grossly inadequate. She championed instead the idea of a colony for freed slaves in the West, where they would have a better chance of becoming self-supporting and self-reliant. She garnered many signatures for her petition urging the government to provide land for this endeavor. Although she presented it to President Ulysses S. Grant, her dream never materialized. Nevertheless, when a large migration of freed southern slaves made their way west in the fall of 1879, despite her advanced age, she traveled to Kansas to help them get settled.

Sojourner died in Battle Creek, Michigan, on November 26, 1883. While many laud her remarkable work in abolition and women's rights, Sojourner was also an evangelist who "testified of the hope that was in her—exhorting the people to embrace Jesus, and refrain from sin . . ."

Notes

1. Olive Gilbert and Frances Titus, *Narrative of Sojourner Truth; A Bondswoman of Olden Time, Emancipated by the New York Legislature in the Early Part of the Present Century; with a History of her Labors and Correspondence Drawn from her "Book of Life"* (Boston: Sojourner Truth, 1875), 26.
2. The correct spelling is Van Wagenen. Isabella took it as her last name until she changed her name to Sojourner Truth.
3. Pingster (Pinkster) is the Dutch word for Pentecost, the season of the Christian year that celebrates the coming of the Holy Spirit as detailed in Acts 2:1–4. The Pinkster festival was a week-long party, full of "frolic and abandon. Booths were set up where fish, cakes, fruit, meat, cider, and beer were sold. Slaves dressed up in finery. A 'king' usually led a parade. Slaves sang, danced, drummed, fiddled, gambled, smoked, and drank heavily." Margaret Washington, "Introduction," *Narrative of Sojourner Truth* (New York: Vintage Books, 1993), xxv.
4. Numbers 14:3–4; Acts 7:39.
5. 1 Corinthians 15:52.
6. Psalm 139:7–10.
7. Psalm 46:1.
8. Psalm 139:7–8.
9. Isaiah 1:6.
10. George Washington (1732–1799) was Chief of the Continental Army during the Revolutionary War and the first President of the United States of America.
11. The Marquis de Lafayette (1757–1834) was a Frenchman who greatly aided the colonists during the Revolutionary War by volunteering as a soldier and by securing funds and troops from his native country.
12. Deuteronomy 4:24, 9:3; Hebrews 12:29.
13. Song of Solomon 5:16.
14. Gilbert and Titus, *Narrative of Sojourner Truth*, 64–68.
15. "In her lifetime, Isabella changed names twice. Not wishing to be known by the name of her previous slaveholders, she adopted the last name Van Wagenen. She again changed her name as the 'voices' instructed her in 1843

when she became 'an instrument of God' and began her life as a traveling preacher. At that point Isabella Van Wagenen became Sojourner Truth, a woman whose proclaimed mission was to 'sojourn' the land and speak God's 'truth.' " Washington, "Introduction," *Narrative of Sojourner Truth*, xv.

16. Gilbert and Titus, *Narrative of Sojourner Truth*, 100.

17. See n. 8, chapter 1.

18. Gilbert and Titus, *Narrative of Sojourner Truth*, 100–01.

19. In the early nineteenth century, camp meetings rose to the fore as the venue for evangelistic services, particularly on the American frontier. Participants in these outdoor meetings would literally camp nearby in order to attend the daily and nightly services that lasted anywhere from several days to several weeks. At these meetings, where the openness and freedom of the great outdoors replaced the strictures of church structures, the emotional side of evangelism rose to its height. Fervent preaching at all hours of the day and night, spirited singing of hymns and gospel tunes, and impassioned exhorting of awakened sinners, evoked various physical responses in the participants, such as groaning, crying out, falling down, jerking, barking, and snapping teeth. For more on camp meetings, see Ann Taves, *Fits, Trances, & Visions: Experiencing Religion and Explaining Experience from Wesley to James* (Princeton, NJ: Princeton University, 1999), 114–17; Charles A. Johnson, *The Frontier Camp Meeting: Religion's Harvest Time* (Dallas: Southern Methodist University, 1955; 2nd. edn., 1985); Kenneth O. Brown, *Holy Ground: A Study of the American Camp Meeting* (New York: Garland, 1992); and for women's participation in camp meetings, see Catherine Brekus, *Strangers & Pilgrims: Female Preaching in America, 1740–1845* (Chapel Hill, NC: University of North Carolina, 1998), 140–42, 267–68.

20. Nell Irvin Painter, *Sojourner Truth: A Life, A Symbol* (New York: W. W. Norton, 1996), 113.

21. Daniel 6:20.

22. Deuteronomy 32:30.

23. Sojourner wrote this hymn herself. For more on her singing, see Carleton Mabee, with Susan Mabee Newhouse, *Sojourner Truth: Slave, Prophet, Legend* (New York: New York University Press, 1993), 219–31.

24. Matthew 25:31–46.

25. Gilbert and Titus, *Narrative of Sojourner Truth*, 115–20.

26. The timing of the publication of Gage's account of the speech is curious. It appeared less than a month after Harriet Beecher Stowe's immensely popular article on Sojourner in the 1863 *Atlantic Monthly* titled, "Sojourner Truth, the Libyan Sibyl." Although it catapulted Sojourner into the limelight, the article was highly stylized and incorrect. As a recent biographer of Sojourner comments, "Mining the vein that had produced her black characters in *Uncle Tom's Cabin*, Stowe makes Truth into a sort of quaint and innocent exotic who has little to say about slavery beyond the chronicle of her own experience. Stowe's Truth disdains feminism.... The 'chief delight' of this Truth, who is far more preacher than radical, is 'to talk of glory and sing hymns.' " [Painter, *Sojourner Truth*, 154.] Gage no doubt capitalized on Stowe's article and Sojourner's fame and "reached back to a different setting and invented 'and ar'n't I a woman?' " [Painter, *Sojourner*

Truth, 164.] "Gage's rendition of Truth far exceeds in drama Marius Robinson's straightforward report from 1851. Through framing and elaboration, she turns Truth's comments into a spectacular performance four times longer than his." [Painter, *Sojourner Truth*, 169.] For other historians who support Robinson's account as most accurate, see Washington, "Sojourner Truth's 'Ar'n't I a Woman' Speech," *Narrative of Sojourner Truth*, 117–18 and Mabee, *Sojourner Truth*, 67–82.

27. Genesis 3:1–24.

28. John 11:1–44.

29. Luke 1:26–2:20.

30. Marius Robinson, "Editorial" Salem (Ohio) *Anti-Slavery Bugle*, 21 June 1851; cited in Mabee, *Sojourner Truth*, 81–82 and Painter, *Sojourner Truth*, 125–26.

31. Spiritualism was a nineteenth-century religious movement whose emergence can be traced to 1848 and the "rappings" heard by the Fox Sisters in their home in upstate New York. Central to this movement were the trance mediums through whom the spirits spoke a message for the gathered audience. Since trance mediums were usually women, spiritualism offered a leadership role to women but ironically, the spirits could only speak if the mediums were passive. For more on spiritualism, see Ann Braude, *Radical Spirits: Spiritualism and Women's Rights in Nineteenth-Century America* (Boston: Beacon, 1989). Sojourner encountered Spiritualism in the early 1850s, and several of her closest friends were Spiritualists. The community of Harmonia was a comfortable setting for Sojourner because it attracted many liberal-minded Quakers turned Spiritualists, who advocated a progressive stance on race and gender issues.

32. For more on her photographs, see Painter, *Sojourner Truth*, 185–99.

33. The first edition of *Narrative*, published in 1850, was written by Olive Gilbert as Sojourner's amanuensis. They met at the Northampton Association in 1845–1846. Frances Titus, who edited later reprints of the *Narrative*, was Sojourner's closest companion during the last decades of her life. The later edition, "written communally, by Truth, Olive Gilbert (her 1850 amanuensis), and Frances Titus," included a "collection of articles, letters, anecdotes, and commentaries written by various white people about Truth." [Richard J. Douglass-Chin, *Preacher Woman Sings the Blues: The Autobiographies of Nineteenth-Century African American Evangelists* (Columbia: University of Missouri, 2001), 66.] Because of the *Narrative*'s communal authorship, scholars recognize that the women vie with each other for the prominent voice. "At the end of the *Narrative*, the voices of Gilbert and Truth become one; we are no longer able to discern where one ends and the other begins . . ." [Douglass-Chin, *Preacher Woman*, 92.] Most likely, Sojourner got the idea for selling her lifestory from Frederick Douglass, whose 1845 autobiography, *Narrative of the Life of Frederick Douglass, An American Slave*, sold "4,500 copies in less than six months . . ." [Painter, *Sojourner Truth*, 103.] Sojourner began telling her story for the *Narrative* in 1846.

Ever Yours in love
Phoebe Palmer

Methodist holiness evangelist, author of several books, including *The Way of Holiness, Promise of the Father*, and *Tongues of Fire on the Daughters of the Lord*, leader of the Tuesday Meeting for the Promotion of Holiness, founder of Five Points Mission in New York City, editor of *The Guide to Holiness*

CHAPTER 4

PHOEBE PALMER (1807–1874)

P hoebe Worrall is unusual in this anthology because she was raised in a prosperous family and lived her entire life in a large, urban center. Her father, Henry Worrall, owned an iron foundry and machine shop in New York City. Both of her parents, Henry and Dorothea Wade Worrall, were active members of a Methodist Episcopal church in the city. Religious activities saturated the daily regimen of her childhood home. The family gathered both morning and evening, when the bell sounded, to read the Bible, sing a hymn, and pray, and grace was said before and after meals. At the age of thirteen, Phoebe experienced her conversion and joined the Methodist church. Her third person account of her conversion is noteworthy for its brevity. "When about thirteen, she acknowledged herself before the world as a seeker of salvation, and united herself with the people of God."[1] Shortly after this event, she expressed dissatisfaction with her religious experience, and she longed "for the full assurance of faith."[2]

When she was nineteen, she married a homeopathic doctor, Walter Clarke Palmer, who had also been raised in a devout Methodist home. Their first two children, Alexander and Samuel, did not survive infancy. In her grief, Phoebe concluded that she had neglected her "religious activities" in favor of her children. "After my loved ones were snatched away, I saw that I had concentrated my time and attentions far too exclusively, to the neglect of the religious activities demanded. Though painfully learned, yet I trust the lesson has been fully apprehended. From henceforth, Jesus must and shall have the uppermost seat in my heart."[3] She then gave birth to Sarah who lived to adulthood. When her next child, Eliza, died at eleven months in a nursery fire, she once again interpreted the death of a child as a clarion call to seek a more intense spiritual experience. On her "day of days," July 26, 1837, she experienced sanctification, "the full assurance of faith," for which she had been searching.

On Her Sanctification

I went to the evening meeting. Our dear brother S———preached, but I scarcely heard a word. I had resolved to *die* in the struggle to believe rather than give up my confidence; and it seemed as if the matter had now come to a climax. I felt, after wrestling some time, that the Lord permitted me to come near the throne, and in much simplicity of heart, even as a little child to a tender parent, make known my grievances.

I said, "O Lord, Thou knowest that I would not believe merely because I *will* believe, without having a proper foundation for my faith. And now, in condescension to my constitutional infirmities, my proneness to reason, O give me this blessing in some such tangible form, that the enemy of my soul may never be successful with the temptation, that I believe merely because I will believe. Thou knowest that I would not believe, without a proper foundation for my faith; and now let me have this blessing in some such *tangible* form, that I may know the *precise* ground upon which I *obtained*, and also upon which I may *retain* it."

The answer came. New light burst upon my soul. The Holy Spirit took of the things of God, and revealed them unto me. It was by the unfolding of this passage to my understanding: "I beseech you, brethren, by the mercies of God, that ye present your bodies a living sacrifice, holy, acceptable unto God, which is your reasonable service." (Rom. xii. I.)

I now say that I had *obtained* this blessing, by *laying all upon the altar.*[4] I had *retained* it, by still *keeping* all upon the altar, "*a living* sacrifice." So long as it remained there, I perceived that both the faithfulness and the justice of God stood pledged for its *acceptance.* While kept upon this altar, it *must be* cleansed from all unrighteousness; for the blood of Jesus *cleanseth;*[5] not that it *can* or *will* at some *future* period, but *cleanseth now, just when the offering is presented.*

By this I saw that I could no more *believe* for the *future* moment, than I could *breathe* for the future, and perceived that I must be contented to *live by the moment*, and rely upon God to sustain me in spiritual existence just as confidently as for sustainment in natural existence. So long as the offering was *kept upon the altar*, I saw it to be not only a privilege, but a *duty*, to believe.

I also saw that just so soon as I should begin to lean to my own understanding, feeling that I cannot do this or the other duty, just in the degree in which this is indulged in, the offering would be taken from off the altar, and I should have no *right to believe* the offering "holy and acceptable," inasmuch as it is not such an offering as God has declared acceptable by the voice of the written word.

The infinitely efficacious blood was represented as ever flowing. And it is thus that the soul, laid upon the altar, is *cleansed* and *kept clean.*

O my soul, mayest thou ever remain upon the altar of sacrifice; and Thou, my strength and righteousness, forbid that any unhallowed act should ever cause its removal! It is by Thy power alone, O God, that I am kept. Here shall

I ever feel the cleansing efficacy. Here shall my soul fill and expand—fill and expand—till it shall burst its tenement, and faith shall be lost in sight.[6]

Phoebe's older sister, Sarah Lankford, was leading women's prayer meetings at two Methodist churches in New York City. In 1836, Sarah combined the meetings into one, which convened in Phoebe's home. The meeting was held on Tuesday afternoons, and it eventually became known as the Tuesday Meeting for the Promotion of Holiness. Phoebe assumed the leadership in 1840 when Sarah moved away, and the meeting grew in number and stature. Lay men and women from every denomination attended. "Here we see Methodists, Baptists, Presbyterians, Episcopalians, Quakers, United Brethren, and Jews in Christ, forgetting creeds, confessions, hair-splittings, and party distinctions, sitting side by side, drinking deeply of the one living fountain."[7]

Also in 1840, Phoebe began in earnest her evangelistic work, in which she "preached"[8] primarily about the experience of sanctification. For well over a decade, she traveled alone while Walter remained in New York City, maintaining his medical practice and their home. By the late 1850s, Walter began to accompany Phoebe and participate in the meetings. Their fame rose to such heights that in 1859, the Palmers embarked on a four-year evangelistic tour of Great Britain, where they often preached to crowds of several thousands.

On Her Evangelistic Method: Camp Meetings[9]

This excerpt, taken from Phoebe's letter to her sister, Sarah, described a typical day at a camp meeting for Phoebe and Walter.

July 6th, 1857

To Mrs. S. A. Lankford:

Suppose you follow us for one day, and you take it mostly as a specimen of the manner in which many of our other days are spent, during our repeated absences from home. We arose about six o'clock, after having closed a meeting before the preachers' stand, near midnight, the night previous. Dr. P. is always, in this region, given in charge of all the meetings before the stand.[10] We sleep about one-third of a mile from the encampment. Soon after we arose, a conveyance was brought to the door, to take us to the ground. But the kind brother with whom we abide, who is the owner of the ground, was resolved that we should remain, and breakfast with the family at the house, and therefore, the vehicle is kept standing until after we have dispatched our breakfast. . . . And now we go to the encampment. The eight o'clock preaching service is already in progress. The servant of Christ is preaching from the text, "God sent not his Son into the world, to condemn the world, but that the world, through Him, might be saved."[11] The discourse finished, we are called upon to address the congregation. With a feeling of conscious, and absolute dependence on the Holy Spirit, we speak of the

Christian's high calling—of the glory of the present dispensation,[12] and its responsibilities on individual professors. We speak of the day of Pentecost,[13] as fully come—no need of waiting, in view of the fact, that He who baptizeth with the Holy Ghost, and with fire, is in the midst.[14] Conscious of the Spirit's impellings, I speak on, and on, till a half hour passes, as though it were but a few moments. Dr. P., now in an earnest exhortation,[15] invites all who will, to draw nigh, and partake of the gospel feast, assuring them, in the name of the heavenly Provider, that all things are now ready,—Pardon, and Holiness, and Heaven. From sixty to eighty present themselves. God's Spirit is poured out in such copious measure, in the conversion of sinners, and the sanctification of believers, that the measurement of time is forgotten. Preachers, and people unite as one. Victory succeeds victory, till, ere we are aware, it is one o'clock, and we are urged to take something to eat, and find, that the time for the ten o'clock service, has passed by without our having taken note of time. One case after another presses upon us, and we find it difficult to release ourselves, so as to get time to eat. And now we dine. . . . We have just finished our repast. I rise to make room for another table, when we were asked to converse with a daughter-in-law of our host. For quietness from intrusion, we take her a little distance in the woods. She tells us that from her childhood, she has been a seeker of religion. We find her case so similar to our early condition of perplexity, and have so learned from what we have suffered, that we do not find it difficult to point her the way of faith. And by the same marks, by the way, by which we ourselves entered upon a life of unperplexed, and assured faith, she enters, and not only quietness and assurance, but holy joy at once fills her soul, and we hasten with her back to the tent to tell what great things the Lord has done for her soul. We find quite a large number present. Several are sitting around the table. She flies to her husband and friends, and with tears of exultant joy, embraces them. Praises and tears abound, and others are announced as seeking the Lord. And here we remain in an informal meeting, numbers having gathered in, and a crowd surrounding the door, the trumpet again calls us to stand. And here we have a sermon from a devoted ambassador for Christ, on the passage, "We would see Jesus."[16] This finished, we are again called upon, from the minister in charge, to address the congregation. We have made it a point never to refuse. For we have pleaded in faith that the Master of assemblies will take the direction, otherwise, we would not consent to address the people after every service, with the exception of the evening, as we now do, in view of the number of ministers present. There are three superintendents of circuits here,[17] beside rather a larger number of other ministers than usual. But this is the order of nearly all the camp-meetings we have attended, in these regions, for the last four or five years. I once, about three years since, after having been called upon publicly, at a previous meeting, to speak after almost every service, and without previous consultation, gave way to the temptation that it was perhaps not using me just right. I therefore spoke to the minister in charge of the next meeting we went to, and asked that I might not be announced thus publicly, without previous consultation. But so keenly did the

Holy Spirit reprove me, that I have never dared to do anything of this sort since, but have left the time and manner of my laboring, all with God, believing that He will guide the minds of others toward me, and thus direct me into His will. And to the praise of His grace, I feel that I ought to record my hearty belief, that I have thus been divinely directed. Dr. P., again, in an earnest exhortation, invites all seeking either pardon or purity, to present themselves, when again, scores come forward, and many receive the grace for which they supplicate. Alternate prayer and praise resound. Would that I could portray before you, in living, truthful characters, these alternate scenes of earnest, intense implorings, bringing such speedy returns from the throne of grace, and answering praises. That angels are hovering around us, carrying the news to heaven, of repenting sinners, and redeemed spirits newly saved and washed, seems scarcely a matter of faith, but a living verification. But again I must check my pen.

It is not till about six in the evening that we can again leave the scene of so many bloodless victories, in front of the stand, and permit ourselves again to be torn away, in order to refresh the outer man with the food that perisheth. We go to yet another tent, seldom taking food twice at one tent. Scarcely have we supped, and rise from the table to leave, feeling that demands from without are calling us, when we observed one sitting near the tent-door, as we are about to pass out, who arrests our attention. She is of a sorrowful countenance. "Why of a sorrowful countenance," I ask, "when you have such a gracious Saviour?" etc. We have conversed but a few moments, when her sorrow is turned to unutterable rejoicing and she is unable to bear the weight of glory, and she sinks down overpowered, in her husband's arms. A crowd again gather around the tent. Seekers of full salvation,[18] and also seekers of pardon, again congregate, and kneeling all around by the table, in unutterable groanings, plead for the promised grace. Another, and yet another is blest, and then again the garment of praise is given, and loud Alleluias ascend. And thus ascends the alternate voice of supplication and triumph, till again the trumpet sounds[19] for a rallying of Israel's hosts, at the stand.

But here my portrayings must end; my time and also my sheet forbid my saying more, with the exception that we generally have remained on the ground till near midnight.[20]

Along with her evangelistic work and leadership of the Tuesday Meeting, Phoebe was also active in urban mission work. In the 1840s, she distributed tracts in New York City slums and visited in the city prison. Then in 1850, she founded the Five Points Mission, one of the first urban mission centers. The mission consisted of a chapel, schoolroom, baths, and rent-free apartments for twenty needy families. Additional outreach facilities were added to the mission, including the Five Points House of Industry, which employed 500 people, a day school, and other social service programs.

Phoebe was also a prolific writer. For many years she edited the journal, *The Guide to Holiness*, which featured the testimonies of men and women who had experienced sanctification. Under her editorial leadership, the circulation of *The Guide* rose from 10,000 to 40,000.[21] She also wrote several books, including *The Way of Holiness* (1843), *Entire Devotion to God* (1845), *Faith and Its Effects* (1848), *Promise of the Father* (1859), and its shortened version, *Tongues of Fire on the Daughters of the Lord* (1869).

On Women

In her 400-page book, *Promise of the Father*, Phoebe argued on biblical grounds for women's right to speak in public. Her favorite verse came from the story in Acts 2 known as Pentecost, when the Holy Spirit in the form of "tongues of fire" descended on a crowd in Jerusalem. In the midst of the story, the biblical author quoted from the Old Testament prophet, Joel, who proclaimed that when the Spirit was poured out, *all flesh*, including women, would prophesy: "And it shall come to pass, after those days, that I will pour out my Spirit upon all flesh, and your sons and your daughters shall prophecy" (Joel 2:28–29; Acts 2:17–18). Phoebe considered this the paradigmatic verse because it encapsulated the *promise of the Father* who has imparted to women, in the last days of this present age, the power to bear witness to the saving and sanctifying gospel of Jesus Christ.

The opening lines of the excerpt clarified Phoebe's perspective on the "woman question." She remarked that she would not push for women's ordination; she distanced herself from proponents of women's rights and sanctioned women remaining in their prescribed sphere. Nevertheless, she recognized that there may "occasionally" be exceptions to this norm. Phoebe, herself, was an exception, and by her example, she emboldened scores of women to speak in public. In addition, central to her teaching was the belief that if men and women did not testify to their experience of sanctification, then they might lose it. As a result, many women, particularly in the holiness movement, raised their voice to speak about their sanctification. Phoebe's influence can be traced directly to several notable women, such as Catherine Booth, cofounder of The Salvation Army with her husband and mother of Evangeline Booth,[22] Frances Willard, author of *Woman in the Pulpit* and long-time president of the Woman's Christian Temperance Union, and Amanda Berry Smith.[23]

Do not be startled, dear reader. We do not intend to discuss the question of "Women's Rights" or of "Women's Preaching," technically so called. We leave this for those whose ability and tastes may better fit them for discussions of this sort. We believe woman has her legitimate sphere of action, which differs in most cases materially from that of man; and in this legitimate sphere she is both happy and useful. Yet we do not doubt that some reforms contemplated in recent movements may, in various respects, be decidedly advantageous. But we have never conceived that it would be subservient to the happiness, usefulness, or true dignity of woman, were she permitted to occupy a prominent part in legislative halls, or take a leading position in the orderings of church conventions. Ordinarily, these are not the circumstances where woman can best serve her generation according to the will of God. Yet facts show that it is in the order of God that woman may occasionally be brought out of the ordinary sphere of action, and occupy in either church or state positions of high responsibility; and if, in the orderings of providence, it so occur, the God of providence will enable her to meet the emergency with becoming dignity, wisdom, and womanly grace.

Examples of modern and ancient days might be furnished of women who have been called to fill positions involving large responsibilities, both civil and ecclesiastical. . . . And when, in the order of God, woman has from time to time been called to sustain positions of momentous trust, involving the destinies of her country, facts show that she has not been wanting in ability to meet the demands of her station in such a manner, as to command the respect of her constituents or the homage of her subjects. Look at Her Most Gracious Majesty Queen Victoria, the reigning sovereign of the most mighty, intelligent people of this or any other age. Who questions her ability for her station, and talks of her as having transcended the bounds set by public opinion of the sphere of woman?

And is it in religion alone that woman is prone to overstep the bounds of propriety, when the impellings of her Heaven-baptized soul would lead her to come out from the cloister, and take positions of usefulness for God? Whence has the idea obtained that she may not even open her lips for God in the assembly of the pious, without being looked upon repulsively, as though she were unwomanly in her aims and predilections?

And where is the beloved female disciple of any denomination, truly baptized of the Holy Ghost, but feels the Spirit's urgings to open her mouth for God? We do not now speak of that cold, worldly conformed professor, who has never, in obedience to the command of the Saviour, tarried at Jerusalem, as did Mary and the other women, on the day of the Pentecost.[24] We speak of that consistently pious, earnest, Christian woman, whose every-day life is an ever-speaking testimony of an indwelling Saviour, and on whose head the tongue of fire has descended. And it is of the power of an ever-present Jesus that the Spirit would have her testify; but the seal of silence has been placed on her lips. And who has placed the seal of silence on those heaven-touched lips? Who would restrain the lips of those whom God has endued with the gift of utterance, when those lips would fain abundantly utter the memory of God's great goodness? Not worldly opinions or usages, for these reprove. Think of a refined social gathering of worldlings, to which invitations have been extended to ladies with the expectation that the seal of silence would be imposed! No, it is not the world that forbids; for due consideration will constrain us to acknowledge that in this regard "the children of this world are wiser in their generation than the children of light."[25] Who is it then that forbids that woman should open her mouth in either prayer or speaking in the assemblies of the saints?[26]

And here we come to the point, and are forced to an answer to which in the name of the Head of the church we claim a rejoinder. Our answer is this: The Christian churches of the present day, with but few exceptions, have imposed silence on Christian women, so that her voice may but seldom be heard in Christian assemblies.[27]

These next three paragraphs from her book, *Tongues of Fire on the Daughters of the Lord*, a shortened version of *Promise of the Father*, continued in a more pointed way her critique of the church that has buried women's gifts in a Potter's Field.[28]

Again we repeat that it is our most solemn conviction that the use of a gift of power delegated to the Church as a specialty of the last days has been neglected,—a gift which, if properly recognized, would have hastened the latter-day glory. We believe that tens of thousands more of the redeemed family would have been won over to the world's Redeemer if it had not been for the tardiness of the Church in acknowledging this gift. . . .

We believe that the attitude of the Church in relation to this matter is most grievous in the sight of her Lord, who has purchased the whole human family unto himself, and would fain have every possible agency employed in preaching the gospel to every creature. He whose name is Faithful and True has fulfilled his ancient promise, and poured out his Spirit as truly upon his daughters as upon his sons.[29]

God has, in all ages of the Church, called some of his handmaids to eminent publicity and usefulness; and when the residue of the Spirit is poured out, and the millennium glory ushered in, the prophecy of Joel[30] being fully accomplished in all its glory, then, probably, there will be such a sweet blending into one spirit,—the spirit of faith, of love, and of a sound mind; such a willingness to receive profit by any instrument; such a spirit of humility, in honor preferring one another,[31]—that the wonder will then be, that the exertions of pious females to bring souls to Christ should ever have been opposed or obstructed.[32]

Phoebe experienced serious health problems throughout her life, due no doubt to her grueling schedule, and she often had to rest and recuperate for lengthy periods. By September of the year she died, she was confined to bed with blindness, kidney disease, and heart trouble. She died on November 2, 1874, at the age of sixty-six. After Phoebe's death, Walter wrote these words about her in a letter to some close friends. "She was an angel on earth. She was the model mother, the loving wife, the perfect Christian lady. She was God's chosen one, and faithfully did she obey the instructions of His word. . . . But, dear sister, forgive me, my dear Phoebe made up the most of me, and what there is left of me on this side of the river I want you to pray for as never before. I am not rebellious, but, O, the wound is so deep!"[33]

Notes

1. Phoebe Palmer, *The Way of Holiness, with Notes by the Way: Being a Narrative of Religious Experience, Resulting from a Determination to be a Bible Christian* (New York: Piercy and Reed, 1843), 53.

2. Richard Wheatley, *The Life and Letters of Mrs. Phoebe Palmer* (New York: W. C. Palmer, 1881); reprint edn. (New York: Garland, 1984), 21. Her desire for this "full assurance" would not be resolved until she reached the age of thirty and had lived through the death of three children.

3. Palmer, *The Way of Holiness*, 26.

4. The altar was a significant metaphor for Phoebe based on Matthew 23:19: "the altar sanctifieth the gift." The act of "laying all on the altar" was the first step, in her understanding, to the experience of sanctification. "Placing all on the altar illustrated the active role individuals played in seeking sanctification. The gift that was to be laid on the symbolic altar of Christ was comprehensive, requiring complete consecration." [Susie Stanley, *Holy Boldness: Women Preachers' Autobiographies and the Sanctified Self* (Knoxville: University of Tennessee, 2002), 72.] The next step was then to have faith that God accepted the gift and sanctified the giver. For more on Phoebe's altar metaphor, see Stanley, *Holy Boldness*, 69–79 and Diane Leclerc, *Singleness of Heart: Gender, Sin, and Holiness in Historical Perspective*, Pietist and Wesleyan Studies, No. 13 (Lanham, MD: Scarecrow, 2001), 116–21.

5. 1 John 1:7.

6. Hebrews 11:1–3. Palmer, *The Way of Holiness*, 103–05. *The Way of Holiness* was Phoebe's first and perhaps most influential book, since it "went through three editions in its first year of print and was still being issued—by then in its fifty-second edition—some twelve years after Palmer's death." Harold E. Raser, *Phoebe Palmer: Her Life and Thought*, Studies in Women and Religion, vol. 22 (Lewiston, NY: Edwin Mellen, 1987), 58.

7. Wheatley, *Life and Letters*, 251.

8. When she addressed a gathered audience, Phoebe did not consider what she was doing as preaching. Instead she called it "bearing witness," "prophesying," or "exhorting." Preaching had a negative connotation for her; she considered that it was oratory based upon "metaphysical hair-splittings in theology." When she spoke, she was simply telling the good news. "We have nothing more to do than Mary, when, by the command of the Head of the Church, she proclaimed a risen Jesus to her brethren. [John 20:18] . . . We occupy the desk, platform, or pulpit, as best suited to the people in order that all may hear and see." [See Wheatley, *Life and Letters*, 614. For a discussion of her "preaching," see Raser, *Phoebe Palmer*, 76–79.] Phoebe did not feel inclined to seek ordination or even a license to preach.

9. See note 19, chapter 3.

10. Lest this phrase be interpreted that Walter was the primary preacher of the two, a contemporary account of one of their meetings described their respective roles in this way. "It is not the custom of Mrs. Palmer to name a text, but when the meeting is under her direction she desires her husband to open the services with reading the Scriptures, from which, after a few easy and pertinent remarks by the Doctor, she derives her theme. She may occupy twenty minutes or even an hour." Rev. J. A. Roche, "Mrs. Phoebe

Palmer" *The Ladies' Repository* (February 1866): 68; cited in Raser, *Phoebe Palmer*, 118.

11. John 3:17.

12. She accepted a doctrine of dispensations, most likely as iterated by John Fletcher (1730–85), that considered divine grace and revelation as being progressively poured out as God's salvation history moved along. "This doctrine of dispensations entails the belief that there are normally four stages of faith which believers pass through in the course of their lives. These personal stages of development are abstracted from the public history of salvation as typified in the ages of Noah (Gentilism), Moses (Judaism), John the Baptist (and the disciples of Jesus during his earthly life), and the risen Lord (the post-Pentecostal period)." [Laurence W. Wood, *The Meaning of Pentecost in Early Methodism: Rediscovering John Fletcher as John Wesley's Vindicator and Designated Successor*, Kingswood Books (Nashville, TN: Abingdon, 2002), 6, 159 n. 2; see also Randy Maddox, "Wesley's Understanding of Christian Perfection: In What Sense Pentecostal?" *Wesleyan Theological Journal* 34.2 (1999): 78–83.] Phoebe considered the present dispensation to be almost at an end and anticipated Jesus' soon return.

13. Acts 2:1.

14. Matthew 3:11; Luke 3:16.

15. See n. 8, chapter 1.

16. John 12:21.

17. Methodist superintendents, or presiding elders, are overseers of a group of ministers in an annual conference. These church officials function as the "de facto bishop" for a geographical area. The office of presiding elder was officially recognized in 1792, though it had been in place unofficially in American Methodism prior to that time. See James E. Kirby, *The Episcopacy in American Methodism*, Kingswood Books (Nashville, TN: Abingdon, 2000), 54–55, 87–88.

18. Full salvation is another name for sanctification.

19. Matthew 24:31; 1 Corinthians 15:52.

20. Wheatley, *Life and Letters*, 318–22.

21. Raser, *Phoebe Palmer*, 71.

22. For more on Evangeline Booth, see chapter 12.

23. For more on Amanda Berry Smith, see chapter 6.

24. The reference here is to Mary, mother of Jesus. See Acts 1:14; 2:3.

25. Luke 16:8.

26. 1 Corinthians 14:34.

27. Phoebe Palmer, *Promise of the Father; or A Neglected Speciality of the Last Days* (Boston: Henry V. Degen, 1859), 1–5.

28. The Potter's Field was a tract of land near Jerusalem where strangers and foreigners were buried. In the New Testament, the field is associated with Judas, the disciple who betrayed Jesus. According to Matthew 27:1–10, after Judas betrayed Jesus, he was filled with remorse and returned the thirty silver coins to the Jewish leaders who had paid him to lead them to Jesus. With the rejected coins, the leaders bought the Potter's Field as a burial place for strangers and foreigners. Phoebe's application of this term to the burying of women's gifts by the church is particularly poignant.

29. Joel 2:28–32; Acts 2:17–21.

30. Joel 2:28–32; Acts 2:17–21.
31. Romans 12:10.
32. Phoebe Palmer, *Selected Writings*, Sources of American Spirituality, ed. Thomas C. Oden (New York: Paulist, 1988), 39.
33. George Hughes, *The Beloved Physician, Dr. Walter C. Palmer, M.D., and His Sun-Lit Journey to the Celestial City* (New York: Palmer and Hughes, 1884), 223–34; cited in Raser, *Phoebe Palmer*, 73. Two years after Phoebe's death, Walter married Phoebe's sister, Sarah.

Methodist holiness evangelist, leader in the Woman's Christian Temperance Union, organizer of women's home and foreign missionary organizations in The Methodist Episcopal Church, founder of the New York Evangelical Training School and Settlement House, Professor of English Language and Literature at Illinois Wesleyan University, and author of 200 articles and 17 books, including *God's Great Women, How to Win Souls,* and *The Potential Woman*

Jennie Fowler Willing, author of *How to Win Souls* (Chicago: Christian Witness, 1909).

CHAPTER 5

JENNIE FOWLER WILLING
(1834–1916)

J ennie Fowler, one of three children born to Horatio and Harriet
Ryan Fowler, was raised on a farm in Illinois. At the age of two-
and-a-half, she fell into a well, struck her head against the side,
and sustained severe nerve damage. Her injury caused chronic health problems that in turn affected her schooling. Although she was not able to
attend school after age nine, she continued her education, during the periods when she was free from pain, by teaching herself with the help of her
parents.

Jennie was converted in her youth during an evangelistic service held in
her town, but she wrote little about that experience. She referred more
often in her writing to her experience of sanctification at the age of
twenty-eight.

On Her Sanctification

I shall never forget the hour when I made that surrender. One afternoon when
the Holy Spirit sent His light into the depths of my soul, I discovered, hidden
away, like the wedge of gold in Achan's tent,[1] a determination to work, and
study, and make something of myself. Not that I might win the wealth and honors of the world, but I would make for myself a dainty, little snuggery into which
I would bring a few fine books and pictures, some good music, and a coterie of
choice friends. The loud, rough, coarse old world might wag its way, and not a
whit would I care for its tinsel and show, nor its troubles, either,—do you see?
The Lord in kindness threw a picture upon the canvas that day, that gave me
to see how wickedly selfish was my little scheme. I saw myself in a hospital with
scores of people who were dying, and there was no one to give them their
medicine, or even a cup of cold water. I had been sent there under orders to
help all whom I could possibly reach; and there I was, planning to fit up my
exquisite little room, in one corner, its walls padded to shut out the groans, and
to shut in the delicacy and beauty that I hoped to gather about me. I saw that
selfishness like that could never get into Heaven. . . . When I saw that, I was
enabled to say, "I give it all up. Henceforth for me, only thy will, and thy work."

The pain of the surrender was so severe that a knife seemed to pierce my heart, and the tears leaped from my eyes. Let me add that all these years, just in proportion as I have held myself loyal to that surrender, has God given me richly to enjoy the things that I put aside to accept His will.[2]

In this next excerpt, Jennie made the connection between her sanctification and her dedication to her self-education method, which was so successful that she was hired as a teacher by a local school and later by Illinois Wesleyan University as Professor of English Language and Literature. Although she wrote it in the third person, it clearly described her own situation.

I know a woman who had many a battle, sharp and bitter, because she was hedged by ill health and poverty from the studies in which she delighted. At twenty-eight she gave herself fully to the Lord, and trusted Him to cleanse her from all sin. Then, with purified motives, she asked God to help her get the education for which her heart had always clamored. She asked it for His glory, that she might do more for Him. Everything seemed to be in the way of the answer. Her physician told her that even a light degree of brain work would probably result in paralysis. An oculist, one of the best on the continent, told her, after a close examination of her eyes, that if she would give them perfect rest for six months, and then come back to him, he would tell her if there was any hope for her to escape the threatened paralysis of the retina. God did not work any signs or wonders[3] in answer to her prayer, but He gave her strength for work, day after day. She began a course of reading, and to write for the papers, in a darkened room, with a little light coming in over one shoulder. She also took up the study of German, though she could not tell a "B" from a "V" without turning the book sidewise. She could not afford a teacher, and she could spare only fifteen minutes a day for her German, because she did her own house-work, light, heavy and all; the sewing for her family, and everything possible for her church and Sunday-school, beside entertaining no end of company. She made one little rule when she began, and she adhered to it rigidly. She held herself under bonds for an actual fifteen minutes of study each day; and if she failed one day she had to make it up as soon as possible. She could read German readily before she was in circumstances to study a single hour without work in her hands. She did not go through all the text-books of a college course, but she had the result of the drill as certainly as she would if she had graduated in her youth. At forty she was carrying a heavy benevolent work, editing a monthly paper, and filling a professorship in a university. She had learned to hold herself inexorably to a given duty at a given time, as if she obeyed the call of a college bell four years. She could fix her attention on the thing in hand as well, probably, as if she had been under the stimulus of class emulation and professorial influence a given period. She could make the shuttle of her thought fly as nimbly through the web of affairs, as if she had translated the college Greek and Latin, with the German and French thrown in. If many others have tried to do the same thing and failed, it is possibly because they did not trust God as she was driven to do when everything was against her. [4]

In 1853, she married a Methodist minister, William Cossgrove Willing. Most of their married life was spent in Illinois, where William pastored Methodist churches while Jennie taught at Illinois Wesleyan University and was active in mission and temperance organizations. Their marriage was a partnership of equals with each supporting the other's work. An example of such reciprocity occurred when William, the presiding elder in the district,[5] issued Jennie a license to preach in 1873.[6] In turn, she served a small church in William's district. In a letter to Jennie, William wrote of his commitment to her ministry in a manner that poked fun at the double standard that accepted a man's prolonged absence from home, but not a woman's.

> We men are a selfish lot. Everyone of us will avail himself of the help in evangelistic or temperance work that some other man's wife can give, but it is quite another thing when it comes to having our comfort interfered with. . . . Everybody pities me because you leave me alone so much. I don't know whether they think I'm too delicate, or that I can't be trusted to stay alone. If I were a bishop, or a brakeman on a freight-train, or anybody between the two, I might leave you months at a time, and nobody would make a fuss about it.[7]

Jennie committed herself to three areas of church-related ministries: mission, temperance, and evangelism. First, in terms of missionary work, she served as an officer in both the Woman's Foreign Missionary Society (WFMS) and the Woman's Home Missionary Society (WHMS) of The Methodist Episcopal Church. From 1886–1890, as Secretary of the Bureau for Spanish Work of the WHMS, she oversaw its work in New Mexico and Arizona. Then, their shared commitment to city mission work prompted Jennie and William to move to New York City in order to work in inner city churches.

Second, in terms of temperance,[8] Jennie gave a stirring speech on women and temperance in 1874, which prompted many who heard it to consider forming a national temperance organization. She then chaired for a year the meetings which eventually gave rise to the national Woman's Christian Temperance Union (WCTU).[9] In addition, she served in several other capacities for the WCTU, including vice president of the national organization, editor of its first periodical, and president of the Illinois Woman's Temperance Union. The WCTU also provided a forum for combining her commitments to temperance and evangelism. From 1895 until her death, she was a WCTU Evangelist, and she also served for several years as Secretary of the Department of Evangelistic Institutes and Training for the WCTU. Under the umbrella of this department, she founded the New York Evangelical Training School and Settlement House in 1895 and ran it until 1910, when the Pennsylvania Railroad Company closed the school and tore down its building in order to build tunnels underneath it. Her training school's publication, *The Open Door*, was an important venue for bringing together "all her causes in one magazine for a combined frontal attack on the evils of this world."[10]

Third, in terms of evangelism, she preached at camp meetings, in churches, and city missions. She founded the aforementioned training school to train workers in evangelism, and she was its principal, teacher, and the regular preacher for its nightly services.

On Her Evangelistic Method: *How to Win Souls*

Jennie wrote extensively on evangelism in several venues, including a monthly column entitled, "Women and Gospel Evangelism," in the periodical, *Guide to Holiness*, as well as a book on evangelistic methodology, *How to Win Souls*. This book was first given as a series of lectures at her training institute. When the school closed, she published the lectures in a book, so that more workers might be trained in evangelism. In the book's introduction, a Methodist bishop, Willard Mallalieu, described in glowing terms the import of this book from "a woman's pen."

> . . . many books great and small, have been written in regard to revivals, evangelism, and soul winning. . . .
>
> But how rarely has a woman's pen given us a book on these important themes. In due time another is added to the scanty list. And why should not women write books of this kind. . . .
>
> Thank God that now we have one more book, and that the product of a woman's hand, and brain, and heart, that ought to attract the attention of all who covet the wisdom essential to be successful soul winners. . . .
>
> If the seventy thousand, more or less, Protestant clergymen in the United States, and as many more Christian men, and as many more Christian women would read this book, catch its spirit, follow its suggestions, and work out, in daily life, its soul winning methods, this whole land of ours would speedily become the prepared inheritance of the Lord Jesus Christ.[11]

Chapter XXV
ONE WORD MORE.

Many are saying, "Yes: we agree with all that is written here. Soulwinning is certainly the most glorious work ever committed to human beings. What can be higher, or nobler, than being coworkers with Christ in saving souls from eternal death? But cannot some one give us to see just how it can be done?"

In a general way we have laid down the axioms that govern evangelistic success. We may add another, a little more personal. An evangelist must not only have deep devoutness of spirit, but sound, common sense. Then, enlightened and guided by the Holy Spirit, one will find the right thing to be done and the right way to do it. Thoughtful observers may wonder at the "generalship"; but the one who has been shut away, alone with God, will understand fully that Spirit-guided common sense is in control.

A few practical hints may help the human side of the work.

An evangelist must be kept, during services, in the best condition of spirit, mind, and body. One who is fit for the place must think out and pray out, the spiritual, mental, and physical, hygienic laws that must be observed, to that end.

One must believe, "I am in His hand to be used for this work, at this time; and I must be at my best, and do my best for His sake."

One must know that of the calls that have come for service, this engagement was made according to the Divine will: and this work must be done heartily, as unto the Lord. Engagements must not be carelessly made, or lightly set aside, for fear of a loss of reputation for stability and reliableness.

A good evangelist, like a good general, plans every detail, before the actual conflict....

One must plan in advance how to capture the children, the young people, the church members, the singers, the townspeople, and get them all immediately, interested in the work. Committees must be appointed to look after all these items, as well as for printing, finance, temperance, social purity, and all other special lines that ought to be brought in as departments of the services.

While the laborer is worthy of his hire,[12] it is usually better to leave one's personal remuneration entirely with the Lord, to save the temptation and accusation of mercenary motives. A commercial spirit is at swordspoints with the gospel: and an evangelist must keep utterly clear of it. If one can trust the Lord to give a hundred souls as the fruit of a revival, he can certainly believe for the care of his own small, personal finance.

One must be careful of his entertainment during the services. When the best has been done to secure the privilege of being shut away, alone with God, no matter how charming, or how chilling the hospitality, one must remember that there is but one thing to do, the winning to Christ, of all souls within reach.

One with sufficient common sense for so great a work, would not need more than a hint to guard against depleting sociality, undue familiarity with persons of the opposite sex, carelessness in dress, manners, or speech keeping the pastor from his rightful place before the congregation, remembering that he must stay, and do, by far, the heavier part of the work, after the evangelist is gone, and similar properties and improprieties, that will prejudice people for, or against the work....

All through the services, the evangelist must have a steady, simple faith that the Lord's hand is on the helm. The answer for victory must be had, before the work is opened, and held through thick and thin. . . .

Every revival work has its "ups and downs." The evangelist's faith is most needed when it is in the "downs." Anybody can be in good spirits when it is "up."

One who had been holding meetings sometime at different points in her husband's District, came to see that it must be settled whether or not she had a Divine "call."[13] She did not fully believe that a woman ought to do "public work;" but if He called one, He might call many: so the main question would be settled. Then, if He called them, He was bound to fit them for the service, no matter how incompetent they felt.

After nearly a week of prayer, she found herself in a little country church, where the pastor had been holding "meetings" for six weeks without one convert. In the low-ceilinged lecture room, the old saints sat in the front rows looking discouragedly down their noses, while their revival-hardened sons and daughters behind them, were in all sorts of mischief. When she gave the "alter call,"[14] not a sinner came forward, and the young people hardly stopped their fun.

Then the evangelist gave a second invitation, throwing herself back on the Lord's promise so resolutely, that she took no note of what was going on around her. While she exhorted mechanically, her soul cried to the Lord, "Thou didst send me here: and Thou must stand by Thine own work!"

She was recalled to what was passing, by the moving of the chairs, and there were those giddy, young people, on their knees about her, praying God to have mercy on their souls.

That was Saturday evening. The next afternoon she went into the audience room, and seeing the organ in front of the alter, she asked the sexton to move it to one side "Because," she said, "it will be in the way of the seekers when they come to the alter." Through her blind faith, the Lord was pleased to work, and forty came "forward" that evening.

The eyes of the evangelist must be closed to obstacles, and held steadily wide open, upon the promises of God. "Who is blind as he that is perfect, and blind as the Lord's servant?"[15]

It takes months and years of training to prepare one to excel in business, scholarship, athletics; how much more important it is to work hard to prepare one's self for every item of soulwinning service?

After all is said and done, it is "God who giveth the increase."[16] The motto of success must ever be,

"HAVE FAITH IN GOD."[17]

On Women

Jennie adamantly exhorted women to be active in doing work for God, and she considered the first line of women's work to be in their home. "Let the home, where she does her best work, have her strongest thought, her main strength, her most devout prayer."[18] If she were a mother, then a woman's greatest work for God was to raise children in the faith. She reasoned, "Among the mightiest of undiscovered forces, the mother's power for good ranks all."[19] Whether mothers or not, Jennie urged all women, as in the excerpt below, to "use their strength for the world's bettering." She chastised women who allowed laziness or vanity to deter them from their work for God. In particular, she named women who wasted money on dressing their dogs in "satins, ermine and jewels," or who wasted their time on "queer bits of fancy work," or on "neighborhood tangles that yield only a harvest of gossip and ill-feeling." After all, in Jennie's opinion, every woman was a missionary.

Every Woman a Missionary

While we remember that the woman was the first sinner,[20] we must not forget that she was the first penitent, and that the first promise of a Saviour from sin was given to her.[21] He who in aftertime should redeem the race, was to be born of a woman, though the Eternal Son of God.

Women ought to do their best to get sin out of the world, for they have always been the greatest sufferers from the Fall.[22] Not that the physical ills that come from their being kept delicately by those whose passions are pleased by their beauty, were a special curse for the leading part taken by Eve in the dire disaster;[23] for heathen women, the very last ones to escape a moral blight, are usually free from those sorrows, especially when they bear a part in the masculine malediction of eating bread by the sweat of the brow. Not of necessity from mental or social inferiority, for God thrusts into their hands the finest and best work that He trusts in this world at all—the shaping of the mind and destiny of little children. But, in the disordered condition of things arising from the dominance of men and the shirking of women, it has come about that every load that sin lashes upon human shoulders falls most heavily upon the woman.

Women are the greatest debtors to grace. Jesus, the son of Mary, is the best friend they ever had, or ever will have. The Bible is their one book of emancipation and privilege. Every woman ought to be loyal to God to the heart's core. Every one ought to do her utmost to bring everybody that lives to know her Lord.

We are shocked when money-mad women waste thousands on their dogs, dressing them in satins, ermine and jewels. To be sure, that is a harmless fad compared with the club life, races, smoking, drinking and kindred vices, upon which men throw away, not only their money, but their life and their chance of salvation. The woman's whim shocks us, because we have a right to expect better things of her. She may shape the life of her child, an immortal, for whom all heaven cares. She is its teacher during the susceptible years, when lessons are learned that last to the end of time.

But not all women are mothers. No; but all women may teach little children, if they will. The care and money that designs a trousseau for an ugly little pug, and keeps a nurse for it, would take a street waif from the gutter, and start it toward heaven.

Women are designed and fitted for evangelism. From the nature of the work that usually falls to them, the care of children and old people, ministering beside cradles and sickbeds, they learn easily the small, sweet courtesies that help on the effort to reach diseased souls. They have the habit of close attention to minute details, so essential to successful character building. Character is not made by a lucky hit on 'Change, nor a brilliant *coup d'etat*. It depends, like a masterpiece of genius, on infinitesimal strokes and touches, not one of which seems to amount to much, but every one of which is necessary to the result. A woman is trained to carefulness and accuracy, fitting her to become the true character-builder.

Women are the trustful half of the human family. From long clothes to shroud they find themselves in places where they live only as kings claim to rule, by the grace of God. So two of them become our Lord's followers where one man trusts Him for salvation. They must be devout. With their hearts' strings tangled about feet that wander to the world's end, many of them exist only by faith. Self-denial is their daily bread,[24] living for others their luxury.

They do the bulk of the teaching, so they become skilled in finding ways by which human hearts can be opened to the Spirit of truth. Owing to the hedging in of the "dolorous, accursed centuries," they have few chances to reach directly many souls, so they are apt to make the most of their opportunities. They learn what Andrew Murray[25] calls the "greater things" which our Lord promised His disciples that they might do if they would believe:[26] they learn to share the work that now occupies Him, intercessory prayer.

Women are sensitive. A true woman never attempts to force a way for the truth with which she is entrusted. As dumb things know when the weather will change, she knows when it will do to crowd a plan, and when she must wait. She enters into the sorrows and joys of others, and so gains power over them. Her quick sensibilities enable her to make common cause with others, so that she can lead them to what is right.

Women who have not the crown and glory of motherhood must use their strength for the world's bettering. I knew one who had been ill in bed for thirty years, much of the time in severe pain, unable to use even her hands. How could she reach the outside world? Where there is a will there is a way. People of affairs were glad to spend an hour in her room now and then, for it was a suburb of heaven. No means of grace brought the Holy Spirit more surely to the soul than did her whispered words of counsel, prayer and praise.

Woman has the home-making instinct. Give her half a chance, and she will use this power most beautifully for the Master. I used to know a woman whose only child died in infancy, and she mothered twenty-one waifs and strays. They were all set at work, and they were all soundly converted. It was amusing to hear them tell where they first found the Lord's love. One stood at the sink washing dishes. Another knelt in the manger after he had fed the horses. A third was saved while Uncle Austin was praying at the family altar. Surely those people were home missionaries of the right sort. When our Lord came to the door in the person of one of the least of His little ones, they took Him in; hungry, they fed Him; naked, they clothed Him.[27] I am afraid in heaven I shall hardly catch a glimpse of those dear, plain, farmer people, they will be so near to the throne.

All women can "do the next thing" for the Master. One may write or say elegant sentimentalisms about caring for the masses while she neglects the soul of her cook, and has never a nod of kindly recognition for the shabby lad who brings her groceries. Home mission work must begin at home, or it dies the death it deserves.

If a woman has executive force over and above what her family needs— and many a one has,—she had better not waste it on queer bits of fancy work, and certainly not on neighborhood tangles that yield only a harvest of gossip and ill-feeling. We would not advise her to pour out on one victim of vice, pity and effort enough to reform a whole community. If she has the gift of doing a great deal quickly and well, which the Yankees call "facukty," she can use it to advantage in rescue homes, industrial homes, training homes that seek far and near for matrons such as she. Let her make herself thoroughly capable, and the Lord will open for her a door which no man can shut. Our noble Woman's Societies have the best mechanism, always needing steady nerve, clear thinking and a loyal purpose. Those who are not called to foreign fields must support the work of those who go. A deal of prayer is needed by those who are at the front, and who have never a prayer meeting to brighten their spiritual life. Women do their full share of that work. Their supplications may be a mallet to drive the wedge to the heart of the log that has resisted the tornadoes of centuries. And in the final day they will not fail of their reward. In these days the prophecy of the Psalmist is being fulfilled: "The Lord gave the word: great was the company of women that published it. Kings of armies did flee apace; and she that tarried at home divided the spoil."[28]

Jennie lived true to her motto, *plus ultra*—more beyond.[29] When she died at age eighty-two, she was president emeritus of the 18th Street Methodist Episcopal Church Woman's Foreign Missionary Society, president of the Frances Willard Woman's Christian Temperance Union of New York City, and organizer for the New York State Woman's Christian Temperance Union.[30]

Notes

1. Achan was an Israelite who disobeyed God's command not to take spoil from conquered Jericho. He hid gold, silver, and "a goodly Babylonish garment" beneath his tent (Joshua 7:12).

2. Jennie Fowler Willing, *From Fifteen to Twenty-five* (Boston: McDonald and Gill, 1885), 75–77.

3. Acts 2:22.

4. Willing, *From Fifteen to Twenty-five*, 70–72.

5. See n. 17, chapter 4.

6. Seven years later, the 1880 General Conference of The Methodist Episcopal Church revoked all preaching licenses previously issued to women, including Jennie's.

7. Jennie Fowler Willing, *A Prince of the Realm* (Cincinnati: Cranston and Curts, 1895), 42; cited in Joanne Carlson Brown, "Shared Fire: The Flame Ignited by Jennie Fowler Willing," in *Spirituality and Social Responsibility: Vocational Vision of Women in The United Methodist Tradition*, ed. Rosemary Skinner Keller (Nashville, TN: Abingdon, 1993), 100.

8. Temperance, in this case, refers to abstinence from intoxicating beverages.

9. Brown, "Shared Fire," 101.

10. Brown, "Shared Fire," 104.

11. Willard F. Mallalieu, "Introduction," *How to Win Souls* (Chicago: Christian Witness, 1909), 5–7.

12. Luke 10:7.

13. As before, Jennie utilized a third-person style to tell a story about herself.

14. The altar, generally a railing of some sort, was in the front area of the worship service. Following the sermon and/or the exhortation, those who were affected and under conviction were called forward to the altar, hence the term, altar call, where they would be prayed over and encouraged toward conversion.

15. Isaiah 42:19.

16. 1 Corinthians 3:7.

17. Jennie Fowler Willing, *How to Win Souls* (Chicago: Christian Witness, 1909), 213–20.

18. Jennie Fowler Willing, *The Potential Woman* (Boston: McDonald & Gill, 1886), 182.

19. Jennie Fowler Willing, "The Mother's Power in Evangelism," *The Guide to Holiness* (December 1896): 220.

20. The reference is to Eve. See Genesis 3:1–24.

21. The reference is to Mary, the mother of Jesus. See Matthew 1:18–25; Luke 1:26–38, 2:1–7.

22. The Fall refers to the disobedience of Adam and Eve who, despite God's command against it, ate fruit from the tree of the knowledge of good and evil (Genesis 2:17). Because of their action, they "fell" from innocence and immortality and were expelled from the garden. See Genesis 3:1–24.

23. Genesis 3:1–24.

24. Matthew 6:11; Luke 11:3.

25. Andrew Murray (1828–1917) was a missionary and minister in South Africa who wrote many books on the Christian life. In this context of intercessory prayer, most likely Jennie was referring to his book titled, *With Christ in the School of Prayer*.

26. John 1:50.

27. Matthew 25:40, 45.

28. Psalm 68:11–12. Jennie Fowler Willing, "Every Woman a Missionary," *The Guide to Holiness* (November 1896): 178–79.

29. Joanne Carlson Brown, "Jennie Fowler Willing (1834–1916): Methodist Churchwoman and Reformer," Ph.D. Dissertation (Boston University, 1983), 39.

30. Brown, "Jennie Fowler Willing," 38.

Amanda Smith

African Methodist holiness evangelist, emancipated slave, founder of the Amanda Smith Orphanage and Industrial Home for Abandoned and Destitute Colored Children, author of *An Autobiography: The Story of the Lord's Dealings with Mrs. Amanda Smith, The Colored Evangelist*

Courtesy of the American Antiquarian Society.

CHAPTER 6

AMANDA BERRY SMITH
(1837–1915)

Amanda Berry was the oldest girl in a family of thirteen children, five of whom were born into slavery. Her parents, Samuel and Mariam Berry, were slaves on adjacent farms. Samuel worked overtime, "in the fields until two o'clock at night, or making brooms" in order to buy himself and his family out of slavery.[1] Eventually, the Berry family relocated from Maryland to York County, Pennsylvania, where they settled on a farm owned by a prosperous, white family. The underground railroad was active in the county, and Amanda's parents frequently harbored runaway slaves. In her autobiography, Amanda recounted how her father labored by day in the fields and then led slaves by night to the next underground railroad station. Her formal education was severely limited due to her race, so she was mostly educated at home by her parents. When she was eight, an abolitionist opened a school nearby for African American children, but it only operated for six weeks. Five years later, when she was thirteen, she and her brother walked five miles each way to school. This second attempt at a formal education lasted a scant two weeks because the teacher taught them only after she had finished with the white children. Amanda left home shortly after to work as a live-in domestic.

In her new surroundings, Amanda attended a Methodist church and joined a class meeting,[2] but the class leader, like the schoolteacher, made her wait until last to be taught. This practice made her late for preparing her employer's Sunday dinner, so she quit the meetings to keep her job. In 1854, at the age of seventeen, she married Calvin Devine. In a brief but telling description of her husband, Amanda wrote, "He could talk on the subject of religion very sensibly at times; but when strong drink would get the better of him, which I am sorry to say was quite often, then he was very profane and unreasonable."[3] Calvin joined the Union army when black soldiers were admitted, and he never returned from the war. One of their two children, a daughter named Mazie, survived.

Amanda's interest in religion was intermittent until she became deathly ill in 1855. In her weakened state, she had a dream that she was preaching at a camp meeting.[4]

Then, it seemed, I went to a great Camp Meeting and there seemed to be thousands of people, and I was to preach and the platform I had to stand on was up high above the people. It seemed it was erected between two trees, but near the tops. How I got on it I don't know, but I was on this platform with a large Bible opened and I was preaching from these words:—"And I if I be lifted up will draw all men unto me."[5] O, how I preached, and the people were slain right and left.[6] I suppose I was in this vision about two hours. When I came out of it I was decidedly better. When the doctor called in and looked at me he was astonished, but so glad. In a few days I was able to sit up, and in about a week or ten days to walk about. Then I made up my mind to pray and lead a Christian life. I thought God had spared me for a purpose, so I meant to be converted, but in my own way quietly. I thought if I was really sincere it would be all right.[7]

About a year later, on Tuesday, March 17, 1856, Amanda experienced her conversion in the basement of her employer's house, a Quaker family named Mifflins.

On Her Conversion

After I had got out to Mr. Mifflins', I began to plan for my spring suit; I meant to be converted, though I had not given up at all, but I began to save my money up now. There were some pretty styles, and I liked them. A white straw bonnet, with very pretty, broad pink tie-strings; pink or white muslin dress, tucked to the waist; black silk mantilla; and light gaiter boots, with black tips; I had it all picked out in my mind, my nice spring and summer suit. I can see the little box now where I had put my money, saving up for this special purpose. Then I would pray; O, how I prayed, fasted and prayed, read my Bible and prayed, prayed to the moon, prayed to the sun, prayed to the stars. I was so ignorant. O, I wonder how God ever did save me, anyhow. The Devil[8] told me I was such a sinner God would not convert me. When I would kneel down to pray at night, he would say, "You had better give it up; God won't hear you, you are such a sinner."

Then I thought if I could only think of somebody that had not sinned, and my idea of great sin was disobedience, and I thought if I could only think of somebody that had always been obedient. I never thought about Jesus in that sense, and yet I was looking to Him for pardon and salvation.

All at once it came to me, "Why, the sun has always obeyed God, and kept its place in the heavens, and the moon and stars have always obeyed God, and kept their place in the heavens, the wind has always obeyed God, they all have obeyed."

So I began, "O, Sun, you never sinned like me, you have always obeyed God and kept your place in the heavens; tell Jesus I am a poor sinner." Then when I would see the trees move by the wind, I would say "O, Wind, you never sinned like me, you have always obeyed God, and blown at His command; tell Jesus I am a poor sinner."

When I set my people down to tea in the house I would slip out and get under the trees in the yard and look up to the moon and stars and pray,

"O, Moon and Stars, you never sinned like me, you have always obeyed God, and kept your place in the heavens; tell Jesus I am a poor sinner." One day while I was praying I got desperate, and here came my spring suit up constantly before me, so I told the Lord if he would take away the burden that was on my heart that I would never get one of those things. I wouldn't get the bonnet, I wouldn't get the dress, I wouldn't get the mantilla, I wouldn't get the shoes. O, I wanted relief from the burden and then all at once there came a quiet peace in my heart, and that suit never came before me again; but still there was darkness in my soul. On Tuesday, the 17th day of March, 1856, I was sitting in the kitchen by my ironing table, thinking it all over. The Devil seemed to say to me (I know now it was he),

"You have prayed to be converted."

I said, "Yes."

"You have been sincere."

"Yes."

"You have been in earnest."

"Yes."

"You have read your Bible, and you have fasted, and you really want to be converted."

"Yes, Lord, Thou knowest it; Thou knowest my heart, I really want to be converted."

Then Satan said, "Well, if God were going to convert you He would have done it long ago; He does His work quick, and with all your sincerity God has not converted you."

"Yes, that is so."

"You might as well give it up, then," said he, "it is no use, He won't hear you."

"Well, I guess I will just give it up. I suppose I will be damned and I might as well submit to my fate." Just then a voice whispered to me clearly, and said, "Pray once more." And in an instant I said, "I will." Then another voice seemed like a person speaking to me, and it said,

"Don't you do it."

"Yes, I will."

And when I said, "Yes, I will," it seemed to me the emphasis was on the "will," and I felt it from the crown of my head clear through me, "I WILL," and I got on my feet and said, "I will pray once more, and if there is any such thing as salvation, I am determined to have it this afternoon or die."

I got up, put the kettle on, set the table and went into the cellar and got on my knees to pray and die, for I thought I had made a vow to God and that He would certainly kill me, and I didn't care, I was so miserable, and I was just at the verge of desperation. I had put everything on the table but the bread and butter, and I said, "If any one calls me I won't get up, and if the bread and butter is all that is to go on the table, Miss Sue (the daughter) can finish the supper, and that will save them calling for me, and when they come down cellar after it they will find me dead!"

I set the tea pot on the table, put the tea caddy down by it, so that everything would be ready, and I was going to die; and O, Hallelujah, what a dying that was! I went down into the cellar and got on my knees, as I had done so many times before, and I began my prayer. "O Lord, have mercy on my soul, I don't know how else to pray." A voice said to me, "That is just what you said before."

"O, Lord, if Thou wilt only please to have mercy on my soul I will serve Thee the longest day I live."

The Devil said, "You might just as well stop, you said that before."

"O, Lord if Thou wilt only convert my soul and make me truly sensible of it, for I want to know surely that I am converted, I will serve Thee the longest day I live."

"Yes," the Devil says, "you said that before and God has not done it, and you might as well stop."

O, what a conflict. How the darkness seemed to gather around me, and in my desperation I looked up and said, "O, Lord, I have come down here to die, and I must have salvation this afternoon or death. If you send me to hell I will go, but convert my soul." Then I looked up and said, "O, Lord, if thou wilt only please to help me if ever I backslide[9] don't ever let me see thy face in peace." And I waited, and I did not hear the old suggestion that had been following me, "That is just what you said before," so I said it again, "O, Lord, if Thou wilt only please to convert my soul and make me truly sensible of it, if I backslide don't ever let me see Thy face in peace."

I prayed the third time, using these same words. Then somehow I seemed to get to the end of everything. I did not know what else to say or do. Then in my desperation I looked up and said, "O, Lord, if Thou wilt help me I will believe Thee," and in the act of telling God I would, I did. O, the peace and joy that flooded my soul! The burden rolled away; I felt it when it left me, and a flood of light and joy swept through my soul such as I had never known before. I said, "Why, Lord, I do believe this is just what I have been asking for," and down came another flood of light and peace. And I said again, "Why, Lord, I do believe this is what I have asked Thee for." Then I sprang to my feet, all around was light, I was new. I looked at my hands, they looked new; I took hold of myself and said, "Why, I am new, I am new all over." I clapped my hands; I ran up out of the cellar, I walked up and down the kitchen floor. Praise the Lord! There seemed to be a halo of light all over me; the change was so real and so thorough that I have often said that if I had been as black as ink or as green as grass or as white as snow, I would not have been frightened. I went into the dining room; we had a large mirror that went from the floor to the ceiling, and I went and looked in it to see if anything had transpired in my color, because there was something wonderful had taken place inside of me, and it really seemed to me it was outside too, and as I looked in the glass I cried out, "Hallelujah, I have got religion; glory to God, I have got religion!" I was wild with delight and joy; it seemed to me as if I would split![10]

In 1865, Amanda married James Smith in large part because he expressed, falsely so in order to win her affections, a desire to become an ordained minister. She had hoped to be a minister's wife and, through that position, to find an outlet for ministry.[11] The disappointment of her marriage was "grievous." For several years, they lived in squalid conditions while working odd jobs in New York City. All three of their children died before they reached a year old. Constant conflicts between Amanda and James soured their married life, and they were living separately when James died in 1869.

In the midst of her family travails, Amanda experienced sanctification on a September, Sunday morning in 1868. She described the moment in these words, " . . . I seemed to feel a hand, the touch of which I cannot describe. It seemed to press me gently on the top of my head, and I felt something part and roll down and cover me like a great cloak! I felt it distinctly; it was done in a moment, and O what a mighty peace and power took possession of me!"[12] Not long after, she experienced her call to preach in a vision.

On Her Call to Preach

It was the third Sunday in November, 18[7]0.[13] Sister Scott, my band sister,[14] and myself went to the Fleet Street A.M.E. Church, Brooklyn.[15] It was Communion Sunday.[16] Before I left home I said to Sister Scott: "I wish I had not promised to go to Brooklyn." She said "Why?"

"Oh, I feel so dull and stupid."

We went early, and went into the Sabbath School.[17] At the close of the Sabbath School the children sang a very pretty piece. I do not remember what it was, but the spirit of the Lord touched my heart and I was blessed. My bad feelings had gone for a few moments, and I thought, "I guess the Lord wanted to bless me here." But when we went upstairs I began to feel the same burden and pressure as I had before. And I said, "Oh, Lord, help me, and teach me what this means." And just at that point the Tempter came with this supposition: "Now, if you are wholly sanctified, why is it that you have these dull feelings?"

I began to examine my work, my life, every day, and I could see nothing. Then I said, "Lord, help me to understand what Thou meanest. I want to hear Thee speak."

Brother Gould, then pastor of the Fleet Street Church, took his text. I was sitting with my eyes closed in silent prayer to God, and after he had been preaching about ten minutes, as I opened my eyes, just over his head I seemed to see a beautiful star, and as I looked at it, it seemed to form into the shape of a large white tulip; and I said, "Lord, is that what you want me to see? If so, what else?"

And then I leaned back and closed my eyes. Just then I saw a large letter "G," and I said: "Lord, do you want me to read in Genesis, or in Galatians? Lord, what does this mean?"

Just then I saw the letter "O." I said, "Why, that means go." And I said "What else?" And a voice distinctly said to me "Go preach."

The voice was so audible that it frightened me for a moment, and I said, "Oh Lord, is that what you wanted me to come here for? Why did you not tell me when I was at home, or when I was on my knees praying?" But His paths are known in the mighty deep, and His ways are past finding out.

On Monday morning, about four o'clock, I think, I was awakened by the presentation of a beautiful, white cross—white as the driven snow—similar to that described in the last chapter. It was as cold as marble. It was laid just on my forehead and on my breast. It seemed very heavy; to press me down. The weight and the coldness of it were what woke me; and as I woke I said: "Lord, I know what that is. It is a cross."

I arose and got on my knees, and while I was praying these words came to me: "If any man will come after Me let him deny himself and take up his cross and follow Me."[18] And I said, "Lord, help me and I will."[19]

On Her Evangelistic Method: Camp Meetings[20]

In July 1870, Amanda attended her first camp meeting. She and her daughter, Mazie, earned their room and board by carrying water and cooking meals during the meeting for a white family. Amanda made a favorable impression when she preached and sang at that meeting, and soon she became a regular speaker on the camp meeting circuit. These excerpts from her autobiography described Amanda's participation in two different camp meetings.

I had not been accustomed to take part in the meetings, especially when white people were present, and there was a timidity and shyness that much embarrassed me; but whenever called upon, I would ask the Lord to help me, and take the timidity out of me; and He did help me every time.

I remember one Sunday, between the hours of the morning and evening service, there was a great concourse of people. At that time I had a good voice, and could sing very loud. Mrs. L. asked me to go to her tent, and on my way many crowded round me and asked me to sing. Nearby was a large stump. Brother Smith, a class-leader at old Second Street Church, New York, called out, "Sister Smith, step up on that stump so the people may hear you better." By that time there was a crowd around me of about four hundred people. After I had sung one or two pieces, one of which was very familiar and blessed to many—

"All I want, all I want,
Is a little more faith in Jesus."

Brother Smith said, "Sister Smith, suppose you tell the people your experience; how the Lord converted you."

And I asked the Lord to help me if it was His will that I should honor Him in acknowledging what He had done for me. And I felt He would help me, so I trusted in Him and ventured to speak. As I went on my heart grew warm, and the power of the Spirit rested upon me, and many of the people wept, and seemed deeply moved and interested, as they had never been before. God, I believe, blessed that meeting at that big stump on the old Sing Sing Camp Ground. How real it all seems to me now as I think it over, though it was so long ago.[21]

This next excerpt recalled her first southern camp meeting, held in Knoxville, Tennessee. Her northern white friends expressed concern lest she receive harsh treatment in the South, and they attempted to dissuade her from going.

I do not know who preached Saturday night, but my heart was burdened in prayer. On Sunday morning at eight o'clock, Brother Little was lead [sic] the Love Feast service.[22] I was very glad Brother Little had charge of that meeting, as I knew he would not hinder me from speaking as the Lord might lead. Brother Inskip preached at eleven. So the Lord laid it on my heart very heavily that I was to relate my personal experience of how the Lord led me into the blessing of entire sanctification.

The brother that had been talking and arguing so with Brother Grey sat way back in the congregation. It was in the big tent; I shall never forget it. There was a side where the colored people all sat, specially. So I sat on that side, quite near the front, and I kept looking to the Lord to indicate to me when he wanted me to talk. The testimonies and songs went on. There was a beautiful spirit in the meeting. Finally the time came when the Spirit bade me speak. I arose; a good brother from Philadelphia, I forget his name, sat very near me, and he was watching this brother that had been such an opponent; so, as I related how the Lord had led me, and my struggles and difficulties, the Lord blessed me and gave me great liberty in speaking. My! how my soul triumphed. The Spirit of God seemed to fall on the people; it took hold of this brother; I suppose I talked about fifteen minutes, and when I got through I had not more than taken my seat when this brother sprang to his feet, and holding up his hand he said:

"Hold on, brethren, hold on, hold on!" and walked to the front, weeping like a child. Oh! how he wept! "I want to say one word."

The shouts and amens and hallelujahs were full and free. The brother turned round and faced the congregation, straightened himself up, and braced himself, so as to control his feelings till he could get a start. Finally he said, "Brethren, I have been a Methodist preacher for so many years; I was converted at such a time; I entered the ministry," etc. "I have had a great deal of prejudice against these brethren coming here, and I have fought this subject of holiness." And he went on with his confession. But such a confession! And he ended by saying, "This colored sister, who has given us her experience, God bless her." Then he came over and took hold of my hand and said "Lord bless you, sister." Then he finished his testimony, as follows:

"When I heard this colored sister tell how God had led her and brought her into this blessed experience, the darkness swept away and God has saved me, and I see the truth as I never did before. Glory to God."[23]

Amanda became a celebrity on the camp-meeting circuit for her preaching and also for her singing. This account of a service on the beach for a crowd of 8,000 in 1875 illustrated the power of her singing.

> . . . her wonderful, velvety voice rang out in a vibrant contralto, deep, and so swelling that all could hear, as she sang (beckoning toward the ocean):
> 'There's a wideness in God's mercy like the wideness of the sea,
> There's a kindness in His justice that is more than liberty.'

She went through the whole of that wonderful hymn all alone. Tears came into women's eyes; little children stopped their play, and men pulled their hats down farther over their faces. It was a grand hour, and Amanda put the final touch to it.[24]

Beginning in 1878, Amanda preached for several years in various countries, including Great Britain and India. She then lived in parts of West Africa, where she did some evangelistic work, but for the most part she battled malaria, missionaries, and money worries. Her years in Africa were physically and emotionally draining, and she returned to Great Britain in poor health. "Weakened from malaria and recurring respiratory problems, hobbled by arthritis, and drained from constant travel, a haggard Amanda Smith arrived in Liverpool after eight years of 'hardship, privation, and toil.' "[25]

Amanda was committed to the education of children, particularly black children. While she was in Africa, she adopted two children—Frances (6) and Bob (3). Her hope for both children was that they would become missionaries. Frances was left in the care of a family in Liberia, and Bob traveled with her to England and was educated in a boarding school. Despite her financial constraints, she also provided education for her older daughter, Mazie.

The educational project that consumed the last years of her life was the Amanda Smith Orphanage and Industrial Home for Abandoned and Destitute Colored Children located in Harvey, Illinois, a southern suburb of Chicago. When the school opened in 1899, it was "the only Protestant institution for African American children in Illinois."[26] Amanda's goals were to train the children in the basic skills of cooking, cleaning, raising small farm animals, and gardening.[27] Unfortunately, the school was plagued, as was Amanda's entire life, by a lack of funds. Despite a grueling schedule of fund raising and speaking engagements, she could not raise enough money to improve the school's living conditions, which were perpetually cited as substandard by a state agency. At the age of seventy-five, Amanda left the school and moved into a house provided for her by a wealthy manufacturer, George Sebring, in the Florida town he built and named after himself. She died there at the age of seventy-eight.

On Women

Amanda carried the double burden of her race and gender, and she did not fit in easily anywhere. She was accused by some African Americans of abandoning her race to cater to whites.[28] At the same time, she experienced racism when she traveled and preached in white settings. In her autobiography, she recounted the curious looks that followed her when she, a black woman, traveled as a first-class passenger on a ship from New York to Liverpool, England. The curiosity intensified when it was announced that she would hold services on the ship. "How the smiles and whispers went around among the passengers, 'The colored woman is going to preach.' " After the service, she noticed a difference in attitude towards her. "Oh, how it changed the spirit of the passengers. Ladies and gentlemen that had not even said good morning to me before, came to me and thanked me for what I said, and especially for the prayer."[29]

She expressed her feelings about being a misfit between two races in a letter written at a time when she was deep in debt. "I was ashamed to tell anyone, it would look to white people like bad management on the part of those who were my friends. Then I knew what some of my own people would say, and had said already, that I was a kind of a 'white folks' nigger,' and I knew they would say, 'That is just what I told you it would all come to, can't tell me about white folks.' They wouldn't see God in any of it, so here I was."[30] Yet despite a long list of racist experiences, when she mused about her color, she concluded that she was content as she was. "Yes, thank God, I am satisfied with my color. I am glad I had no choice in it, for if I had, I am sure I would not have been satisfied; for when I was a young girl I was passionately fond of pea-green, and if choice had been left to me I would have chosen to be green, and I am sure God's color is the best and most substantial."[31]

Amanda wrote very little about women in her autobiography; she referred more often to experiences of racism than sexism. She did not press for women's ordination. When the debate on the topic erupted at the 1872 General Conference of The African Methodist Episcopal Church, Amanda resolved not to participate publicly in the debate; she had the inward affirmation that her ordination was from God.[32] Where she did encounter opposition against women's public speaking was in Africa from missionaries of other denominations. This excerpt from her autobiography recorded the opposition she received and her response.

But the good Plymouth brethren were much disturbed, because I was a woman, and Paul had said, "Let your women keep silence in the churches."[33] So they had nice articles in the daily papers; then they wrote me kind letters, and bombarded me with Scriptural texts against women preaching; pointed out some they wished me to preach from. I never argue with anybody—just say my say and go on. But one night I said I would speak on this subject as I understood it. Oh, what a stir it made. The church was packed and crowded. After I had sung, I read out my text: "Let your 'men' keep silence in the church," quoting the chapter and verse (I Cor. 14:28) where Paul was giving directions so as not to have confusion—one to speak at a time, while the others listened. And then one was to interpret, and if there was no interpreter, they should keep silence in the church. So I went on with my version of it. We had an excellent meeting, and the newspaper articles stopped, and the letters stopped, and I went on till I got through.

I have wondered what has become of the good Plymouth brethren in India since the Salvation Army lassies[34] have been so owned and blessed of God. Their work has told more practically on the strongholds of heathenism than all that holy conservatism would have brought to bear in a thousand years.

Oh, that the Holy Ghost may be poured out mightily! Then shall the prophecy of Joel be fulfilled.[35] For are we not living in the last days of this wonderful dispensation of the Holy Ghost?[36]

Notes

1. Clara McLeister, *Men and Women of Deep Piety* (Syracuse, NY: Wesleyan Methodist, 1920), 384.

2. Methodist class meetings were instituted by John Wesley, the founder of Methodism, in order to provide an opportunity for small group fellowship and accountability. Classes met once a week for Bible study, prayer, hymn singing, and discipline. The only requirement for joining a class was "a desire to flee from the wrath to come, and to be saved from their sins." [Thomas Jackson, ed., *General Rules of the United Societies, § 4, The Works of John Wesley* (Grand Rapids, MI: Zondervan, 1958), 8:270.] For more on Methodist class meetings, see Philip F. Hardt, *The Soul of Methodism: The Class Meeting in Early New York City Methodism* (Lanham, MD: University Press of America, 2000) and Thomas Albin, " 'Inwardly Persuaded': Religion of the Heart in Early British Methodism," in *"Heart Religion"in the Methodist Tradition and Related Movements*, ed. Richard Steele (Metuchen, NJ: Scarecrow, 2001), 44–45.

3. Amanda Smith, *An Autobiography: The Story of the Lord's Dealings with Mrs. Amanda Smith, The Colored Evangelist* (Chicago: Christian Witness Co., 1921), 42.

4. See n. 19, chapter 3.

5. John 12:32.

6. The words, "slain," "slain in the Spirit," or "falling," describe the phenomenon of falling to the ground while under religious conviction and lying still for a while before awakening. For more on "slain" in the Methodist tradition, see Ann Taves, *Fits, Trances, & Visions: Experiencing Religion and Explaining Experience from Wesley to James* (Princeton, NJ: Princeton University, 1999), 72–75, 108–09, 234, 239.

7. Smith, *Autobiography*, 42–43.

8. In her autobiography, she included several conversations with the Devil, which occurred at significant points in her religious life. There is another particularly lengthy conversation with the Devil immediately preceding her sanctification. See Smith, *Autobiography*, 73–80. For more on her personification of the devil, see Elizabeth Elkins Grammer, *Some Wild Visions: Autobiographies by Female Itinerant Evangelists in 19th-Century America* (New York: Oxford University, 2003), 94–97.

9. See n. 15, chapter 2.

10. Smith, *Autobiography*, 43–47.

11. Many women found a way to pursue a more active ministry as the wife of a minister. "The nineteenth century saw the minister's wife emerge from the crowd to become the institutional leader of church women and to occupy one of the most coveted careers available to American women." Leonard I. Sweet, *The Minister's Wife: Her Role in Nineteenth-Century American Evangelicalism* (Philadelphia: Temple University, 1983), 3.

12. Smith, *Autobiography*, 79.

13. Her autobiography actually reads 1890, but historians contend that the year, 1870, fits chronologically with other events in her life.

14. The band was another level of John Wesley's small groups. Unlike the class meeting (see n. 2 above), the band was for professed Christians who wanted to deepen their faith by meeting once a week for singing and praying with like-minded people. Bands consisted of one sex, either all men or all women. For more on bands, see Albin, "Inwardly Persuaded," 45–48.

15. The initials, A.M.E., signify The African Methodist Episcopal Church. Jarena Lee was also associated with the AME; see chapter 1.
16. This refers to a Sunday when the sacrament of communion, also known as the Lord's Supper or the Eucharist, was celebrated. In the Methodist tradition, the sacramental elements of bread and wine represent the bread and cup served by Jesus to his disciples at the Last Supper. See Matthew 26:26–30; Mark 14:22–26; Luke 22:15–20; 1 Corinthians 11:23–25.
17. Sabbath School, synonymous with Sunday School, was a time of religious education.
18. Matthew 16:24; Mark 8:34; Luke 9:23.
19. Smith, *Autobiography*, 147–48.
20. See n. 19, chapter 3.
21. Smith, *Autobiography*, 174–75.
22. The love feast was a basic ritual of early Methodism, which commonly followed this pattern: "hymn, prayer, eating of bread and water, testimonies, monetary collection, hymn, prayer, benediction." [Lester Ruth, *A Little Heaven Below: Worship At Early Methodist Quarterly Meetings* (Nashville, TN: Abingdon, 2000), 106; see also Karen B. Westerfield Tucker, *American Methodist Worship* (New York: Oxford University, 2001), 60–64.] Amanda would have spoken during the time set aside for testimonies. During camp meetings, the love feast generally occurred early on Sunday morning, as in Amanda's account.
23. Smith, *Autobiography*, 210–11.
24. Frances E. Willard, "Amanda Smith, the Colored Pioneer," *Union Signal* (20 September, 1888): 7; cited in Adrienne M. Israel, *Amanda Berry Smith: From Washerwoman to Evangelist*, Studies in Evangelicalism, No. 16 (Lanham, MD: Scarecrow, 1998), 61.
25. Israel, *Amanda Berry Smith*, 91.
26. Nancy A. Hardesty and Adrienne Israel, "Amanda Berry Smith: A 'Downright, Outright Christian' " in *Spirituality and Social Responsibility: Vocational Vision of Women in The United Methodist Tradition*, ed. Rosemary Skinner Keller (Nashville, TN: Abingdon, 1993), 70.
27. Israel, *Amanda Berry Smith*, 127–28.
28. An editorial in an African Methodist Episcopal Church newsletter cited this criticism of Amanda. "Where is Amanda Smith? She belongs to us, and we ought to set her to work. Tell me nothing about the work she is doing among our white brethren. They don't need her. They are rich in spiritual gifts and spiritual work. We are poor, languishing and dying. We tell Amanda Smith to come home." "The Mite Society" *Christian Recorder* (4 March, 1875): 4; cited in Israel, *Amanda Berry Smith*, 60.
29. Smith, *Autobiography*, 252–53.
30. W.C. Frazer, letter, "Mrs. Amanda Smith," *Christian Standard* (18 August, 1877): 261; cited in Israel, *Amanda Berry Smith*, 63.
31. Smith, *Autobiography*, 118.
32. Smith, *Autobiography*, 200.
33. 1 Corinthians 14:34.
34. For more on women in The Salvation Army, see chapter 11.
35. Joel 2:28–32; Acts 2:14–21.
36. Smith, *Autobiography*, 321. For more on dispensations, see n. 12, chapter 4.

Faith-healing Pentecostal evangelist, author of *The Life and Experiences of Maria B. Woodworth, Holy Ghost Sermons* and *Spirit-filled Sermons*

Courtesy of the Flower Pentecostal Heritage Center.

CHAPTER 7

MARIA WOODWORTH-ETTER
(1844–1924)

Maria Beulah Underwood was the fourth daughter in a family of eight children born to Samuel and Matilda Underwood in rural, central Ohio. In her autobiography she recalled that her parents had minimal interest in religion, a situation that she lamented. "I was left without the religious teachings and influence with which so many homes are blessed."[1] When she was twelve, her father died, and Maria and her sister had to drop out of school in order to help their mother at home. She desperately desired to remain in school. "I wanted to go to school where I could learn, for I longed for an education; and I often cried myself to sleep over this matter. I would have my books in the kitchen, where I could read a verse and commit it to memory, then read another, and so on, thus improving every opportunity while at my work."[2] A year later she attended a service at a Christian Church (Disciples of Christ), where she was converted and experienced an initial call to evangelistic work.

Maria published at least seven editions of her autobiography between 1885 and 1922. Because the editions vary, often significantly, two excerpts concerning her conversion are included. The earliest was simple and straightforward. By 1912, she had added a baptismal account.

On Her Conversion (Two Versions)

All editions

When I heard the story of the cross my heart was filled with the love of Jesus. My eyes seemed to be fountains of tears.

Subsequent paragraph added in the 1912 edition

I was seated in the back of a large audience, and was the first to make the start to seek the Lord. It seemed so far to the front seat, that it looked like

I could never make it, but I said, "I can but perish if I go. I am resolved to try, For if I stay away I know I shall forever die." The minister took great interest in me, and said many good things to encourage me, and prayed that my life might be a shining light. If he could have looked forward and have seen my life's work for the Master, he surely would have rejoiced to know how kindly he had talked to the poor little orphan girl. But I did not get converted then. They did not believe in a change of heart and nature; but praise the Lord, He did not leave me in the dark. The next day, as they took me down to the creek to baptize me, there was a great crowd around. I heard someone say, "Maybe she will be drowned." It scared me a little. I thought, "Maybe I might," but I said, "Lord, I will go through if I do": so I asked the Lord to save me fully, trusting myself in His hands; and while going into the water, a light came over me, and I was converted. The people saw the change and said I had fainted.

All editions

Then began my new life of peace and joy in a Savior's love. Then I was contented and happy, singing and praising God all the day long. I never went to any place of amusement. I attended four meetings on Sabbath and three or four during the week. I did not stay away from meeting once a year unless I was sick. I was more anxious now than ever for an education, for I wanted to work for Jesus and be useful in the vineyard of Christ. Soon after I was converted I heard the voice of Jesus calling me to go out in highways and hedges,[3] and gather in the lost sheep of the house of Israel.[4] Like Mary, I pondered these things in my heart, for I had no one to hold counsel with.[5] The Disciples did not believe that women had any right to work for Jesus. Had I told them my impressions they would have made sport of me. I had never heard of women working in public except as missionaries, so I could see no opening—except, as I thought, if I ever married, my choice would be an earnest Christian, and then we would enter upon the mission-work.[6]

She did not, in fact, marry an "earnest Christian." Her first husband, Philo H. Woodworth, was converted several years after they married. Philo's poor health in body and mind, including severe mood swings, made their married life quite difficult.[7] Significantly compounding their marital difficulties were the deaths of five of their six children. The toll of these adversities catapulted Maria into frequent bouts of severe illnesses. During these prolonged times in bed, she claimed to have a vision of herself preaching to lost souls. At a critical point, when she seemed to be on the brink of death, Maria promised that if God restored her health, she would then do the evangelistic work to which God had called her years earlier. She reported that at that moment, she began to get better immediately. This excerpt, in its several variations, recounted her experience of an "anointing of power," which propelled her into evangelistic work.

On Her Call to Preach

All editions

Several ministers whom I had never seen before told me, at different times that God was calling me to the ministry, and that I would have to go. I said, "If I were a man I would love to work for Jesus." They told me I had a work to do which no man could do; the Lord was calling me to the West to labor for lost souls. I said, "O Lord! I cannot take Willie with me, nor can I leave him behind." Then the Lord saw fit to take him out of the way; so he laid his hand on my darling little boy, and in a few days took him home to heaven. He was the joy of my life. He was nearly seven years old. He was very bright for one of his age—in fact, far beyond his years. He was the pet of the whole neighborhood. He seemed to know when taken sick that he would not get well. He talked of dying and going to see Georgie, who had been dead three years that month. He said he would have to die sometime, and that he would rather go now if we could go with him; that he would never be sick any more, nor have to take any more medicine. He bid us all goodbye and said he was going to be with Jesus. He died very happy. He had talked and fretted much about his little sister, and said he could not live without her. By faith I could see her meeting him at the beautiful gates and welcoming him into the golden city of God.[8] This sad bereavement nearly took my life. The dear Savior was never so near and real to me before. He was by my side and seemed to bear me up in his loving arms. I could say, the Lord gave and the Lord has taken away; blessed be the name of the Lord. When alone, I missed my darling so much that I wept as though my heart would break. Then I would always pray; and as I prayed I would forget everything earthly and soar away by faith to the Golden City, and there see my darlings all together shining in glory, and looking at me and singing, "Mamma, do not weep for us, but come this way." I would always end in praising and giving glory to God for taking them to such a happy place. Lizzie, my oldest child, sixteen years old, was all that I had left of six sweet children. In all these trials God was preparing me and opening the way for the great battle against the enemy of souls; and now the great desire of my heart was to work for Jesus. I longed to win a star for the Savior's crown. But when I thought of my weakness I shrunk from the work. Sometimes when the Spirit of God was striving and calling so plainly I would yield and say, "Yes, Lord, I will go." The glory of God came upon me like a cloud, and I seemed to be carried away hundreds of miles and set down in a field of wheat, where the sheaves were falling all around me. I was filled with zeal and power, and felt as if I could stand before the whole world and plead with dying sinners. It seemed to me that I must leave all and go at once. Then Satan would come in like a flood and would say, "You would look nice preaching, being a gazing-stock for the people to make sport of. You know you could not do it."

Then I would think of my weakness and say, "No, of course I can not do it." Then I would be in darkness and despair.

I wanted to run away from God, or I wished I could die; but when I began to look at the matter in this way, that God knew all about me, and was able and willing to qualify me for the work ...

1885 edition continues with these paragraphs

... then I began to seek a better experience, and pray for an anointing of power. I made a full conversion and asked for a baptism of fire to take everything out of my heart and cleanse it with the blood of Christ, and fill it with the Holy Ghost.

I promised to let nothing but sickness or death come between me and the work. God accepted the offering, and the blessing and power came, and I went about praising God from morning till night. My heart was full of his love and praise. It was as natural for me to say, "Praise God," as it was to breathe. The Bible was a new book. All desires to sin were gone. I dropped into the arms of Jesus by faith and trusted him to keep me each moment. When I saw a temptation coming I would tell Jesus, and a verse, or promise, like the following would present itself: "Lo, I am with you alway,"[9] "Be not afraid,"[10] or, "Cast all your care on Jesus; he cares for you."[11]

With these words would come such power that I gained the victory every time. I lost all desire for the things of the world. I longed to get ready to enter the work of gathering in the lost sheep of the house of Israel.[12]

1894 and subsequent editions insert this paragraph instead

I want the reader to understand, that at this time I had a good experience, a pure heart, was full of the love of God, but was not qualified for God's work. I knew that I was but a worm. God would have to take a worm to thresh a mountain.[13] Then I asked God to give me the power. He gave the Gallilean [sic] fishermen[14]—to anoint me for service. I came like a child asking for bread. I looked for it. God did not disappoint me. The power of the Holy Ghost came down as a cloud. It was brighter than the sun. I was covered and wrapped up in it. My body was light as the air. It seemed that heaven came down.[15]

1912 and subsequent editions continue with these sentences

I was baptized with the Holy Ghost, and fire, and power which has never left me. Oh, Praise the Lord! There was liquid fire, and the angels were all around in the fire and glory. It is through the Lord Jesus Christ, and by this power, that I have stood before hundreds of thousands of men and women, proclaiming the unsearchable riches of Christ.[16]

On Her Evangelistic Method: Signs and Wonders

Maria's initial forays in evangelism at the age of thirty-five consisted of holding evangelistic meetings in nearby churches and communities. Early on, she received offers from several denominations to pastor one of their churches, but her determination was to be an itinerant evangelist, not a minister. "These [offers] were all within ten miles of home, and I would have received a good salary. But I felt that my mission was that of an evangelist. I felt that my work was not confined to one charge or place, but wherever the Lord was leading me."[17] Within several years, her meetings attracted larger crowds, particularly when trances became a regular phenomenon while she was preaching.[18] Trances first occurred during her meetings in Hartford City, Indiana, in 1885, and many newspapers, including *The New York Times*, covered the events.[19] The following excerpt from her autobiography described in detail the trances and other "displays of God's power" that ensued at Hartford City.

After many invitations from Hartford City, and believing that the Spirit of God was leading that way, I consented to go, and I went believing God would do a great work. I commenced meeting there about the first of January, 1885, in the Methodist Church. The first night it was not known we would be there to commence that evening. They rang the bell and the people came from every direction and filled the church to overflowing.

The church was cold and formal, and many of the best citizens had drifted into skepticism. I knew that it would take a wonderful display of God's power to convince the people, so I prayed for God to display His power, that the sinner might know that God still lives, and that there is a reality in religion, and this might convict him of a terrible judgment. Five of the leading members of the church said they would unite with me in prayer for the Lord to pour out the power from on high, till the city would be shaken, and the country for miles around. We prayed that Christians and sinners might fall as dead men, that the slain[20] of the Lord might be many. The Lord answered our prayers in a remarkable manner.

The class leader's little boy fell under the power of God first. He rose up, stepped on the pulpit, and began to talk with the wisdom and power of God. His father began to shout and praise the Lord. As the little fellow exhorted[21] and asked the people to come to Christ, they began to weep all over the house. Some shouted; others fell prostrated. Diverse operations of the Spirit were seen. The displays of the power of God continued to increase till we closed the meetings, which lasted about five weeks. The power of the Lord, like the wind, swept all over the city, up one street and down another, sweeping through the places of business, the workshops, saloons, and dives, arresting sinners of all classes. The Scriptures were fulfilled. The wicked flee when no man pursueth.[22] Men, women, and children were struck down in their homes, in their places of business, on the highways, and lay as dead. They had wonderful visions, and rose converted, giving glory to God. When they told what they had seen, their faces shone like angels. The fear of God fell upon the city. The police said they never saw such a change, that they had nothing to do. They said they made no arrests and that the power of God seemed to preserve the city. A spirit of love rested all over the city. There was no fighting, no swearing on the streets; the people moved softly; and there seemed to be a spirit of love and kindness among all classes, as if they felt they were in the presence of God.

A merchant fell in a trance in his home and lay several hours. Hundreds went in to look at him. He had a vision and a message for the church. The Lord showed him the condition of many of the members. He told part of his vision but refused to deliver the message to the church. He was struck dumb. He could not speak a word because he refused to tell what the Lord wanted him to. The Lord showed him he would never speak till he delivered the message. He rose to his feet, weeping, to tell the vision. God loosed his tongue. Those present knew he had been dumb; and when he began to talk and tell his experience, it had a wonderful effect on the church and sinners.[23]

One night there was a party seventeen miles from the city. Some of the young ladies thought they would have some fun; they began to mimic and act out the trance. The Lord struck some of them down. They lay there as if they had been shot. Their funmaking was soon turned to a prayer meeting and cries of mercy were heard. The people came to the meetings in sleigh loads many miles. One night while a sleigh load of men and women were going to the meeting, they were jesting about the trances. They made the remark to each other that they were going in a trance that night. Before the meeting closed, all who had been making fun were struck down by the power of God and lay like dead people and had to be taken home in the sled in that condition. Those who came with them were very much frightened when they saw them laying there, and they told how they had been making fun of the power of God on the way to the meeting. Scoffers and mockers were struck down in all parts of the house.

One man was mocking a woman of whose body God had taken control. She was preaching with gestures. When in that mocking attitude, God struck him dumb. He became rigid and remained with his hands up, and his mouth drawn in that mocking way for five hours, a gazing stock for all in the house. The fear of God fell on all. They saw it was a fearful thing to mock God or make fun of His work. Surely, the Lord worked in a wonderful way in this meeting. The postmaster was converted. All classes from the roughs and toughs to the tallest cedars and brightest talents of the city were brought into the fold of Christ. We took the meeting to the opera house, and it would not hold the crowds, so great was the awakening among the people. Traveling salesmen arranged to return to the city each night. The Cincinnati *Enquirer* sent a reporter to write up the meetings and report daily. Every day the newsboys could be heard crying out, "All about the Woodworth revival." Reporters came from many states and large cities to write up the meetings.

Lawyer C., one of the leading lawyers of the city, was convinced of the reality of the religion of Jesus by seeing me under the control of the Holy Ghost power while in a trance. Sometimes standing with my face and hands raised to heaven, my face shining with the brightness of heaven; other times the tears streaming down my face with mute preaching, pleading with sinners to come to Christ; other times lying for hours, sometimes as one dead, and diverse operations of the Spirit, conscious all the time, but entirely controlled by the power of the Holy Ghost. Always while in these conditions in this meeting, and all others, the fear of God would fall upon the people. Sinners would be stricken down over the house. Many would be saved: they would rush to the altar crying for mercy. Sometimes scores would be converted while God would use me in this way. Mr. C. was the leading lawyer of the state. He was a skeptic and had no use for churches. The ministers had given up all hopes of him ever being saved. When he came and invited us to his house to make our home with them while in the city, people were astonished. He asked me if I would tell him my experience while in a trance. He said he did not ask this to satisfy curiosity, but for light. He said he had confidence in me and would believe what I told him. I knew the Lord was leading in this. I told him more of my experience than I had ever told anyone. While talking, the power of God fell upon us all. I was almost blind with the glory of God. My hands looked transparent. He broke down and began to weep. We all got on our knees. This was the first time this strong man, this tall cedar,[24] had ever bowed before the living God. In a little while the news had spread all over the city. But that night when he came boldly into the crowded opera house and bowed at the altar, and in a moment another leading lawyer of the city bowed at his side, the excitement and surprise of the people had no bounds. I praise God for victory at this place through our Lord Jesus Christ.

While at Hartford City, calls came from churches in Cincinnati, Fort Wayne, Union City, and many other large cities. They sent one dispatch after another, urging me to come. But God's ways are not our ways. He does not see as man sees. God looks in the heart; man judges from outward appearances. The Lord showed me I must go to a little town fifteen miles away called New Corner. I rode in a sleigh. When I got there, I was so hoarse I could only speak in a whisper and so tired I could not walk without assistance. It was time for meeting. The house and yard were crowded. I could hardly get through to the pulpit. I commenced singing, trusting God to take away the hoarseness and give me voice. In five minutes my voice was strong and clear. I sang in the strength and power of God. I sang two or three hymns. The power of God fell upon me and remained all the week I was there. It could be seen and heard and felt by all who came to the meetings. I preached that night the only sermon while there. After that night I would be interrupted by sinners falling in the congregation. Then there would be a rush to the altar and shouts by the friends of those who were stricken down. In a few minutes the house would be turned into a mourners' bench.[25]

Several months after the Hartford City meetings, Maria believed that God had given her "the gift of healing, and of laying on of hands for the recovery of the sick."[26] As at other momentous times in her life, her interpretation of God's leading came at a crisis point in her health. She was unable to sleep or rest and had to be helped out of bed. Her health improved when she relinquished herself to what she believed to be God's direction to preach divine healing and pray for the sick. The number of people at her evangelistic meetings continued to increase so that eventually the crowds overflowed her tent, which accommodated 8,000 people. By 1912, she made her way into Pentecostal circles when F. F. Bosworth, a prominent Pentecostal evangelist, invited her to hold evangelistic meetings for six months in his Dallas church. From then on, she was a regularly featured evangelist on Pentecostal platforms across the country.

Previously she had been granted a license to preach by the 39th Indiana Eldership of the Church of God (Winebrenner) until the church revoked her license fifteen years later. According to church polity, she overstepped the boundaries when she, an elder in Southern Indiana, held evangelistic meetings in Pennsylvania. Although she had been invited by one elder in Pennsylvania, she had not secured permission of the entire Pennsylvania eldership.[27] The first time this happened, Maria apologized and retained her license. When she was cited again for a second violation, she retorted that she would preach wherever God led her, church polity notwithstanding, and she left the denomination.

Conflict also circumscribed her first marriage. Not only was Philo often despondent and moody, but he also caused trouble at her evangelistic meetings. He appointed himself as her business manager, but his mercenary enterprises during her meetings were ridiculed in print by reporters.

> The husband of the evangelist is of a thrifty turn, and while the meetings are in progress he and his two assistants operate a peanut, candy and lemonade stand within sixty feet of the pulpit. The other day, as men and women were shouting and going into trances, old Woodworth sat beside an ice cream freezer and cranked it unconcernedly, preparing a supply of the popular refreshment for the weary, sinsick crowd. Sunday morning he was dispensing cigars and plugging watermelons for the million, and the nickels, dimes and quarters flowed into his till in a steady stream, while the wife was laboring with care-burdened sinners.[28]

There was also the matter of his recurrent infidelity. Maria expressed her feelings about Philo in these poignant words, "Living trouble is worse than the trouble of those who are dead."[29] She sued Philo for divorce on the grounds of repeated adultery in December, 1890. Immediately after the divorce, Philo married a sixteen-year-old who had already been married, and then a year later, he died of typhoid fever.

Ten years later, Maria married Samuel Etter who, unlike Philo, was an asset to her evangelistic work. "He takes the best care of me, in and out of the meetings. It makes no difference what I call on him to do. He will pray, and preach, and sing, and is very good around the altar. He does about all my writing, and he also helps in getting out my books, and looks after the meeting, in and outside. The Lord knew what I needed and it was brought about by the Lord, through his love and care for me and the work."[30] They were married for twelve years before Samuel died in 1914. From 1918 until her death in 1924, Maria's headquarters were located in a church she founded in Indianapolis, now known as Lakeview Christian Center.

On Women

Initially, Maria was reluctant to speak in public because she was a woman. Although she had heard the unmistakable call to evangelistic work, she was hesitant to obey. "Like Mary, I pondered these things in my heart, for I had no one to hold counsel with. The Disciples did not believe that women had any right to work for Jesus. Had I told them my impressions they would have made sport of me. I had never heard of women working in public except as missionaries—so I could see no opening . . ."[31] After her experience of the "anointing of power," she reflected further on the subject and set forth this biblical rationale for women preaching.

I was to be the vessel of clay[32] God was going to use to his own glory. I was to be God's mouthpiece. I must trust God to speak through me to the people the words of eternal life. There was all this time a secret monitor within me telling me that I should be calling sinners to repentance. I could not get clear of that reflection by day or by night. Waking or dreaming, I seemed to have a large congregation before me, all in tears, as I told them the story of the cross. Thus for months and years did I debate; and yet did I falter and hesitate, and, like Jonah, trim my sail for Tarshish.[33] I thought if I were a man it would be a pleasure for me, but me, a woman, to preach, if I could, would subject me to ridicule and contempt among my friends and kindred, and bring reproach upon our glorious cause.

Always when I had trouble I would flee to the stronghold of faith and grace and prayer. But when I went in secret to pray, the words seemed to come to me, "You deny me before men and I will deny you before my Father and the holy angels."[34] Then I would go to my Bible and search for teachings and examples. Then who made sport of Miriam when the poet said,

An elder sister led the band,
　　With sounding timbrels in her hand,
And virgins moved in order grand,
　　And after her they shouting danced.[35]

Again, the Lord put his erring people in remembrance of his great blessing to Israel when he said, "Did I not send thee Moses and Aaron and Miriam to be your leaders?" and again the prophets were ordained of God. And when there was trouble on hand Barak dare not meet the enemy unless Deborah led the van. And the noble woman, always ready to work for God and his cause, said, "I will surely go. God's people must not be a prey to the enemy." "Oh, no," call out the men of Israel, "Sisera's mighty hosts are gathering."

As I continued to read my Bible I saw that in all ages of the world the Lord raised up of his own choosing, men, women, and children—Miriam, Deborah, Hannah, Hulda, Anna, Phoebe, Narcissus, Tryphena, Persis, Julia, and the Marys, and the sisters who were co-workers with Paul in the gospel, whose names were in the Book of Life, and many other women whose labors are mentioned with praise. Even the children were made the instruments of his praise and glory. See Romans ii. 6; I. Samuel iii. 4; Jeremiah i. 6; Numbers xxii. 28.

The more I investigated the more I found to condemn me. There was the Master giving one, two, and five talents, and the moral obligation of each person receiving them and their several rewards. I had one talent, which was hidden away.[36] . . .

By the prophet Joel we learn that one special feature of the gospel dispensation[37] shall be, "Your sons and daughters shall prophesy, your old men shall dream dreams, your young men shall see visions; and also upon the servants and handmaids in those days will I pour out my Spirit."[38]

Hence it seems by the Prophet Joel that the last days were to be particularly conspicuous for this kind of prophesying. We can not rebuke God's decree, for it is said, "Heaven and earth shall pass away, but the word of God shall endure forever."[39]

By reference to Acts ii. 16, it is determined that this prophecy by Joel was verified on the day of Pentecost. And it was fully warranted as of divine origin, and that the gift of prophecy was not confined to either sex; for they all began to preach and to prophesy; as the Spirit gave them utterance—both men and women.

Paul in his first letter to the church at Corinth (xiv. 13) defines prophesying, exhorting, speaking, edification, and comfort. If we are able to answer the important questions, First, Whose Spirit was poured out? Second, on whom was it poured? Third, When and for what purpose? then we shall also be able to decide somewhat as to what extent women are required to work for the advancement of Christ's cause upon the earth.

I maintain that by the prophecy of Joel women were to participate in this work with their brethren. Now, as the kingdom, or new dispensation, was set up by our Lord and Savior Jesus Christ, their work was not only recognized at that time in a miraculous manner, but was acknowledged by the apostles, as in fulfillment of said prophecies.

Now, to those who are sensitive upon this point I propose the inquiry: First, Is there not as much to sustain the position that women are called to preach as there is that men are called? If you deny that there is such a call to the ministry, then whence the authority for making the work exclusively for the male sex? What would have been the work of those women who labored with Paul? (Paul's letter to the church at Philippi iv. 3.) Second, How could they obey God and not prophesy? (Acts ii. 18.) Philip had four daughters who did prophesy. (Acts xxxi. 9.)[40] Was that by divine authority, although about thirty-five years after the setting up of the gospel kingdom of dispensation? And is it less becoming for women to labor in Christ's kingdom or vineyard now than it was then?

If you determine that there is no acceptable preaching only through a called ministry, who will arrogate to himself the power to determine the calling, seeing that more are invested with miraculous power?

But should you deny that there is any divine authority by which the word is preached, why not offer the most encouragement to those who may labor the most successfully? There will be time when all good works will meet a just recompense; for it is said, "Every valley shall be exalted, and every mountain and hill shall be made low: and the crooked shall be made straight, and the rough places plain: and the glory of the Lord shall be revealed, and all flesh shall see it together: for the mouth of the Lord hath spoken it."[41]

But without controversy, I am willing to trust in whom I have believed for my justification. I will cling to the cross and trust my Redeemer.[42]

Notes

1. Maria B. Woodworth, *The Life and Experience of Maria B. Woodworth* (Dayton: United Brethren Publishing House, 1885), 15.
2. Woodworth, *Life and Experience*, 16–17.
3. Luke 14:23.
4. Matthew 10:6, 15:24.
5. Luke 2:19.
6. Woodworth, *Life and Experience*, 17–18.
7. In the earliest edition of her journal, Maria confided her difficulties with Philo. "About this time my husband was converted in the Methodist Church, where my little girl had been converted. He was very bright and seemed to speak with other tongues. God had answered my prayer. We had a happy home for awhile; but when trials came he became discouraged. At times he was on the mountain-top, and then again he would be down in the valley in his religious experience. I made a great deal of allowance for him, as everything affected his mind. This made it very hard for me, as I had everything to see to. I had to work very hard. With the disease I had, my nervous system became prostrated, and I lay for three months so that doctor and friends thought I would die." [Woodworth, *Life and Experience*, 28.] These sentences were omitted in later editions of her journal.
8. Revelation 21:15.
9. Matthew 28:20.
10. This phrase occurs more than seventy times in the Bible, from Genesis 15:1 to Revelation 1:17.
11. 1 Peter 5:7.
12. Matthew 10:6, 15:24. Woodworth, *Life and Experience*, 34–35.
13. Isaiah 41:14–15.
14. Four of Jesus' disciples were Galilean fishermen: Simon, Andrew, James, and John.
15. Maria B. Woodworth, *The Life, Work, and Experience of Maria Beulah Woodworth, Evangelist*, revised edn. (St. Louis: Commercial Printing, 1894), 33.
16. Maria Woodworth-Etter, *Signs and Wonders*, revised edn. (New Kensington, PA: Whitaker House, 1997), 32.
17. Woodworth, *Life and Experience* (1885 edn.), 52.

18. Great skepticism and debate surrounded these trances; were they of God or were they a hoax? Many believed the latter, such as a reporter for the *Indianapolis Times* who concluded: "It is absolutely, undoubtedly and beyond peradventure a stupendous deception. There is evidently nothing of divine interposition in it. It is simply as a leading physician of the town told the *Times* reporter, a state of comatose into which any person is liable to fall whose nervous system is severely strained. The evangelist apparently has but little personal magnetism. She relies wholly upon the fear and terror which she instills into the minds of her usually ignorant audience. Almost every one who has been stricken is illiterate." ["The Tipton Revival" *The Indianapolis Times* (May 7, 1885), front page; Flower Pentecostal Heritage Center, Springfield, Missouri.] An alternative opinion was printed the same day in another newspaper, the *Kokomo Dispatch*: "Do I believe that there is such a thing as trance? Yes, I have known of trances through history and from the writings of mental philosophers, but this is my first opportunity of seeing anything of the kind. . . . While in the trance, that portion of the brain through which God's spirit comes to us and teaches us of Him is in supreme control, and all the rest of the brain is dormant, or is held more or less inactive for the time. . . . And to you, Christians of the Methodist and Quaker order, who have been praying so long and loud for the fullness of that religion of which you have been permited [*sic*] to have a little taste, let me say that this woman only has that fullness for which your souls have long panted; so be careful how you treat her when she comes among you . . ." [Dr. T.V. Gifford, "Conversion By Trance" *Kokomo Dispatch* (May 7, 1885), 5; Flower Pentecostal Heritage Center, Springfield, Missouri.] For a recent discussion of her trances, see Taves, *Fits, Trances, & Visions*, 241–47.

19. Three articles on the Hartford City evangelistic meetings in 1885 appeared in *The New York Times* on January 24, 26, and 30. See Wayne Warner, *The Woman Evangelist: The Life and Times of Charismatic Evangelist Maria B. Woodworth-Etter*, Studies in Evangelicalism No. 8, eds. Kenneth E. Rowe and Donald W. Dayton (Metuchen, NJ: Scarecrow, 1986), 43.

20. See n. 6, chapter 6.

21. See n. 8, chapter 1.

22. Proverbs 28:1.

23. A similar occurrence happened to Zechariah, the priest. See Luke 1:5–24, 57–80.

24. 2 Kings 19:23.

25. Woodworth-Etter, *Signs and Wonders*, 51–54. The mourners' bench, also known as the anxious bench, was a seat, pew, or bench in the front of the service area, where those under conviction would come and sit while people prayed for them to move from conviction to conversion. For more on the mourners' bench in early Methodism, see Ruth, *A Little Heaven Below*, 53–55.

26. Woodworth, *Life, Work, and Experience*, 189.

27. For a summary of these events, see Jon R. Neely, "Maria B. Woodworth-Etter and The Churches of God," *The Church Advocate* (August 1975): 2–7. Along with the polity issue, the church hierarchy also considered her revival "successes" to be problematic since her converts, who experienced trances and the like, were deemed unruly.

28. *Weekly Courier* (Wabash, Indiana) August 21, 1885; cited in Warner, *The Woman Evangelist*, 133–34.

29. Woodworth, *Life and Experience*, 33. In later editions of her autobiography, this sentence was removed.
30. Maria B. Woodworth-Etter, *Acts of the Holy Ghost, or The Life, Work, and Experience of Mrs. M. B. Woodworth-Etter, Evangelist* (Dallas: John F. Worley, 1912), 339.
31. Woodworth, *Life and Experience*, 18.
32. Jeremiah 18:4.
33. Jonah 1:3. Although the exact location of Tarshish is not known, it is linked, as in the Jonah story, with sea-going vessels.
34. Matthew 10:33.
35. Exodus 15:20–21.
36. Matthew 25:14–30.
37. See n. 12, chapter 4.
38. Joel 2:28–32; Acts 2:16–21.
39. Matthew 24:35; Mark 13:31; Luke 21:33.
40. The correct verse is Acts 21:9.
41. Isaiah 40:4; Luke 3:5–6.
42. Woodworth, *Life and Experience*, 38–43. A later and altered version was published as a sermon titled, "Women's Rights in the Gospel," in Woodworth-Etter, *Signs and Wonders*, 197–203.

Roman Catholic lecturer and lay evangelist, author of *Woman: Her Quality, Her Environment, Her Possibility*, co-author of *Bolshevism: Its Cure, Campaigning for Christ*, and *Socialism: The Nation of Fatherless Children*

Courtesy of John J. Burns Library, Boston College.

Chapter 8

Martha Moore Avery
(1851–1929)

artha Moore was born into an established New England family whose accomplishments on the battlefields for several generations, beginning with the Battle of Bunker Hill, had accrued for them some fame and recognition. Martha often boasted in the lineage of her "proud sires." Her parents were not religious. She recalled that the first prayer she heard in her home was spoken at the funeral for her younger brother. Nevertheless, from her early childhood, Martha claimed to have a passion for intellectual certainty, especially about religion. She spent her adolescence and much of her adult life on a quest for what she referred to as "the Truth." In that process, she reasoned her way in and out of various religious and secular ideologies, including Spiritualism, Unitarianism, Nationalism, and Socialism. The following paragraphs from her unpublished autobiography, *The Longest Way Home to Rome*, which reaches the considerable length of several hundred hand-written pages, described various stages of her spiritual quest.

On Her Conversion

Private Judgment

Perhaps I was ten years old when I quarreled with my Sunday-school teacher on the subject of miracles. "It is true," said this rather dignified business man of the town, "because the *Bible says* so." The Bible? What if it does, who cares? Common-sense will settle the question for me. I would be ashamed to believe such nonsense. This was my attitude, though I hope my form of speech showed something of the good manners which was due to my breeding.

The next summer when the Methodist minister came to our home on his round of calls through the village, I eagerly listened to the "grown up" conversation. My mother brilliantly resisted the Rev. Strood's importunities to go to church. Just as he was leaving he asked "How many of your children will go to Sunday-school, Mrs. Moore?" My mother's reply was "I don't know how many will go." "But surely you know how many are old enough to attend," he expostulated. "Yes indeed," laughingly. "But they may go or not, as they please." Turning to me the gentleman said kindly, perhaps sorrowfully, "Will you go, little girl?"

My mind was filled to the brim with pride, for my mind had seized the importance of the "liberty" which my mother had conferred upon me by her confidence in my individual judgment. I could not afford to deprive myself of the friendly association with the girls of the village, nor of the opportunity for the intellectual bouts which the Sunday-school afforded. And though I could not appear to think it of the slightest religious consequence, yet once my word was pledged I must stick to what I should say, so I must be cautious. Quick as a flash I had covered all this ground. My good manners lay all in my good words for I was bristling with self-satisfaction as I replied, "I have not yet decided, Sir." Surely private judgment, and my own at that, was firmly grounded as the bed rock of my philosophy. . . .

My maternal grandmother, a devout and goodly Methodist, thinking to influence me by enlisting the highest authority available, no doubt, asked the Presiding Elder[1] on his quarterly rounds to take me in hand. Grandma Leighton had already promised me a double skirted challis dress, trimmed with white satin ribbon if I would read the New Testament, "every word in it."

"Do you love the Lord, my dear?" began this solemn and dignified elder of the Methodist communion.

"I don't know, Sir, I have never seen him."

"The Lord sees you all the time and everywhere. He wants you to love him, will you?"

"I can't love anybody that I haven't seen and don't know."

"But I tell you that the Lord is as truly a person as is your father, can you not believe me?"

"Sir, I believe you think so, but because you think so I do not know that it is so."

"If I should tell you that it is five miles from the Millbridge Post office to Steuben bridge would you believe it?"

"Sir, I should believe that you believe so. But I could not *know* the distance is five miles unless I measured it myself."

My poor dear grandma stood in the sitting room door with a look of holy horror on her placid face. She turned away sorrowfully as I glanced up at her. Truly I was a hopeless case! There was no other standard for me but my very own experimental knowledge. Thus, at the age of ten I had carried Protestantism to its limits in that direction. . . .

The Tempter—Spiritism[2]

Along came the tempter. Spiritism was raging in the little town and those who were near to me if not dear to me were its devotees. Would I join their "circles?" If I would only be *passive* I could soon be "developed" into this that or another "great gun."

No, I could not. It was my pride which saved me; there was too much stir in my blood to take a self effacing road to greatness. I myself wanted to do what I did. Deeper still, I reasoned it out on the moral side. If a spirit were to perform "good works" with the use of my "organism" I should be no better off. I could not keep the credit, for I must in honor give it over to the doer. No, even if it were true that spirits could perform great deeds I would not be "developed." To achieve great things myself? It was a new sensation, I had never met the thought before. It thrilled me and it chilled my heart. No, I could not aspire to public influence. I was a woman, even so, a public woman should be beautiful—without flaw, and noble without fault.

Alas, my standards were so high, and yet I would not pitch them lower. Ah! dear me, dear me! I was homely, ugly and ignorant. I could never be beautiful, nor gracious and I could not be wise; a public career was not to be thought of. And yet I had once made a great hit. Dressed as a little boy I sang a patriotic duet with my uncle; and by waving the stars and stripes I brought down the house. But there was the sting, I was dressed as a boy, I myself was effaced.

Martha lived with her grandfather from the age of thirteen when her mother died and her family dispersed to several locations. Her grandfather set her up as a milliner in Ellsworth, Maine. She became active in The Unitarian Church, and it was there that she met Millard Avery. They married in 1880 and had a daughter, Katherine, the next year.

Membership in the Unitarian Church

Meantime I was giving devoted service to the Unitarian Church. The sermons attracted me and for a time the "higher criticism"[3] of which I heard and read much, satisfied my views as to the demands of reason. . . .

Unitarianism Palls Upon the Taste

Just a year or two longer and the Unitarian faith had grown stale. Its moral vision was too narrow and its intellectual waters were too shallow to hold my allegiance. Grief it was to part, but I was greatly in earnest. A mere collection of cultivated persons assenting to a loosely-jointed set of opinions could not constitute the rock upon which a church must be founded. Truth could not be indifferent to exactness of thought. Truth like the multiplication table must be dogmatic. . . .

As we could worship only at a shrine of our own making it were truer not to waste our time in prayer but to go to work. Better conditions were needed to develop the intelligence of the masses. Work in the place of worship by far suited my conception of duty: I owed nothing to an abstract God, but from an altruistic standpoint I owed to men the best work that was in me. . . .

There must be something of great practical import to do; I must find it out. With the church door shut behind me I must take the open road in quest of the world's work.

She looked for "something of great practical import to do" in Boston, where she and Katherine moved in 1888. It is not clear whether Millard, who died shortly after in 1890, moved with them because the one reference to him in her autobiography suggested that their marriage was troubled. In Boston, Martha quickly became active in a Unitarian Church, but she soon left religion behind in favor of the First Nationalist Club of Boston, an organization committed to economic and social reform. When some of the leaders then decided that Socialism, not Nationalism, offered a better platform of reform, Martha then joined the Socialist Labor Party in 1891. She climbed rapidly through the ranks and became a leading propagandist of Socialism. Within several years, however, friction mounted between Martha and the Party's leadership. When they were not able to resolve amicably their differences, she quit the Party and became a leading antagonist of Socialism.

In the meantime, she had enrolled her daughter, Katherine, in a convent boarding school. Within several months, Katherine announced her decision to become Catholic and to enter the convent. Martha, no doubt prompted by Katherine's decision, engaged in a two-year study of Catholicism with a Physics professor from Boston College. Her search for "the Truth" ended in 1904 when, at the age of fifty-three, she joined the Roman Catholic Church.

Beginning A-new

There was a long—a double process of eliminating error, one intellectual the other experimental. From the darkness of confusion at last my vision became strong enough to bear up against the direct beam of positive light. Like as a mariner after the tempest has spent its force in vain I was full of joy for the rolling clouds had just for a little parted and I was sure of my due course. Truly my own proud sires had sent me out on my journey the longest way round, and in very rough and stormy weather.

Indeed, I would take soundings, constantly, for no half-hearted assent would satisfy me—I must give my all. Rome must prove to be supreme: that central figure in control of the universal design for the perfection of the individual and at once in control of the means by which civil society shall be elevated. Otherwise it were not adequate to meet the demands of the rational mind. The Catholic Church must be found to have possession of all the keys for unlocking all the meanings which are necessary to explain both the inner and the outer, the lower and the higher life of man.[4]

On Her Evangelistic Method: The Catholic Truth Guild

Martha learned about evangelism not from ecclesiastical sources but rather from former Socialist comrades, who taught her an array of communication methods. While a Socialist, she spoke in lecture halls and outside on Boston Commons and public streets. She wrote countless newspaper articles and editorials and distributed literature to educate the populace about the Socialist cause. All of these methods were utilized in the Roman Catholic lay evangelism organization—the Catholic Truth Guild—founded in 1917 by Martha and her closest friend, David Goldstein, another zealous convert to Catholicism from Socialism.[5]

The Catholic Truth Guild was a pioneering organization in the United States for sending out Catholic laity "into the highways and byways in city squares and street corners" to proclaim Catholic truths and to make The Roman Catholic Church "better known and loved" by Americans.[6] The most spectacular feature of the Guild was its customized Model-T autovan, whose decorations were designed to attract a crowd. One side of the car sported a quote from George Washington's Farewell Address: "Reason and experience forbid us to believe that national morality can prevail where religious principles are excluded." Painted on the other side of the car was the refrain from the Holy Name hymn, written by the Archbishop of Boston and the Guild's financial patron, William O'Connell: "Fierce is the fight for God and the right; sweet name of Jesus in Thee is our might." Decorating the hood was a miniature star spangled banner, and a large, lighted crucifix adorned the sounding board. The Model-T itself was painted in the papal colors of yellow and white.

Meetings sponsored by the Catholic Truth Guild began with an informational lecture on some aspect of Catholicism, such as its doctrines, accomplishments, or stance on contemporary issues. The lecture topic was publicized beforehand by each local Catholic community. Following the lecture was a question and answer time, known as the Quiz period, where listeners voiced their objections or asked questions. At the close of the meeting, Catholic literature was distributed and sold. These meetings were designed to awaken interest generally in the Catholic Church, to correct misinformation about Catholicism, to reclaim lapsed Catholics, and to gain Catholic converts. During the summer months, Catholic Truth Guild meetings were held throughout the northeastern United States. The number of meetings ranged from eighty the first summer in 1917 to nearly one hundred and fifty during the last summer of Martha's life. Each summer season began and ended with a rally on Boston Commons. During the winter months, Martha remained in Boston, attending to numerous affairs within Boston Catholicism, while Goldstein and various associates embarked on cross-country tours on behalf of the Guild.

In this excerpt, Martha set forth the rationale for open-air evangelism by Catholic laity. Although she claimed authorship of the article in several letters to her daughter, it was published under David Goldstein's name, a frequent occurrence in their collaboration.[7]

Lay Street Preaching

The effectiveness of Catholic street preaching in America has been tried out and not found wanting. After a test of eight years of carrying the Catholic message to the man in the street it is safe to say that the average American is interested in what Catholic laymen have to say of the faith that is in them.

The Catholic is glad to hear his faith defended and the other fellow is surprised at the clarity with which Catholic claims are set up in proof that Christ's Church—one and the same in doctrine throughout the ages—is as thoroughly qualified to meet the religious needs of the race today as at any other time in her history; that neither scientific discovery, historic research, attainment, or prospect takes from the Church her sure touch as to the ills of mankind, or their remedy.

The confidence of the preaching layman in the catholicity of his faith, in its utter fearlessness in face of problems in any sphere of human knowledge, arrests and holds the attention of masses of men and women in the open spaces in America. The Catholic message is as unfamiliar to the populace as is the technique of broadcasting to the novice in physics. It is not that the opportunity has been wanting for "putting the message across." It is rather the failure of the layman to meet his duty by responding to the call of the Hierarchy to become living echoes of the voice of the Good Shepherd,[8] his failure to realize that our Declaration of Independence and Constitution constitute good Catholic Stamping ground; that our God-given rights as against that of Pagan might shall conquer by the means of free speech so dear to good American hearts.

This being so, all too long our natural forums—the streets, squares and parks of our cities and towns have been monopolized by all sorts of folk not merely preaching doctrine against the true religion but against right reason as well. All sorts of freak religions have been propagated, not to mention the recent activities of Protestant sects who, at best, have Christ's doctrine only in part.

There is a latent interest in things religious on the part of that vast number of Americans who own no Church affiliation. Many of these former Protestants are turning away from the idea that a cure for immorality, rebellion and crime of all sorts lies within the purview of the civil law. Evidently the effort to enforce prohibition has somewhat shaken public confidence in law-made reform. So it is that hope—which springs eternal in the human breast—prompts them to view moral obligation as the quickener of better relations betwixt man and man. This fact, happily, points behind man-made laws back to the constitution of things human as laid down by Almighty God. All this is of course, by the multitude at street meetings, seen but darkly. Yet when the clear light of Catholic understanding is directed to this or that social problem there is an unmistakable response from the crowd that argues well for a further interest in things Catholic. . . .

Indeed, the urge for the laity to do the initial work, to go out and plough the virgin soil of spiritual America, so that it might flower and fruit under the social cultivation of the priests, had found voice long years ago. So although *the call* is not new the first response also was lying fallow for many years. . . .

If then, the laity of the Church, divinely commissioned to teach truth in whole, not in part, the Church commissioned by Christ to hear and to forgive the truly penitent, have been slow in responding to *the call*, it is not too late. For, the American populace will listen to those who echo and re-echo the law and the love of Christ as it has ever been taught by the great doctors of the Christian faith.

Providence left it to the Archbishop of Boston, Cardinal O'Connell, to make the start. His sanction to the inauguration of a layman's outdoor movement has blazed the way for the extension and expansion of a Catholic army of the laity under St. Francis,[9] to bring the old old story of man's salvation in word and in song to the mind and heart of our fellow countrymen who for no fault of their own know not the Bride of Christ—the Catholic Church—as she really is, the Kingdom of Heaven, the salvation of man, the hope of the world![10]

On Women

Martha tirelessly expressed her views on men and women's roles in print and in lectures. She championed vociferously the notion that men and women were different yet complementary. Each sex was assigned by God to different spheres of influence; women were connected to the social and domestic spheres, men to the civic and economic spheres. On the basis of these divisions, she mounted an argument against women's suffrage. Previously, while a Socialist, she had supported women's suffrage and explained her position in her pamphlet, *Woman: Her Quality, Her Environment, Her Possibility.* However when she joined the Catholic Church, she became a staunch opponent of women's right to vote. In the years between 1908 and 1915, the antisuffrage theme dominated her lectures and articles. In this article published in the Catholic journal, *America,* in 1915, Martha explained her belief in separate spheres for men and women as the foundational argument against women's suffrage.

Spread of Social Disorder

NOBODY expects a perfect society this side of heaven. But since both philosophy and practice have so far departed from the moral law, and since women seek to enter on equal terms those spheres for which they are disqualified by their physical being and their natural character, it is worth while to contrast the order within the spheres which women dominate with that existing where men hold the reigns of power. Are the home and social intercourse in a better state of morality than commerce and politics?

If the departments of civilized life over which women rule were strictly in order, then, indeed, they might assist in setting to rights man's world, for there is much to be done. Truly, things are due to Caesar[11] which men deny and things are done to Caesar that stress and strain the civil peace, while the absence of economic justice sets class against class. Yes, it must be said that both politics and trade are in disorder, but men, not women, should set them in order. If men should permit their own work to be done by women, and women were able to do it, who then would do the work which women alone are qualified to do?

The Feminists have the answer, they look to see the woman made more of a man and the man more of a woman. Aye! the philosophy of a great English poet has ripened in these sixty years, for the superman will be not only absolutely soulless but practically sexless.

That the woman's world is greatly in disorder no one can deny. Men are helpless before the task of setting it to rights. The nature of the disorders in the home and in society are such that women alone can cope with them. But "votes for women" merely confounds the confusion. Neither can the votes of men reach to the core of the issue, for it lies in the mental and moral fabric of woman's weaving. Woman may, if she will, heal the sores that are festering within her own dominion. But if she will, she must call upon the Vicar of Christ[12] for her instruction.

Suffragists have so long been weaving public opinion with the warp of mental rebellion and the woof of sex discontent that the very foundations of our Republic are being sapped, because of the failure of a vast number of women to do the work God set them to do. Even the mention of her natural qualifications and their corresponding activities is vexatious to those most advanced in denying the true mission of woman. Their insistent iteration is for freedom from all the *limitations of convention*. Lacking the structure of logic, they read into the meaning of convention those limitations of sex prescribed by nature itself. Moreover, as a consequence of a lack of interior womanliness that is compelling, our country faces the demoralizing influence of vain women, idle women, selfish women, luxurious women with their real rights condemned and their duties unperformed.

Women's legitimate rights, as the second term of mankind, give her control of the home and of society, and her duties are to keep these environments in good order. But the following after strange gods has disordered her provinces and is constantly working havoc to the cause of Christ.

Besides woman's work in the home and in society, she plays a secondary, though very important, part with the civic and exchange spheres. So it is that women's influence is good or bad in civics and in trade in proportion as she keeps or exceeds her proper influence within these extended environments.

In the elevated arts—music, painting, architecture—comparisons are invidious, for men are freely at home upon these fields, while women are but occasional comers. But woman, as well as man, has her creative spheres. Her great art is worked out interiorly in conscious union with the Giver of Life, she moulds her unborn children, dedicating her first-born to the especial service of God. Women build in the hearts of the little ones, in the hearts of men, in the world of emotion and intuition. Masculine building, on the other hand, is exterior: men organize governments and build up the intellectual and moral codes that show the designs of Almighty God. Thus, working together in complementary spheres, men and women lay the foundation in the home and build gloriously those nations which honor God.

No votes are needed for the women to set their half of the world in order. Besides, the most fatal disorders are seen in the home, where even the votes of men, are powerless, for men have not in their keeping the chastity of motherhood. It was to our Blessed Mother[13] that God gave the custody of the Redeemer who was to appear. It is the woman who commits that abomination of desolation, murder of the unborn child, the most ruthless crime ever devised by the ingenuity of wickedness. Votes are not wanted to prevent another vile practice, which leading suffragists advocate. Votes are not wanted to give good care to helpless infants in squalid homes, but rather the early conviction of the mother that a child is a gracious gift from God, and a drill in the best practices known in the care of babes. Votes are not wanted to cure the incorrigible children who crowd our juvenile courts, but, rather, good government at home, where parents are commissioned by the Judge of judges. Votes are not wanted to clear our streets of hoodlums, but mothers who do not hearken to evil counsels. Votes are not wanted to solve the servant-girl problem which is left all untouched while a multitude of illogical women pester men for votes that women need as much as the moon and are as well equipped to use as the baby is to handle the carving-knife. Votes are not wanted to protect the housemaids to whom the wages of sin make almost successful appeal, but rather a training of the young men in the family in Christian chivalry which guards defenseless girls even against their own desires. Votes are not wanted for the prudent spending of the husband's wages in the market place, but rather a sober sense of the fitness of things, which adjusts one's expenditure to one's income. Votes are not wanted to shame the rich bargain-hunter, but rather a sense of fair-play, demanding measure for measure in economic value. Votes are not wanted to better conditions and raise wages for girls working in shops and factories, but a right public opinion.

Neither are votes wanted to empty those theaters and moving-picture houses where pleasure seekers are gorged with the vile trash they feed upon. Women support, largely, the "problem plays" with their false mental concepts and emotions reeking with the sweat of lust. The daughters of mothers are there with their mothers, together breathing in the fire of sex rebellion. The "best sellers" are bought with hard earned cash of husbands and fathers, and read, seducing the mind and capturing the fancy for a life the exact opposite from wholesome ideals. Newspapers carry into every home the most shocking tales of disordered families and social scandals, together with the vagaries of the so-called science of our day, which finds the "same root for man and brute," to borrow a great Pope's phrase. In the ball-room good women stand unabashed in scandalous attire, while luxurious women spare no pains in their appeal to the sensuous in mankind. The tango teas bring heart to heart the panting prig and the newest girl, both bred in the atmosphere of a soft and decadent environment, lurid with passions uncontrolled. On the street, one may be at pains to discover the line between the woman in self-conscious scarlet and the woman merely in the garb of fashion. Vice in schools astounds and alarms the sober-minded. But sex hygiene and eugenics are preparing a stench not yet endured, while the school strike is but a ripe fruit of the revolt against the moral order which subjects children to parental control. For the rod has been long since spared and many a child has long since been spoiled[14] in that home where "the baby is the head of the family," because the father has abdicated his authority and the mother has forgotten that under God she stands at the head in the home.

These disorders within the spheres that women dominate cannot be cured by creating new ones within those departments under the rightful control of men; they must be cured by protecting the family as the unit of society.[15]

Her zeal for disseminating "the Truth," as she understood it, propelled her to the end of her life. The Sunday before she died at the age of seventy-eight of heart trouble, she had addressed a large crowd on Boston Commons. During the eulogy at her funeral service, these remarks were made about her evangelistic work: "And where did she speak His [God's] testimony? To the simple vendor who came to her door; to the intellectuals within classic walls; and to the vast multitude to which she spoke on corner, in park and hall, and public square. She was still a propagandist. For her to possess Truth was to share it. To go out into the open was her ambition . . ."[16]

Notes

1. See n. 17, chapter 4.
2. Spiritualism is the more common name for this movement. See note 31, chapter 3.
3. Higher criticism is a method of biblical interpretation that was developed during the Enlightenment. Its most basic characteristics include: academic inquiry free of church influence, interpretation of the biblical texts with methods that could be applied to any literature, sacred or secular, and, in many instances, a rigorous historical skepticism that called into question the accuracy of the Bible. For a history of this method, see W. G. Kümmel, *The New Testament: The History and Investigation of Its Problems* (Nashville, TN: Abingdon, 1972) and Stephen Neill, *The Interpretation of the New Testament 1861–1961* (New York: Oxford University, 1964).
4. Martha Moore Avery, *The Longest Way Home to Rome*, Beaton Institute, University College of Cape Breton, Nova Scotia. Page numbers cannot be cited for her autobiography since not all the pages are numbered, and when numbers do exist, the sequencing is not correct. For more information on her, see two articles by D. Owen Carrigan, "Martha Moore Avery: Crusader for Social Justice," *The Catholic Historical Review* 54 (April 1968): 17–38 and "A Forgotten Yankee Marxist," *The New England Quarterly* 42 (March 1969): 23–43; see also Debra Campbell " 'I Can't Imagine Our Lady on an Outdoor Platform': Women in the Catholic Street Propaganda Movement," *U.S. Catholic Historian* 3 (Spring/Summer 1983): 103–14.
5. David Goldstein (1870–1958), who was born into a Jewish family, became acquainted with Martha through the Socialist Labor Party. They then traveled the same path out of Socialism and into Catholicism. This common

ground undoubtedly cemented their friendship and enabled them to work closely together. For more on David Goldstein and the Catholic Truth Guild, see David Goldstein, *Autobiography of a Campaigner for Christ* (Boston: Catholic Campaigners for Christ, 1936) and Debra Campbell, "A Catholic Salvation Army: David Goldstein, Pioneer Lay Evangelist," *Church History* 52 (1983): 322–32.

6. "The Origin, Methods, and Results of the Boston Catholic Truth Guild," Beaton Institute, University College of Cape Breton, Nova Scotia. While some priestly orders had been active in evangelism in America for many years, the Catholic Truth Guild was unique as a lay organization.

7. In a letter to her daughter, Martha specifically mentioned writing this article. "Today I wrote the last words of an article—of course to go out in the Secretary's name about lay street preaching for one-third of a book gotten out by Father John A. O'Brien, Ph.D. The other two-thirds is to be written by priests." (Letter from Martha Moore Avery to Katherine, May 15, 1925, Beaton Institute, University College of Cape Breton, Nova Scotia.) In a subsequent letter to Katherine, she expressed her true feelings about not receiving due credit for the article. "A letter comes saying that the M.S. 'reads well'—the one-third of the booklet I told you of. Father wants personal data from *the author*. Sometimes it is hard to maintain the equities, since *the author* is really the woman not the man whose name is attached." Letter from Martha Moore Avery to Katherine, May 25, 1925, Beaton Institute, University College of Cape Breton, Nova Scotia.

8. John 10:11–14.

9. St. Francis of Assisi (1181/82–1226) was born into a wealthy family, but he had a series of religious experiences that convinced him to undertake a devout religious life, which included a vow of poverty. Following the directions which Jesus gave to his disciples (Matthew 10:5–15; Mark 6:7–13; Luke 9:1–6), Francis renounced all possessions, wore a simple, coarse tunic tied with a knotted rope, and became an itinerant preacher. His followers were organized into the Franciscan religious order.

10. David Goldstein, "Lay Street Preaching," in *The White Harvest: A Symposium on Methods of Convert Making*, ed. John A. O'Brien (New York: Longmans, Green and Co., 1927), 209–10, 214–16. For more on the authorship of this article, see n. 7 above.

11. Matthew 22:21.

12. According to Roman Catholic tradition, this is one of the Pope's titles, which proclaims that he is the head of Christ's church.

13. This refers to Mary, the mother of Jesus. See Luke 1:26–38.

14. Proverbs 13:24.

15. Martha Moore Avery, "Spread of Social Disorder" *America* (October 9, 1915): 78–79.

16. "Mrs Avery Is Laid At Rest," *The Boston Globe*, Saturday, August 10, 1929, Beaton Institute, University College of Cape Breton, Nova Scotia.

Holiness evangelist, Quaker minister, copastor with her husband, Seth Rees

Frontispiece, Byron J. Rees, *The Pentecostal Prophetess, or A Sketch of Her Life and Triumph, Together With Seventeen of Her Sermons* (Philadelphia: Christian Standard, 1898).

CHAPTER 9

HULDA REES (1855–1898)

H ulda A. Johnson, the third child of four born to Nathan and Malinda Johnson, grew up in rural Indiana in a Quaker family. Little is known about her early life since she did not author an autobiography, as did most women in this anthology. Information on her life comes from a biography written by her son, Byron, including the first two excerpts on her conversion and sanctification.

On Her Conversion

Even the days of her childhood were not without tokens of the character of her future life and work. Her sisters recall distinctly child sermons which, in innocent fun, she preached to her playmates, and she frequently conducted play-meetings with great zest and keen enjoyment. But there were more serious glimmers in her youth of coming brightness and usefulness. Although of a bright and merry temperament, she was at the same time capable of the deepest religious feeling. Even as a child, the Spirit of God made profound impressions upon her spiritual nature. Jonathan Johnson, her grandfather, a man of rare insight and of more than ordinary devotion, firmly believed and said that "Hulda would be a minister, and, if faithful, would accomplish much good." When in her tenth year, she arose in a meeting and gave in a testimony. This was the more remarkable because, at that time, children rarely took any part in the meetings of the Quakers.

At the age of eleven she attended the public funeral of her grandmother; and although the silence of the occasion was profound, she knelt by the open coffin and offered vocal prayer. Thus, as a child, she felt and frequently obeyed the promptings of the Holy Spirit.

At the age of sixteen she was truly converted. The great revival was sweeping over the meetings of Western Friends.[1] The services, in many cases, were pentecostal in power and depth. A God-honored preacher came to Cherry Grove Meeting, the Johnsons' home meeting, and began services in harvest-time. The people came in throngs. The evangelist preached in his characteristic, but always effective, way. Hulda Johnson, in company with a number of her girl friends, attended the meetings. For days she felt no conviction whatsoever. She sat well forward in the meeting, undisturbed by the Knox-like[2] declarations of God's servant. One day, while he was preaching, the mind of the evangelist was moved to pray for her. He poured forth his scatching message, his heart meanwhile ascending to God for the thoughtless girl before him. Suddenly, as she afterward related, she was seized with profound conviction, and dropped her head upon the back of the seat before her. The preacher stopped speaking, and then, after a moment, cried out in gratitude, "Thank God, her head is down!" Instantly, pride asserting itself, she raised her head and sat perfectly erect in her place throughout the remainder of the service. She told herself that she had been insulted. She determined *never* to enter the meeting house again. Her parents might entreat and persuade, but she would not cross the threshold of the building again. The moment the meeting "broke up" she started for the door; but the preacher, divinely impressed that a soul was in peril, passed out another door, and met her in the yard. He grasped her by the hand, exhorted her to seek the Lord, dropped upon his knees and began to pray. When he had ceased a Christian young woman, deeply interested in the salvation of the proud girl, also prayed. God heard his servants, and by the time opportunity came, Hulda Johnson, thoroughly penitent, kneeling upon the grass in the old meeting house yard, cried to the Lord, and was clearly converted.

Immediately after her conversion she began to preach; but, although she was frequently blessed and often enjoyed manifestations from the Lord, her Christian life was more or less vacillating for three years, the memory of which gave her great pain in after-life.

But the spiritual shadows were soon dispelled forever. She was fully reclaimed in a series of meetings held at Cherry Grove, in December, 1875. From this on her course was one of unwavering fidelity to her Lord. The monthly meeting, of which she was a member, recognizing her earnestness and appreciating the gift which God had bestowed upon her, soon recorded her a minister.[3]

In December, 1876, Hulda married Seth C. Rees, who also was a Quaker minister. Together they began to hold meetings in their home state. At first, preaching was difficult for Hulda because her natural timidity was heightened in public settings. "She has been heard to say that, at this time in her life, when sitting in the pulpit, waiting for the time to come to preach, she often closed her eyes, simply to avoid seeing the congregation. Then the cares of home, and her responsibility as the wife of a minister, and as a preacher herself, weighed upon her."[4] Through her experience of sanctification, as this excerpt indicated, she found release from her anxieties and a renewed power for preaching.

On Her Sanctification

About this time, a dream came to her which made her very hungry for a better experience. In her dream it seemed to her that she was a child again, at the old home, perfectly happy and free from care. She was sitting in her favorite seat, in the willow tree, near the springhouse. She could hear the bees humming in the sweet locust flowers, and the birds were singing with their old-time beauty. She looked up and saw her mother standing in the door at the house, and she said to herself, contentedly, "By and by, when I get hungry, I will go to the house and mother will give me something to eat." There were no cares or responsibilities to oppress her. She need take no thought for anything. The dream passed, and she sighed when she remembered that it was merely a dream. Then it seemed as if the Lord spoke directly to her:

"Wouldn't you like to be as free from care as when you were a little girl?"

"Yes, Lord, could I?" she said wistfully.

"Would you be willing to be childlike and happy and contented, and just be my little girl and do errands for me?"

"Oh, I would be so delighted!" Thus the Lord led her along to seek sanctification.

Other things revealed to her the extreme need of her soul. Sometimes the feeling that she could not measure up to the expectations of the people well-nigh crushed her. On one occasion she was expected to preach at a First-day morning meeting, at Westfield, Ind. A large anticipative audience came together. She arose, took her text, and in ten minutes had said all that she could possibly think of to say. She sat down feeling, as she said afterward, "like a fool." It was a great humiliation to her. She felt extremely mortified. She determined that she would never preach again. She "had not done herself justice," and "wished that she was not recorded a minister." Suddenly she found herself, naturally enough, in great darkness. God convicted her deeply for her lack of humility and her want of deafness to the opinions of other people. She began to seek holiness. A series of meetings was in progress. One night she remained home in order to be alone and pray. She locked the door of her room and faced the Lord. As she prayed, God gave her such a revelation of her own heart that she arose from her knees, went out of the room, and closed the door, unable to endure the sight.

But she could not rest, and finally, after a long struggle, she made a complete and entire consecration of herself to God, and was sanctified wholly.

. . . She no longer feared congregations, but preached "in the power of the Spirit." Consequently, it was said that she was "not so humble as before." Some thought that she "was not so modest and womanly"; but God, on the other hand, began to honor her with souls, and used her in His work as never before. Her ministry gained in effectiveness and force by her sanctification.[5]

On Her Evangelistic Method: Evangelistic Meetings

Hulda and Seth established a routine of copastoring churches for nine months through the fall and spring and then itinerating as evangelists during the summer. With this schedule in place, they served a church in Ohio for four years and a Friends' Meeting in Michigan for two years and held summertime meetings throughout the midwest and northeast. These letters, written by Hulda to her mother and sister, provided a unique glimpse into the life of an itinerant evangelist, a life that required long periods away from home and family. The topics in her letters ranged from descriptions of their meetings to the activities of their sons, Byron and Loring, to inquiries into her family's health and activities.

Portsmouth, R.I.
July 3, 92

My Darling Sister Jane,

I was *so glad* to get thy good long letter it had been so long since thee had written. I tried not to build up any hopes about Father and Mother coming for fear I would be disapointed [sic] but I did hope in spite of it. It seemed such an *unusual* chance and I found myself getting my work arranged and looking forward to what they would say. Oh, it would *have been so nice*—but I leave it all with the Lord. I do believe it is for his sake I live so far from you all . . . Tomorrow is the 4th and Seth asked everybody to come to the campground, men to bring teams, women to bring dinner and sewing machines and we expect to get a great deal done getting ready for the meeting. We are to have a large tent. It is such a rest to get away from home and live in a picnic way—37 tents have been engaged already which with 8 large tents and the *large tent Tabernacle* which will seat 400 and the cook and eating house make quite a town. Seth has a great part of the responsibility of it all.[6]

Bloomingdale, Ind.
1-16-97

Sister Jane,

I can't tell thee how glad I was to get thy letter tho' so *sorry* to hear that father was poorly again—Seth wrote to father while we were at Spiceland and I wrote a card after we came here—we are now in the second week of meetings at this place. It's a beautiful country here, the village of Bloomingdale is small but it is a thickly settled neighborhood mostly Friends. . . . The meetings here have been large and interesting from the first. They were exceedingly interesting to us—it's an old fashioned quarterly meeting house—only they have taken out the gallery seats and put a platform clear accross [sic] the side of the house, left the partition in, part of the time both sides have been open because one room would not hold the people, but usually we all sit in one room, there are about 50 middle aged people who sit up on the platform. I hardly ever saw such a body of concurred and weighty friends in one peticular [sic] meeting, and so nice and quiet. *Oh' dear* but it was cold seemd [sic] like there *never, never* could be a revival but we began preaching and praying the best we could. For days not an *amen* or anything, at last it began to break and these dear friends began making confessions to bondage and hunger for salvation and there has been such a breaking up we seldom see. 60 at the altar in two days—many backsliders[7] reclaimed and several conversions—two converted last night—there is a Friends

Academy here and the fire is spreading among the students for several days. I was sick, pain in my head, no appetite but am feeling better now. Byron has been at Gadley holding meetings or rather helping. . . . He is working under the Evangelistic Committee of the yearly meeting. He stopped with us our first day on his way to Ills [Illinois]. He is well and *so happy* in his work. Loring is getting on well in school. We expect now to return East early in the spring. Seth expects to go in next month. I have not quite decided to go so early. We will perhaps close here about the 28th then after a few days rest begin at Bridgeport 9 miles out from Indianapolis—hold perhaps two weeks—that will close our evangelistic work. We have other calls one in Ills [Illinois] and one in Ind [Indiana]—yearly mtg—but have not cared to take more believing the Lord calls us back to Rhode Island. The sad thing about it is to leave our folks especaally [sic] our *precious parents*.[8]

Portsmouth, Va.
9-23-97

My Precious Mother,

How is thee and what is thee doing? I think of thee *so much.* I guess being with thee so much last spring spoiled me. . . . Our meetings here are held in the Friends meeting house it will seat 600 people and has been well filled most of the time of evenings. The attendance in the day is good and many are getting saved. We make our home at Frank Halls he is the pastor of the church. Has a wife and one child. The meetings at Wilmington Del [Delaware] closed with an all day meeting. House packed and altar crowded. We got much attached to the people there. I wrote thee about this place when we were here a real southern city. So many darkies they have just had a great revival in their churches *800* converts. They are nearly all Baptist. They shouted in the streets so that the mayor of city [sic] warned them if they did not stop it he would have them arrested. So they had to shout in the church or in their houses. The boys are both well and doing well. Loring is much better satisfied this year. Byron has moved on to the university grounds which makes it much easier for him. He wrote yesterday that he had dropped his watch and broke it all to pieces. Loring is well has got back his flesh. He did get *so poor,* he looked like he would not live long. Got so he hardly even *walked* about, but the Lord healed him so that afterward he never suffered a pain with the reumatism [sic] or missed a meal. Oh we have *so much* to be thankful for. I am feeling real well. . . . How I would love to see you all. What of weather have you had. [sic] How are the crops? The yellow fever may prevent us going South. We could not go *now* on account of yellow fever. They sell no tickets there, may be it will be better before time for us to go. We go from here to Norfolk for ten days. Did thee get any new clothes during the summer. [sic] I must close and get ready for meeting.[9]

On Women

From their beginning in the seventeenth century, Quakers have believed that men and women are equal and that they should exercise equal roles in the family and in church. Their principle of gender equality arises from their doctrine of the inner light, or "that of God" in every person. The inner light is the ultimate religious authority for Quakers. Through the inner light, God might move any person to speak, male or female. Before a person was recorded as a minister, he or she would have to possess a clear conviction of God's calling through the inner light, and then that call would be evaluated by the Quaker community. Only when the members were convinced of the call's validity would the person be recorded as a minister. In Hulda's case, her grandfather, also a Quaker, predicted when she was only a girl that she would be a minister.

In this sermon, "The Gift of the Holy Ghost," Hulda delineated the Holy Spirit's gifts to the church, one of which is women's right to preach.

The Gift of the Holy Ghost

"The gift of the Holy Ghost."—Acts ii: 38

The Holy Ghost is a gift to the Church. Jesus was a gift to the world for the salvation of the world, and the Holy Ghost is likewise a gift to the Church. He is as much a person as is Jesus. But we will not speak at this time so much concerning Him as His work. We will not deal at this time with the doctrine and theory of holiness, though there is much on this line in the Bible. But we wish to speak of the results and effects of his work.

He was not a gift for the apostles exclusively. In proof of this we find that at one time one hundred and twenty persons received Him, and among them were disciples, such as Mary and the brothers of Jesus. All with one accord in one place, in perfect readiness to receive Him whom Jesus had promised to send.[10] Suddenly He filled them.[11] He did not now take His place as the Shekinah[12] in the Temple, but in the hearts of these believers.

One of the first results which followed His coming was: "They began *to speak.*"[13] The Holy Ghost makes witnesses out of us. These newly-endued people never dreamed they could "live and never say anything about it." They knew they could not live Him if they did not let Him speak. It was He who spake. This was not simply "speaking in meeting," or quoting a text, but it was speaking "as the Spirit gave them utterance."

It was "noised abroad."[14] Certainly! They never tried to keep this great effusion a secret. The Holy Ghost, like Jesus, "cannot be hid." The people will see the effects and learn the cause. The man at Bunker Hill who thought it was only a sham battle suddenly realized when wounded that there were genuine shot.

The baptism with the Spirit drew the people together. He can do this, and does do it, when He comes. He excels all the brass bands and flowery preaching. And when the crowd comes the Holy Ghost at once convicts them. That is His mission. When He comes to the Church as its sanctifier, then He radiates out and powerfully takes hold of the sinner. This occurs whenever He can get possession of a people for a base of operations.

Another effect was boldness. Peter changed from a timid disciple who denied his Saviour into a bold preacher of not only repentance, but holiness. The Holy Ghost always gives boldness when He comes. "Perfect love casteth out fear;"[15] and the fearful, cringing believers who are afraid of the word "holiness" do not have the Spirit, for He gives boldness in using God's own words and terms.

He gives woman the right to preach. "Your daughters shall prophesy," says Peter, and Joel tells us that the prophecy was fulfilled on the day of Pentecost.[16] And if women on whom is laid the burden for souls and the work of God, instead of complaining that they "can't preach," their "church or pastor forbids it," would open their hearts to the Holy Ghost, they would preach. They would do it kindly, but they would preach, and no regulation or rules would stop them from it.

The gift of the Holy Ghost made and kept the church orthodox. They continued in the apostle's doctrine steadfastly.[17] There is no one like the Holy Ghost to make and keep the church sound in doctrine. He has been very properly termed "the conservator of orthodoxy." After all, doctrine is very important. The most theologically sound person is a thoroughly sanctified one, for the presence of the Spirit clears up theological difficulties. The divinity of Christ, the importance of the blood, the personality of the Comforter—all these matters straighten themselves under His tutelage; but so long as He does not come and inbred sin is present, so long will it plead for unsoundness in doctrine.

But these sanctified, Spirit-endued people not only continued steadfastly in the apostle's doctrine, but also in fellowship.[18] They not only had the theory and were sound theologically, but they had real Holy Ghost fellowship with each other. It is thus to-day. People of different denomination, with different theories and beliefs, meet on a common platform and enjoy real fellowship.

There was steadfastness "in prayers."[19] Preachers are asking: "How can I get my members to prayer meeting?" Some advertise that there will be a "short, spicy service" and "good singing," etc. But if the Holy Ghost comes to a church, He will put the praying into the people and He will add all the spice needed. This spice in prayer will be sweet to the one who knows Him, but will probably bite the tongue and throat of the indifferent Christians.

The Holy Ghost brought fear upon the people round about the Pentecostal Church.[20] Holy Ghost experience always does that. He brought also to the heart of the disciples great gladness. Joy is not the Holy Ghost, but He brings it when He comes.

"Singleness of heart."[21] Ah! here is a most valuable result! Pentecost makes our hearts to love God with singleness of affection. We adore Him and worship Him with undivided love. Not only is the eye single, but the heart is a unit for God. Glory!

February 13, 1892[22]

Hulda died in 1898 at the age of forty-three. These stanzas from a poem written as a tribute to her life, memorialized her evangelistic work.

> We remember her zeal for the cause she loved,
>   Her labors for perishing souls;
> And the courage grand that remained unmoved
>   Through breakers, and storms, and shoals.
> And as we remember our eyes o'erflow,
>   Though our hearts feel so strangely glad,
> For she rests from her labors—and well we know
>   That she would not have us be sad.
>
> We have seen her stand in the battle shock,
>   'Midst the enemies of our Lord,
> With her feet placed firmly upon the Rock,[23]
>   As she wielded the Spirit's sword;[24]
> We have seen her prostrate upon the ground,
>   Regardless of sneer or of stare
> From the wondering throngs who gathered round
>   While she won the fight through prayer.[25]

Notes

1. Another name for Quakers is the Society of Friends, which is often shortened to Friends.
2. John Knox (1513–1572) was a Scottish Protestant reformer known for his zealous preaching.
3. Byron J. Rees, *Hulda A. Rees: The Pentecostal Prophetess, or A Sketch of Her Life and Triumph, together with Seventeen of Her Sermons* (Philadelphia: Christian Standard, 1898), 12–16.
4. Rees, *Hulda A. Rees*, 17–18.
5. Rees, *Hulda A. Rees*, 18–20.
6. The Lydia J. Pegg Papers, Indiana Historical Society. The campground she described became known as the Portsmouth Camp Meeting, and Hulda and Seth were instrumental in its establishment. She served as a member of its executive board until her death.
7. See n. 15, chapter 2.
8. The Lydia J. Pegg Papers, Indiana Historical Society.
9. The Lydia J. Pegg Papers, Indiana Historical Society.
10. Acts 1:14–15.
11. Acts 2:1–4.
12. *Shekinah*, generally translated as the "presence" of God, comes from a Hebrew word whose root means "to dwell."
13. Acts 2:4.
14. Acts 2:6.
15. 1 John 4:18.
16. Joel 2:28–32; Acts 2:17–18.
17. Acts 2:42.
18. Acts 2:42.

19. Acts 2:42.
20. Acts 2:43.
21. Acts 2:46.
22. Rees, *The Pentecostal Prophetess*, 75–79.
23. Psalm 40:2.
24. Ephesians 6:17.
25. Mrs. E. E. Williams, "Hulda A. Rees" in *The Pentecostal Prophetess*, 9.

Holiness evangelist, founder of The Pillar of Fire, first woman bishop in the United States, author of many books, including *The Story of My Life, The New Testament Church*, and *Why I Don't Eat Meat*

Courtesy of The Pillar of Fire.

Chapter 10

Alma White (1862–1946)

Alma Bridwell was one of seven daughters, who along with four sons, comprised the family of William and Mary Ann Bridwell. They lived in rural Kentucky, where the already burdened economy felt even more the impact of the Civil War. According to her autobiography, her parents anticipated that she would be a boy who could work to help support the family. Their disappointment in her gender added fodder to what she recalled as an unhappy childhood. Her Methodist mother and her Baptist father were the main religious influences on the children since the closest church was five miles away. At the age of twelve, Alma became a member of the Methodist church, though she had not yet experienced conversion; that happened several years later when evangelistic meetings were held in her neighborhood.

On Her Conversion

The Lord had answered my prayers for a hymn book and a Bible, and had saved my brother and raised him from a bed of sickness, and I believed prayer would be answered for a preacher to come who would hold special revival services, giving the people a chance to seek the Lord. I was not disappointed. Mr. Carter's successor was the Rev. W. B. Godbey, since known as a world-famed author and evangelist.[1] He began meetings in our neighborhood November 5, 1878. I was away from home and did not attend the first service. The second evening I went forward with others on the first invitation. Our hired man, whom I thought to be very wicked because he attended balls and places of worldly amusement, knelt near me. After a short struggle he leaped to his feet shouting. On the other side of me was a worldly neighbor girl who went to shows and dances. She broke through and began to praise God for deliverance from sin. These conversions were a great surprise to me. I had supposed it would take them longer than it would me to find acceptance with the Lord. I had to learn that through faith in the atoning blood[2] grace will reach as far as sin has gone, when conditions are met.

I found no relief that evening, and left the house in great distress. I could almost hear the wails of the lost, and felt that one more step would take me over the brink into the abyss below. Everything hitherto had failed to bring relief, and I knew now that it was not in the power of the preacher or anyone to bring peace to my soul. All desire for food was taken from me.

The next day, as far as possible I remained out of sight. The cry of my soul was, "I must be saved tonight or be lost forever!" On entering the meeting house that evening I found the seats all taken. There were two benches near the speaker that were used for the mourners.[3] I sat down on one of these, near the end, and held tightly to keep from falling to the floor, for I was almost prostrated under my load. The text was Romans 6:23, "For the wages of sin is death; but the gift of God is eternal life through Jesus Christ our Lord." Breathing became difficult as the preacher thundered the terrors of the law. The old serpent[4] tightened his coils about me. Conviction settled down with such power on the congregation that some persons turned ill and went out. One of my uncles, who had been trying to be a Universalist, went out and threw up his supper, and returned. Hell was uncapped; people looked into it and became desperately sick of their wages. The call for seekers brought many to the altar.[5] Demons were clutching at my heart-strings as I sank to the floor. A sister in the church came to talk to me, but I wished to be alone. When she left, the preacher came and knelt at my side and asked me to repeat the following familiar lines, from which he thought I might receive benefit:

> But drops of grief can ne'er repay
>   The debt of love I owe:
> Here, Lord, I give myself away,—
>   'Tis all that I can do.

My reply to him was that I had repeated them over and over. I felt that the Savior was far away and could not hear me; I was so inwardly absorbed and crushed I could scarcely hear the voice of the preacher who was speaking in his usual tone. Trying to arouse me from this death-like stupor, he said, "Daughter, will you take Jesus for your Prophet, Priest, and King; your Prophet to teach you, your Priest to forgive you, and your King to rule over you?" I told him that this was the desire of my heart. He asked me then to rise to my feet. I said, "I must be saved tonight, and I cannot leave the bench until the work is done, if I have to stay until morning." "But you have taken Jesus, have you not?" I hesitated, but finally said, "Yes." He helped me to rise to my feet. Instantly my burden rolled away, my heart opened, and heaven came down and filled and thrilled me until my whole being was tremulous with new life. The power of the Holy Spirit was so great upon me I was unable to stand without support. Everybody around me seemed to be changed; the faces of some were radiant with light, while others were very dark. Some said, "Shout"; others said, "Sing"; but all I could do was to laugh, wondering if heaven could be any better. A young man who apparently had been unmoved until this time turned to Mother and said, "I can never doubt again after seeing the change in your daughter." Three days later he was converted.[6]

After her conversion, Alma resolved to become a preacher, but she soon changed direction and decided to become a missionary. To prepare for mission work, she earned a teacher-training certificate and began teaching at a local school. At the age of nineteen, Alma moved to Montana with her aunt and uncle, where she continued to teach school. In 1887, Alma married Kent White, who was training to be a Methodist minister. The birth of their first son, Arthur, left Alma in poor health. Their second son, Ray, born three years later, almost died of pneumonia as a baby. Alma attributed Ray's recovery to her promise to God that she would preach, "regardless of the opposition she faced."[7] However, there was still her innate shyness that had to be overcome. As with other evangelists in this anthology, when she experienced sanctification, Alma found the courage to speak in public.

On Her Call to Preach

It was during this revival that the Holy Spirit moved me to exhort.[8] My husband had tried to get an evangelist to come and help him, but had failed. On a certain evening at the close of the sermon, an exhortation was badly needed. I felt that I should get up and give one, inviting the people to come forward to the altar, but I hesitated, and the opportunity was gone. I spent that night in prayer and weeping.

Satan tried to ease my conscience by telling me that women had no recognition in the Methodist Church and that I should have been out of place had I given an exhortation and an altar call. I was so troubled I awakened my husband to talk with him on the subject. He said, "If you want to speak, I will open the way for you at any time."

A few evenings later I was again moved by the Holy Spirit to speak, this time more strongly than before. Just as I was about to rise to my feet the enemy said, "You will make a great blunder if you attempt to speak now." I hesitated, and again the opportunity passed. The revival closed and left me heartbroken; the class meeting[9] was the only place now where I could have another chance to speak. On the following Sunday I made an attempt to break through the powers that held me, but utterly failed. My health had been improving, but after this I seemed to lose what I had gained....

From day to day my body was racked with pain; burning fever was followed by hard chills, and as death seemed to be near I felt more and more my unfitness for eternity. During short intervals of restless sleep I dreamed I was a child again, climbing up to break the icicles from the eaves of a house to quench my burning thirst. Just as I was ready to grasp them my feet would slip and they were never reached. A literal fire seemed to be consuming me and I was well aware of the fact that there was no hope for me if God did not undertake. Through all my suffering my mind was perfectly clear. I was thankful for this, for I wanted to hear the Lord speak to my soul....

The baby would often stand by my bedside and draw my arm around his neck as much as to say, "You must not leave me." The thought of his being left motherless was heart-breaking. I had heard of mothers who, when seriously ill, had become resigned to leaving their children, but it was not so with me....

My temperature reached one hundred and six degrees, and then dropped to below normal in fifteen minutes. While thinking of the child and making one more earnest plea to be spared for his sake, I heard a gentle, chiding voice say, "Is not that a selfish prayer?" I could see it then, and said, "Yes, Lord." The Christ of Calvary[10] was bending over me. A vision of a greater work than simply living for my own child was flashing upon my soul. I had thought nothing in that hour of the other motherless children in the world, and the multitudes of men and women who were in the tombs of spiritual death, who needed the resurrection power of Christ. Could it be possible that I had been so selfish? Another moment and the following familiar lines were going through my mind and heart:

> I will sing the wondrous story
>   Of the Christ who died for me;
> How He left His home in glory
>   For the cross of Calvary.
>
> He will keep me till the river
>   Rolls its waters at my feet;
> Then He'll bear me safely over
>   Where the loved ones I shall meet.

The assurance came that my life would be spared, not only to sing, but to preach the Gospel. After this I sank still lower and became unconscious. On regaining consciousness I wanted to tell the nurse that she need not be anxious about me, for the Lord would spare my life to preach the Gospel. She was slightly deaf and I was not strong enough to make her hear, and did not tell her until the next day.[11]

On Her Evangelistic Method: Founding a Denomination and a Community

Kent and Alma held evangelistic meetings throughout Colorado and became active in the Colorado Holiness Association. Coincident with an increase in Alma's popularity, prominent holiness leaders strengthened their opposition to women in ministry and refused to let her speak at their gatherings. After several years of such conflict, Kent, Alma, and their boys relocated to Denver, where they set up an independent mission and held street and tent meetings. They also opened a training school to educate workers for the mission. Despite Kent's resistance, the mission was formally organized as a church—The Pentecostal Union Church—on December 29, 1901. Alma oversaw about forty pastors and evangelists and had missions in four states. Because she was now heading up a church, she sought ordination several months later when Seth Rees[12] was holding evangelistic meetings in Denver. This independent church eventually grew into The Pillar of Fire denomination.[13]

In this excerpt, Alma explained that she felt compelled to begin a church because she wanted to continue to nurture and educate those who had been converted at her meetings and to put them to work in evangelism.

During the weeks of my absence the Lord spoke to me definitely about organizing an independent church. The difficulties of such an undertaking were inconceivably great, especially since my husband and many of our people thought it would be a great mistake. The experience I had had in missions where false shepherds would use every available means to carry off the lambs—capture my converts—was sufficient to show me what we should have to contend with in taking a definite step toward organization. For years I had faithfully preached against the apostasy of the old denominations, and God's word had been hammering in pieces the rock, and much of the opposition to an independent society had given way among our patrons, even though there were still mountains of difficulty to be removed. To delay now when the crisis had come I knew would be perilous. I had asked the Lord many times to put me in a hard place if He could trust me, but when I prayed this way I had but little comprehension of what would be involved.

The question of how to save those who were converted under my ministry had been a great problem for seven years. In spite of all efforts to keep them satisfied with mere membership in the missions where most of them had been converted, some had been persuaded by false shepherds that this was not sufficient and were drawn away into the cold, formal churches where they soon died spiritually.

When I spoke to our people about organizing, I found that a few of them were prepared and waiting for it, while others were on the fence, halting between two opinions. Some who had clear light drew back and stayed with the dead mother from whose breast they could get no nourishment.

Two weeks after my return from the Coast, fifty persons were ready to cooperate with me and unite with the new church, the organization of which was effected December 29, 1901. Two years later (1903) a four-and-a-half story building for a Bible school and church auditorium was erected at 1845 Champa Street, Denver. In 1906 operations were begun in New Jersey, where later grew up the national headquarters of our organization.[14]

However, even an independent church was not sufficient, in Alma's opinion, to prevent converts from being tainted by worldly influences. She then founded a self-sufficient community, a town in New Jersey, which she named Zarephath.[15] At Zarephath, residents lived, worked, worshipped, and ate vegetarian meals. There was also a school for every level of student, from elementary age through college. Building Zarephath from the ground up was an arduous task requiring financial equity, executive foresight, and physical labor. Numerous reports cataloguing its growth were included in her five-volume work, *The Story of My Life*. This short description related some features of the community in 1913, six years after it began.

The summer of 1913 was one of the most remarkable in the history of our organization. Important business and other transactions were taking place almost every day that took a miracle of faith to meet, and we were enabled to do so only by the help and power of God.

We had made application for a third class post office to take care of our own business at Zarephath so that we might be saved all the trouble of taking truck loads of papers and books to Bound Brook [a nearby town], besides all the other mail that had to be handled. We felt that the establishment of a post office on our own grounds would be a great achievement and if we were so favored it would be in direct answer to prayer. There had been opposition to it from the post office at Bound Brook on the supposition that it would greatly curtail their business. On the nineteenth of July a government official came for further information. Later (October 4) our application was granted and F. W. Borough, one of our brethren, was approved as postmaster.

The name, Zarephath, had been given to me of the Lord, and it would now become official. There was no other locality or city in the United States with this name....

During the latter part of July a contract was made for the purchase of an engine and boiler at Tarrytown, New York.... We were now to have a power plant of our own to furnish light and heat for the buildings and to operate the machinery in our new printery. From time to time the hand of the Lord was thus opened to us in providing material for the construction of buildings and in giving us other supplies.

In July negotiations were begun for the purchase of an adjoining farm across the canal. The securing of this farm was another step of faith. It had become necessary to increase the acreage at Zarephath, with our schools and fast-growing constituency, and the purchase of an adjoining farm was the only way by which it could be accomplished satisfactorily.[16]

Along with building up Zarephath, Alma's work in other areas was tireless. She continued to expand The Pillar of Fire's membership through evangelistic meetings and the distribution of gospel literature in cities across the United States and in Great Britain. To mark her authority over the denomination, in 1918, at the age of fifty-six, she became the first woman bishop in the United States. The same minister who was present at her conversion, the Rev. William B. Godbey, did the consecration service. She also found opportunities to support the Ku Klux Klan during the height of its popularity in the 1920s. She concurred with the Klan's anti-Catholic and anti-immigration sentiments, all of which seemed quite patriotic to Alma.[17] Finally, because of her commitment to Christian education, by the 1940s, she had opened eighteen schools in American cities, including Cincinnati, Baltimore, Los Angeles, Jacksonville, and Denver.[18]

All was not so well in her personal life. She and Kent had an unhappy marriage. Even though she preached her first sermon in Kent's pulpit and they had shared evangelistic meetings for several years, their marriage and evangelistic partnership began to dissolve when Alma became the more popular preacher. They separated not long after Kent gravitated toward Pentecostalism, and they were never reconciled. Their sons, Arthur and Ray, embraced their mother's work and became Pillar of Fire leaders. When Alma died in 1946, the same year Ray died, Arthur became president and general superintendent of the denomination. Then Arthur's daughter, Arlene White Lawrence, followed her grandmother's footsteps as head of The Pillar of Fire.[19]

On Women

Alma stands out in this anthology as one of the most outspoken on women's rights. She supported the platform of the National Women's Party, including the Equal Rights Amendment. She believed wholeheartedly that men and women were equal and that their equality must be institutionalized in every realm—political, religious, familial, social, and economic. She based her egalitarian position on biblical passages, particularly the creation story in Genesis. "In the beginning God gave men and women co-partnership and control of all that He had created. But His order has been reversed and woman has become man's servant or slave, and as a result the social fabric is going to pieces and the world is well-nigh wrecked. Before lasting peace can be expected, woman must be accorded the place designed for her."[20] She published her feminist teachings, including this poem that critiques the church, family roles, the fashion industry, and men in general, in her periodical, *Woman's Chains*.

Woman's Place in Church and State

Our woman's cause must now be heard,
And true to light and God's own word
The truth herein we now present,
That further wrongs man may prevent.

Woman as well as man should preach;
This Bible standard men should teach
The word is plain, none can deny,—
Then why should they the truth belie?

This Bible truth is set aside
And woman of her place is denied;

The church is run with half a force,
And homes are broken by divorce.

Since with the home man draws the line
Of her influence and use of time,
A standard new shall be our theme,
Till woman's cause man shall redeem.

Since dark clouds hang o'er church and state,
And fearful things it yet may take
To make men see the wrongs they do,
To their souls now we must be true.

Without cooperation, men
The world can't save by tongue or pen;
With wars they've drenched the ground with blood,
And fear and darkness o'er us brood.

If woman's help man now would take,
The chains of tyrants soon would break;
It takes two to draw a load
On God's highway or Caesar's road.

The morale of the Church she'd raise,
And legislators would amaze,
If all her shackles men would break,
And ne'er her place would try to take.

The nations then would serve the Lord
And build upon God's holy Word;
They'd beat their swords into plowshares,[21]
And use no more their guns and spears.

Though ages come and ages go,
The truth of God all men should know;
'Tis not in man this world to lift
Above its tendency and drift,

When woman's help has been denied
To break and stem the awful tide
Of immorality and crime
Increasing now in ev'ry clime.

Pulpits are barren of the truth,
And children stray in early youth,
And long before maturity
They've lost their childhood purity.

Without restraining hand they go
To any place or ev'ry show,
Until their minds are so corrupt
They break our laws and homes disrupt.

When to the vices they have turned
And ev'ry law of home have spurned,

The state responsible must be,
And only God the end can see.

Should fathers who their duty shirk,
Who go each morning to their work,
And mothers leave with all the care
Of children whom they helped to bear,

Have any argument to make,
Where office could a woman take,
Because of inefficiency,
Or that she lacked ability?

If she our statesmen all must train,
The argument will still remain
That capable and true she'd be,
As ev'ry one can plainly see.

The pulpits women are denied,
And filled with men ofttimes untried,
Who have, unfaithful to their trust,
Brought on disgrace through greed and lust.

No argument is there to prove,
In all the earth or from above,
That men from women should withhold
The place accorded her of old.

'Tis in the home of sad neglect
That men should now try to correct
The many evils fostered there
Because of long-neglected prayer.

With family altars broken down,
The crime wave spreads from town to town;
The preachers have no power to stay
Or turn calamity away.

Since they the throne have not besought,
And inequality have taught,
Responsibility of men
Must now be told by tongue and pen.

If social evils they'd correct,
Men on this subject should reflect,
And learn from Genesis, the Book
Where God would now have all men look.

'Tis there equality is taught
For which the women long have sought;
To this end then we will contend
Till men their rights to them extend.

Then will a change be brought about,
And God's word men no more will doubt;

The nations all shall be at peace
When inequality shall cease.

When God made men out of the dust
He gave to him a sacred trust;
'Twas that the woman, near his heart,
Of his own life should be a part.[22]

A helpmeet not alone was she,
But man's own equal she should be,—
In partnership with him to rule
O'er everything on God's footstool.

When Satan would them both deceive
He came first to our mother Eve;
And by his subtlety and power
He captured her in that dark hour.[23]

Secure her first, he would prefer,
So as not to risk losing her;
She was the stronger citadel,
And what she'd do he could not tell.

So at the task the tempter went,
That her escape he might prevent;
The man heard all that Satan said,
And into sin he, too, was led.

Not e'en a protest did he make,
But from her hands the fruit did take.
From Eden then both had to go,
Since good and evil they did know.[24]

The penalty must then be paid,
And heavy burdens on them laid;
In sorrow Eve should children bear,
And none with her the pain could share.[25]

If God's word she would not refuse,
Her seed the serpent's head should bruise;
A Savior of the world must come
To lift the curse from heart and home.

The curse brought on mortality,
And thenceforth man's brutality;
Woman would be subordinate,
And make her an unequal mate.

God said the man must till the soil,
That his life should be one of toil;
Because he hearkened to his wife
He must the ground till all his life.[26]

The ground was cursed for man's own sake,
And ne'er to this would he awake;

The penalty he now would shirk,
And make the woman do the work.

Besides the children she must bear
In pain and suff'ring ev'rywhere,
The burden of the home she takes,
And washes, irons, scrubs, and bakes.

The sewing by her hands is done,
And sympathy she finds from none
Who could her burdens help to bear
While ills of others she doth share.

In ev'ry country you may go,
In sunshine, rain, or falling snow,
You'll find the woman with a load
Trudging along on some rough road.

Ofttimes the women work the farms,
They sow the seed, and fill the barns,
While men seek easy things to do,
And oft leave home and children, too.

Where'er on earth is found the curse,
'Twould seem God's plans man would reverse.
A woman's place he'd try to fill
And her with burdens help to kill.

May seem unjust to charge him thus,
And no doubt some will make a fuss;
But Bible truths none can deny,
Then what's the use for man to try?

Look you, I pray, to heathen lands,
Where none there are to break her bands,
Subordinated to a brute
Whose life each day brings forth the fruit;

The woman lives beneath the rod
Of man, who is her tyrant god;
A slave to beat, abuse, or sell,
Is woman in the tyrant's hell.

The property of foreigners,
In rendezvous of white slavers,
The woman pines her life away
Where lust of Sodom's vine holds sway.[27]

These pens are fed from public halls
Where slavers lure girls from the balls;
A long or shorter route they take
To get them to their dens of fate.

The fashion dame is in the town
With rouge and frill and silken gown,

The butterfly of flattery,
Man thinks her a necessity.

To keep the social structure up,
Where men devoted to the cup
Would have a toy with which to play,
To keep more serious thoughts away.

They lure her on in revelry,
And into their own deviltry,
And when her character is gone
They find someone else to blame this on.

The Christ-hating commercial men,
Supporters of the white slave den,
The arts of Satan now employ
Morals of women to destroy.

The fashions men design and make,
And then the blame must women take
For garments Satan could not beat,
For winter's cold or summer's heat.

The skirts are short, the necks are low,
You'll see it ev'rywhere you go;
No matter what a woman thinks
Of fashions bold from which she shrinks,

She must the latest "togs" all wear,
Must paint her face and bob her hair,
So that a market may be had
For ev'ry vain and foolish fad.

Her neck and arms they would have bare,—
A place for jewels rich and rare;
And thus you see that woman's made
The dupe of all the tricks of trade.

But what has she to do or say?
When man decrees she must obey.
He is the power upon the throne,
And naught can she say is her own.[28]

Notes

1. William B. Godbey (1833–1920) was a Methodist pastor and evangelist. After he experienced sanctification in 1868, he became a zealous advocate of the experience. He wrote a pamphlet titled, *Woman Preacher*, in which he presented biblical arguments in favor of women preachers.
2. Romans 3:23–25.
3. See n. 25, chapter 7.
4. Genesis 3:1.
5. See n. 14, chapter 5.

6. Alma White, *Looking Back From Beulah* (Zarephath, NJ: Pillar of Fire, 1902), 18–22.

7. Susie Cunningham Stanley, *Feminist Pillar of Fire: The Life of Alma White* (Cleveland, OH: Pilgrim, 1993), 20.

8. See n. 8, chapter 1.

9. See n. 2, chapter 6.

10. Calvary is a name for the site of Jesus' crucifixion.

11. White, *Looking Back From Beulah*, 123–24, 131–35.

12. Seth was married to Hulda Rees, see chapter 9. After she died, he married another woman evangelist, Frida Rees. Seth and Frida both signed Alma's ordination papers, as did Alma's husband, Kent. Stanley, *Feminist Pillar of Fire*, 47.

13. God led the Israelites, after their exodus from Egypt, with a pillar of cloud by day and a pillar of fire by night. See Exodus 13:21–22.

14. White, *Looking Back From Beulah*, 374–75.

15. Zarephath was the name of the town where the prophet, Elijah, was miraculously fed during a famine by a widow and her son who were down to their last crumbs when Elijah arrived (1 Kings 17:8–9). Alma explained her rationale for naming her community, Zarephath, in these words, "The famine in Israel in Elijah's time is a symbol of the spiritual famine in Christendom today. There is also significance in the name as it relates to the work of our society in trying to raise the old standards of true religion that have been broken down." Alma White, *The Story of My Life and the Pillar of Fire*, vol. III (Zarephath, NJ: Pillar of Fire, 1936), 340.

16. White, *The Story of My Life and the Pillar of Fire*, vol. III, 339–41.

17. For more on Alma and the Klan, see Stanley, *Feminist Pillar of Fire*, 85–98.

18. Stanley, *Feminist Pillar of Fire*, 80–81, 116.

19. Stanley, *Feminist Pillar of Fire*, 120.

20. Alma White, *Woman's Chains* (Zarephath, NJ: Pillar of Fire, 1943), 41.

21. Isaiah 2:4; Joel 3:10; Micah 4:3.

22. Genesis 2:7, 18, 21–23.

23. Genesis 3:1–7.

24. Genesis 3:22–24.

25. Genesis 3:15–16.

26. Genesis 3:17–19.

27. Sodom, an ancient city, was characterized in the Hebrew Bible as a wicked place (Genesis 13:13). It was destroyed by God because of its depravity (Genesis 19:1–29).

28. White, *Woman's Chains*, 78–86.

Holiness evangelist, minister in The New Testament Church of Christ, which merged with The Church of the Nazarene, author of *The Life and Work of Mary Lee Cagle: An Autobiography*

Courtesy of The Church of the Nazarene Archives.

Chapter 11

Mary Lee Cagle (1864–1955)

Mary Lee Wasson was born on a farm in rural Alabama. She attended school sporadically, three months in winter and two in summer. Her father was Presbyterian and her mother was Methodist, but she remarked in her autobiography that neither were religious. When Mary was fifteen, she was converted at a Methodist evangelistic meeting. During the next year, she evangelized her fifteen classmates, all of whom experienced conversion. She sensed a call to Christian work, but her family's hostile response eventually quelled her enthusiasm. Her mother "bitterly opposed her," and her brother-in-law declared that if she ever preached, his children would not be allowed to acknowledge their aunt. About five years later, she heard an evangelist, the Rev. R. L. Harris, preach on the doctrine of sanctification. "Holy Ghost conviction" seized her heart during his message, as did her "old-time call to preach . . ."

On Her Conversion and Call to Preach

Early in life I had a longing desire to be a blessing to the world.

When fifteen years of age I was truly converted to God and with this change of heart, the longing to carry gladness and sunshine to darkened hearts and homes became more intense. I felt assured of a Divine call to engage in Christian work. On account of the teachings of that time regarding woman's ministry, I decided there would be no opening for me in my home-land. I came to the conclusion that my call was to the foreign field where I supposed a woman would have freedom in preaching Christ to the heathen. Many dreams I had of crossing the waters and preaching to them.

I opened up my heart to my mother, telling her of my call and of my intention to obey it. She gave me no encouragement, but on the contrary bitterly opposed me, saying she would rather have me go to my grave than to the foreign field as a missionary.

Finally I became discouraged and a spirit to disobey the call came into my heart and thus I lost the joys of salvation. Although backslidden[1] in heart my outward life was consistent and I kept up the form of religion but without power. My name was on the church record and my pastor considered me a true, loyal Christian.

While in this backslidden condition, a preacher filled with the Holy Ghost came to our Church to conduct a revival meeting. Holy Ghost conviction seized my heart and the former joyful experience was restored to me. With the restoration came the old-time call to preach; but God by His Holy Spirit revealed to me that my work was not across the waters, but here in my home-land. What a struggle I had. I plead with God to release me from the call. It seemed it would have been so easy for me to say "Good-bye" to loved ones and native land and pour out my life among the heathen. The thought of remaining at home to preach the Gospel brought trouble to my heart. I knew there was not so much reproach attached to going as a missionary.

On my face before God, with tears, I would plead to be released. I knew to go out in this country as a woman preacher would mean to face bitter opposition, prejudice, slanderous tongues, my name cast out as evil, my motives misconstrued and to be looked upon with suspicion.

Besides this, I was so conscious of my inability. My educational advantages had been very limited. I was reared a timid, country girl and had never been out in the world—in fact until twenty-seven years of age, had never been outside of my native county in the State of Alabama. It seemed very strange God would call me when all these things were considered.

So often as I would plead my inability, the following verses of Scripture would be presented to my mind: "Then said I, Ah Lord God! behold I cannot speak: for I am a child. But the Lord said unto me, Say not I am a child: for thou shalt go to all that I shall send thee, and whatsoever I command thee thou shalt speak. Be not afraid of their faces: for I am with thee to deliver thee, saith the Lord. Then the Lord put forth His hand, and touched my mouth. And the Lord said unto me, Behold, I have put My words in thy mouth."—Jer. 1:6–9. Many times, as I would take my Bible to read it, it seemed it would open where this passage is, I wished in my heart it was torn out of my Bible.

During this struggle I am thankful I did not say, "*I will not preach,*"—but I said, "*I can not preach.*"

In 1891, at the age of twenty-seven, Mary married the Rev. R. L. Harris. They held evangelistic meetings throughout Tennessee, Mississippi, Alabama, and Texas. R. L. preached, and Mary assisted with the singing and prayer meetings.

While debating in my mind about the call, I became engaged to and married Rev. R. L. Harris, the Texas Cow-Boy Preacher. I married him thinking that by becoming a preacher's wife, I could more easily do the work God called me to.[2] But instead of this, I found it so easy to shift the work upon him, and I thought by so doing that God would release me and I would conduct the singing and women's prayer meetings and would assist in the altar work in our revival meetings.

During all this time my heart was not satisfied. God still pressed upon my heart *the call to preach.*

After three short years of married life, my husband was seized with that dreadful disease—consumption of the lungs. It was a great source of grief to me.

After some months of suffering he told me his work was done and that God was going to take him to his home in Heaven.

I refused to entertain such a thought. We were so devoted to each other, I felt that I could not submit to such a separation.

One day I went all alone with God to have a season of secret prayer. In my desperation I said: "Lord, if you will heal my husband, I will preach," and God answered me with these words: "Will you do what I want you to do whether I heal your husband or not?" These words came as a thunder clap to my soul.

There on my knees the inward struggle was long and heated. Finally by the help of God I was enabled to say from my heart: "Yes Lord, whether my husband lives or dies, I will do what you want me to do." What joy flooded my soul! From that hour to this, that question has been settled.

Shortly before his death from tuberculosis, R. L. founded a church which grew into a denomination, The New Testament Church of Christ. A central belief of the movement was its strict standards for holiness in dress and habits; members were not allowed to smoke, drink, or wear jewelry or any ornamentation.

About two months after this my husband was promoted to Heaven. At the time of his departure God did a most gracious work in my soul. He sanctified me wholly, thus fitting me to go out on the battlefield as an Evangelist to win souls.

Shortly after husband's death I entered the open doors in Kentucky, Tennessee, Alabama, and Arkansas. God graciously put His seal upon my ministry in rewarding my efforts with many precious souls brought into His Kingdom.[3]

With her husband's mantle now placed on her shoulders, Mary tentatively accepted invitations to speak, but she was quite timid at first. She prayed that God would turn her loose. Her prayer was answered.

[God] absolutely broke every fetter . . . It was the first time in her life that she could turn the pulpit loose—she ran from one end of the large platform to the other and shouted and praised God, and preached with the Holy Ghost sent down from above. . . . It was a permanent loosing from that day, and she has never been bound again. Although of a shrinking, backward disposition, she has never seen a crowd since that day large enough to make her knees tremble, and she has preached to thousands.[4]

Mary, along with several other women evangelists, held evangelistic meetings in Arkansas, Kentucky, Tennessee, and Texas, and then organized their converts into churches associated with The New Testament Church of Christ.

On Her Evangelistic Method: Evangelistic Meetings

Mary's evangelistic meetings were often held in out-of-the-way places, where the poor and oppressed lived. She accepted invitations to hold meetings for African Americans in the South, even though her family and others disapproved. Her message was always one of personal holiness, following R. L.'s example. These two aspects of her ministry, an identification with the poor and an emphasis on personal holiness, were intertwined. "Even the legalistic emphasis of her preaching was shaped partly by her identification with the dispossessed. Though her sermons against the worldliness of rings and jewelry strike later generations as narrow, her practice was to sell jewelry and use the money to support food and orphanage ministries in India."[5]

This excerpt from her autobiography, written in the third person, described her meetings and the opposition she faced.

After being in Alabama a short time and her mother getting better, she decided, after being requested and urged time and again by the people, that she would hold a meeting. Her friends asked for the use of the Methodist church where she had been a member in girlhood and where her father had put in as much money in the building of the church as any one man and where she had worked with her own hands and helped to paper it; but the opposition to holiness and also to women preachers was so great, that she was promptly denied the use of the building. The Missionary Baptists, of their own accord, offered her the use of their church, and in a few days of their own accord decided that she could not have it. She kept sweet in her soul and said nothing . . . In a few days a member of the Christian church sent her word that she could use their church building and was as welcome as could be and to go right ahead and make herself perfectly at home and preach just as long as she wanted to. This was the largest and best furnished in the county . . . She passed some tests and trials there that she had never faced before. She was at her childhood home where she had lived for twenty-seven years and had taught school and worked among the people, and was known and loved by all till she professed sanctification. Then she was as a speckled bird among them. As she had all her life been timid and backward and no one thought that she could ever preach, they came in throngs to see what she could do. The house was packed to overflowing— all standing room was taken. It was so warm that the window sashes were taken out from top to bottom, and throngs were standing around the church trying to catch a word. God was present in power, and soon curiosity gave way to conviction and after preaching a week an altar call[6] was made, and there was a rush for the altar. Such crying and praying, confessing and straightening up of lives as is seldom seen these days took place as they began to pray through to victory and to rejoice. Their friends and loved ones joined in and when shouting was at its height, the floor gave away and went down with a crash, but she did not feel very badly about it, for it was mostly the members of the church that were shouting. The meeting ran for two and one-half weeks, and there were more than one hundred professions. She had no human help at all—no one to even start the songs, so God got all the glory.

One morning while there, as usual, she had to preach on "Women's Right to Preach." The house was packed and the people were all attention. She had gotten about half through her message, when a Baptist lady, whom she had known all her life, jumped up and began to wave her handkerchief and say, "Go it, Mary, go it. God bless you, go it." With that she began to shout and others took it up, until the preacher had to stand for ten minutes before it was quiet enough to proceed. After the service, someone asked the husband of the lady who started the shouting, what he thought about women's right to preach. He answered, "I think Mary has a right to preach." . . .

At the close of the Landerville meeting, she was given a pressing invitation by the colored people to come to their church and preach for them, which she was glad to do, as she had known many of them from her childhood when they had worked for her father on the farm. She was a favorite with the colored people. Some of her relatives opposed her preaching for them; but she felt it was of the Lord and said that she must go, and she did. It was a day long to be remembered by her as she preached the Word of God to them and saw their black faces light up with the blessings of heaven. When the ones who objected saw the results they gladly withdrew all objections.

At the close of the Newberg meeting she preached again to the colored people with very gratifying results. In this meeting she saw her eldest brother sanctified wholly, and in the Landersville meeting she saw one of her sisters reclaimed, which was a great cause of rejoicing to her. Under her ministry she saw her sinner brother converted—her mother sanctified and a host of other relatives and friends brought to God . . .

She went back to Milan, Tennessee, which was then her home, and there she met Miss Trena Platt, a fine young woman and a most excellent musician. Their devotion to each other was something like that of David and Jonathan,[7] and during the four years they labored together, they were separated only one time. That four years represented some of the best work of Sister Harris' life as well as some of the most difficult. The two workers continued summer and winter—using a tent in the summer and preaching in schoolhouses and courthouses in the winter; thousands came flocking home to God for either pardon or purity.

They worked in Tennessee, Arkansas and Texas and traveled in all kinds of conveyances, from the wagon to nice carriages (autos had not been heard of then). Many young people were called into the work and some are in the foreign field at this writing; and the churches planted at this time are among the best in the movement.[8]

During her meetings in Texas, a cowboy named Henry C. Cagle was converted, sanctified, and experienced a call to preach. He had been a "wild and woolly cowboy . . . known in those early days as 'Battle Axe' because he rapaciously chewed vast cuds of tobacco of that brand."[9] In 1900, Mary and Henry were married. For over forty years, they held evangelistic meetings and organized churches together and separately across the south and into the west, from Tennessee to Wyoming. In 1927, she cited these statistics for one year's work. "Our work has not been with the larger churches, but with the weak struggling ones. I have held 13 revival meetings, preached 175 times, saw 216 converted and 118 sanctified, and . . . have traveled about 10,000 miles in a car and have made a few trips on the train. I have visited practically all of the churches in the district and some of them more than once."[10]

On Women

The denomination that R. L. Harris founded, The New Testament Church of Christ, grew largely through the efforts of Mary and several other women evangelists. In 1908, The New Testament Church of Christ merged with The Church of the Nazarene, a Wesleyan/Holiness denomination with Methodist roots. At that time, women comprised 13 percent of the ordained ministers in The Church of the Nazarene, a statistic due in large measure to Mary and her sister evangelists.

Whenever Mary held two-week-long evangelistic meetings, at some point she would preach a lengthy sermon on "Woman's Right to Preach." A portion of the sermon was excerpted for this chapter.

Woman's Right to Preach

Now we are going to look into the Bible and see what it has to say on the subject. We are going to take this up entirely from a biblical standpoint and see what women were allowed and what they were not allowed to do. I am persuaded that what they were allowed to do when the New Testament was written will be all right for them to do now.

1. They took part in public prayermeeting. Acts 1:13, 14.

This is an account of the first prayermeeting after Jesus went away and there were some women in it, and best of all the mother of Jesus was there. I don't believe that she would have been there if it was wrong; neither do you. Some would say, "Yes, the women were there, but they were not taking part publicly." They were doing just what the men were doing for, "They all continued in prayer and supplication with the women." . . .

2. They prophesied. Luke 2:36–38.

3. Acts 21:8, 9, "And the next day we that were of Paul's company departed, and came unto Caesarea: and we entered into the house of Philip the evangelist which was one of the seven; and abode with him. And the same man had four daughters, virgins, which did prophesy."

This brings us to the consideration of his girls: What kind of girls do you suppose that a man like that would bring up? "Oh," says one, "I suppose that they were leaders of society, and followed all the latest fads of fashion, had bobbed hair, painted faces and skirts above their knees, and went all the gaits and adorned themselves with gold." No! No! Never! Never!

We know that they did not have bobbed hair, for women in those days were not allowed to speak in public with short hair (1 Cor. 11:4, 5).

We know that they did not paint their faces, for in Bible times a painted face signified a harlot: 2 Kings 9:30, "And when Jehu was come to Jezreel, Jezebel heard of it; and she painted her face, and tired her head, and looked out at a window." Jer. 4:30, "And when thou art spoiled what wilt thou do? Though thou clothest thyself with crimson, though thou deckest thee with ornaments of gold, though thou rentest thy face with painting, in vain shalt thou make thyself fair; thy lovers will despise thee, they will seek thy life."

They could not have worn their skirts above, or to their knees, for women in those days were commanded to dress modestly, and also not to wear gold: I Tim. 1:9, 10, "In like manner also, that women adorn themselves in modest apparel, with shamefacedness and sobriety; not with braided hair, or gold, or pearls, or costly array; but (which becometh women professing godliness) with good works."

By this time we are anxious to know what kind of girls they were.... We find that all four of Philip's daughters were prophesying. Now, if we can find the meaning of the word "prophesy" it will help us some.... Read I Cor. 14:3, 4, "But he that prophesieth speaketh unto men to edification, and exhortation, and comfort." I throw out the challenge: is not that what every Bible preacher does? (see v. 12) (1) He teaches the people what God says; (2) he exhorts the people to obey God; (3) he comforts the people with promises of God.

... Philip had a family of four girl preachers, and there is no record given in the Bible that any man had a family of four boy preachers. There is nearly always a black sheep among the boys.

4. "They labored in the gospel." Phil. 4:3.

Here, Paul admits that these women were his fellow-laborers in the gospel. Once while I was preaching on this subject, I read the above quotation and as I was making the point that they labored with Paul, someone in the audience spoke up and said, "They cooked and washed for Paul." But I informed the person that the Book did not say that they labored in the kitchen, and over the wash tub, but in the gospel; whatever Paul was doing they were doing.

5. They served the church. Rom. 16:1, 2.

Here was this woman Phebe, who Paul declares was a servant of the church. The church sent her to Rome on business for the church. Paul wrote this letter to the church and sent it down there by her. And for fear that some might forget that respect due a woman worker he urged them to receive her in the Lord as becometh saints; in other words, treat her as your equal, and assist her in the business that she has been sent there to do.

We want to notice that word "Servant," a little. If I should come to your town a stranger and would get in conversation with a Methodist concerning the work of God there, and I should ask him, "Who is serving your church this year?" whose name do you suppose he would call? Of course we all know that he would call his pastor's name, the only thing to do, and the same thing would occur in regard to any or all of the different denominations. What was Phebe? None other than the pastor at Rome; and the great apostle certainly regarded her very highly....

6. A woman was the first to preach Jesus after he arose from the dead. John 20:16–18 is where we will read in a few minutes, but we want to notice a few things preceding the quotation. Jesus had been crucified, had died and had been buried. The men had gone away but the women were still lingering around the tomb of their precious Lord, their all was buried there. We women are free to admit that the men are our superiors in almost every sense of the word. They are our superiors physically and mentally. They can excel us in sermonizing and they may excel us in preaching, but there is one

thing that it is impossible for them to excel us in, and that is, loving Jesus. When you get a woman's heart, you get her all. A man does not love like a woman. Of course a man loves, but not like a woman.

Mary Magdalene came and told the disciples that she had seen the Lord and that he had spoken these things unto her. The first sermon that was ever preached on the resurrection was preached by a woman and she got her call, her commission and her message from Jesus himself, and He sent her to the brethren. Women may not be able to sermonize much, but when they see Jesus and He gives them a message they can deliver it.

7. Jesus first declared his Messiahship to a woman: John 4:25, 26.

The Jews tried to get him to say that he was the Christ. His disciples had tried to get him to say that he was the Christ, but the first time that he said it was to the woman at the well of Samaria. The woman got scared, left her water-pot, ran back to town, told what the Lord had done for her and a revival broke out; the record says that many believed because of the sayings of the woman.

8. They are as divinely authorized to preach as men. Joel 2:28, 29.

Some say that women have a right to preach, but not the same right as a man has, but I contend that if they have any right at all they have the same right to preach as men have. . . .

Now we will consult Acts 2:14–18, to find the fulfilment: . . . Just as much the daughters as the sons, just as much the handmaiden as the servant, one is just as divinely authorized as the other. . . . And had there been no such gifts bestowed on women the prophecy could not have had the fulfillment.

No matter what men have to say about women preaching, God said, "She shall." And when God says, "She shall,": by the grace of God "She will." Joel said, "They shall prophesy," and Peter said that on the day of Pentecost the prophecy of Joel was fulfilled, and if such was the case (and there is no *if* about it), women were prophesying or preaching (I have already shown you the meaning of prophesying), just like the men; if they were not, then the prophecy was not fulfilled; Peter said that it was fulfilled.

9. The grace of God knows no sex. Gal. 3:28.

God is not looking for a man or woman to do His work, but He is looking for someone wholly consecrated to Him, and when He finds someone like that, He will use him or her, regardless of sex. We are too near the judgment now and too many souls are lost to quibble about who shall reach them. I have said for years and I still say that if a little black dog could come to our town and stand on the street corner and bark and get people under conviction and to God I would stand by and say, "Sick him, Tige," and take him home with me and feed him.

10. Why did God give women such a talent to talk, if not to be used for Him? If God did not intend for women to use their tongues for Him He certainly did give the devil a great advantage in the beginning, for women can talk. The men are generally our superiors; but there are some things that we can excel them in. And one of them is talking: You can put a half-dozen women in one room and they can all talk at once and no one listen, and yet when they get out of the room each one can tell everything the other said. Men could

not do that if their lives depended upon it. They have to talk one at a time and then they can't tell it correctly across the street. How many men are there who never went down town and phoned back and asked the wife what it was she told him to get? All that never did that keep your seats. It is no wonder to me why the devil has tried and in a large measure succeeded in keeping women from using their tongues for God, for he knows that if the women get filled with the Holy Ghost and turn their tongues loose on him he will have to hunt cooler quarters, or in other words will have to vacate.

11. Woman brought sin into the world.[11] Why not let her help put sin out of the world? One bad woman can do more to damn souls than a half-dozen bad men can do; on the other hand, often one good woman does more to save souls than half a dozen good men.

The Bible says, I Tim. 2:14, that the man was not deceived, but the woman. It was one single transgression by one person that opened up the floodgates of depravity and damnation that has been sweeping souls to hell for the last 6,000 years. If one woman under the power of the devil did so much to damn the world, it stands to reason that woman, under the power of the Holy Ghost, can and will do much to save the world.[12]

Mary continued to preach regularly until she was eighty-four; after that she preached only on occasion. On her eighty-ninth birthday, she preached her final sermon. Although she was blind and needed to be supported as she stood, she still managed to preach for half an hour. She died the following year.

Notes

1. See n. 15, chapter 2.
2. See n. 11, chapter 6.
3. Mary Lee Cagle, "My Call to the Ministry," in *Women Preachers*, ed. Fannie McDowell Hunter (Dallas: Berachah Printing, 1905), 70–73.
4. Mary Lee Cagle, *The Life and Work of Mary Lee Cagle: An Autobiography* (Kansas City, MO: Nazarene Publishing House, 1928), 29.
5. Stan Ingersol, "The Ministry of Mary Lee Cagle: A Study in Women's History and Religion," *Wesleyan Theological Journal* (Spring-Fall, 1993): 192. For more on Mary, see Robert Stanley Ingersol, "Burden of Dissent: Mary Lee Cagle and the Southern Holiness Movement," Ph.D. Dissertation (Duke University, 1989).
6. See n. 14, chapter 5.
7. 1 Samuel 18:1–5, 20:41–42.
8. Cagle, *Life and Work*, 60–63.
9. Hamilton Wright, "Mrs. Mary Lee Cagle Of Buffalo Gap, Assisted By Husband, Active As Evangelist At Age Of 80" *Abilene (TX) Reporter News*, no page cited, The Church of the Nazarene Archives, Kansas City, Missouri.
10. Wright, "Mrs. Mary Lee Cagle Of Buffalo Gap," no page cited.
11. The reference is to Eve. See Genesis 3:1–24.
12. Cagle, *Life and Work*, 160–176.

Fourth General of The Salvation Army, Commander of The Salvation Army in the United States, Territorial Commissioner for The Salvation Army in Canada and Newfoundland, author of *Love Is All* and *Toward a Better World*, recipient of honorary degrees from Columbia University and Tufts College

Courtesy of The Salvation Army National Archives.

CHAPTER 12

EVANGELINE BOOTH (1865–1950)

E vangeline Cory Booth, the seventh child of Catherine and William Booth, cofounders of The Salvation Army, was born on Christmas Day in London, England. Although christened as Eveline, she was called Eva, after a character in Harriet Beecher Stowe's well-known novel, *Uncle Tom's Cabin*. Years later when she moved to the United States, Eva changed her name to Evangeline. The Booth children were immersed from birth in The Salvation Army and were encouraged to take up its work at a young age. "By age five she [Evangeline] was preaching to her dolls, and several years later William Booth discovered his young daughter propped on a chair, exhorting the kitchen staff."[1] Every one of the eight Booth children and all three sons-in-law worked at least for a time in The Salvation Army.[2] Evangeline's official Army work began as a young teenager when she sold the Army's newspaper, *The War Cry*, on the streets of London. Prior to that, as this excerpt related, she experienced a call to ministry among the "poor, the wicked, the helpless, the little children who had none to care for them."

On Her Call to Ministry

The Picture

Perhaps it was because of my delicate health—I cannot say. I have always been puzzled over the fact that when Doré's[3] paintings came to the Art Galleries in London my mother decided that, out of her family of eight, I was the one she wished to be taken to see them. I had not reached my tenth birthday, and up to that time, as far as memory serves me, the most unmistakable evidence I had demonstrated of an artist's propensity was a decided objection to the vivid red of our cook's hair. When corrected by my mother for being too outspoken upon the matter, I said, "Well, I won't mention it again, but will you not ask her to wear a black dress instead of a brick-colored one?" Now it may be that although I was young my mother could discern I had a vague idea of correct background and felt this should be encouraged.

However, with my hand holding fondly the hand of the housekeeper, in whose care I was placed and whom I promised my mother to "cherish and obey," I found myself gazing, with that wonder that alone belongs to the awakening of the soul, upon Doré's masterwork of "Christ Standing Before Pilate." The exquisite blending of the unyielding majesty of Jesus, combined with the infinite patience and tender forbearance spoken in the firm but silent lips; the tall, slender figure in the seamless robe; and the eyes that looked upon the screeching, maddened mob with fathomless compassion, made me shiver as though I were very cold.

Then the Crucifixion—and I burst into tears. My dear mother had often told me about it, and told me with realistic description; but looking upon the scene of agony as portrayed by the magic skill of Doré's brush was different. I thought upon my own endeavors to defend the sheep being cruelly driven through the crowded traffic street, and asked again and again would no one come out to help Him? Could not some strong man shoot them down?

Seeing I was physically affected, the kind Miss Berry advised that I leave the picture. "Come look at this other beautiful painting," she said, "no one is hurting Jesus here," and I was led to Doré's "*Vale of Tears.*"

Here was the painting that had a great deal to do with life's work. Jesus, with His arms outstretched toward a motley throng depicting almost every condition of sorrow, want, decrepitude and misery that can destroy the bodies and souls of men.

The first figure my eyes fell upon was that of a man torn by evil spirits. So realistic was the artist's conception that I felt I must go to his aid.

"Why does he not throw them away from himself?" I asked.

"He cannot do so. You can't throw evil things away from you without the help of Jesus Christ," replied the good Miss Berry.

"Do they cling too hard?"

"Yes," was the simple reply.

There was the poor woman lifting her crippled baby to Jesus! The lame on crutches, struggling with the crowd. The little girl, so small, leading her blind father. A group of mothers, poor and ragged, pressing their little families close up to Him that He might lay His hands on them and bless them. The sick, on stretchers made of newly-hewn trees, the bearers so frail they appeared as if they themselves should be carried.

Entranced by the picture, I felt a charm so lovely, so high, so new to me that I became indifferent to all else—to all that was going on around me. My indefinite, childhood idea of religion was exalted into a passionate understanding. In this picture was the reason for the cruelty of Pilate's hall. Here was the reason for the Crucifixion. And here was my future spread out before me. My life should be lived for the poor, the wicked, the helpless, the little children who had none to care for them. They should have it, they should have it all!

Looking at the picture, I could see that it was for the helping of people like these I came into the world. This was why I was born on Christmas Day, while the bells were ringing, and the snow coming down, making everybody and everything white. I can definitely recall the trembling and stupendous longing to do some good that surged through my young soul as I gazed upon the portrayal of the Savior of men. Something that would abide because of the good in it. Something apart from *me*. Something that would be God. Oh, how early in life we can experience the noblest and highest spring of excellence in this lovely impulse to do good!

And so it was that, when young in years, I stood by the altars upon which burned the sacred and never-dying fires of service to humanity. My young soul prayed—the more passionately because silently—and I received something that day—something like Heaven. Perhaps it was Heaven, for is not Heaven the receiving of what each most desires? And is it not that glowing, yielding spirit toward what we most want that makes it ours? "They that hunger and thirst, shall be filled."[4]

"Come," said Miss Berry, "I will take you now to get some lunch."

With eyes fastened on the picture, and with a voice as determined as ten years could make it: "I am not coming," I replied.

"Oh," pleaded the housekeeper, "you must! You promised your mother you would do as I asked you."

"I'm not coming"—with intensified determination, and eyes still fastened on the picture.

A lady, sweet and gentle of voice and manner, broke in:

"Excuse me," she said, "can I be of any assistance? Can I take care of the little girl while you run out and get her something to eat?"

"Will you stay with the lady, Eva?" Miss Berry anxiously inquired.

"Yes, I will—if the lady will stay with the picture!"

My father and mother were thrilled by my childhood description of *The Vale of Tears*; how with flushed face and trembling with emotion I confessed that, although I was hungry, I could not go out to get lunch because I would have had to leave the picture.

....

Many years afterward, I was confronted with a great temptation. A temptation which gained attraction as I looked upon it. Wealth, jewels, court life, passionate devotion—all a young heart could desire.

It was then that my father thought upon my experience with Doré's paintings and told me the story as we sat under an old tree in our home garden. A departing sun drove a scarlet flame across the sky. With that flame there came the memory of the burning passion of the childhood revelation, bringing the strength divine expressed in, *"I'm not coming."* When for me the Gates open on a fadeless morning, I shall be with the Picture![5]

By her late teens, Evangeline had an Army post of her own in a destitute London neighborhood. On occasion, she explored the slums dressed in rags in order to blend in among the poorest. These ventures earned her the nickname, "White Angel of the Slums." She quickly moved through the Army ranks, serving as Principal of the Army's International Training College in London, the Army Field Commissioner for Great Britain, and then at the age of twenty-three, she moved to Canada to take up the post of Territorial Commissioner for Canada and Newfoundland.[6]

Her longest tenure, 1904–1934, was spent as Commander of the American branch of The Salvation Army headquartered in New York City. During these thirty years, Evangeline indelibly shaped the Army's image, such as the well-known Army ministry by female Salvationists, nicknamed Sallies, to American soldiers in Europe during World War I. The Sallies set up huts near the front lines and made coffee and cooked "doughnuts for doughboys." "As their proficiency grew, Sallies turned out as many as 9,000 a day—along with pies, biscuits, flapjacks, cookies, and cakes."[7] Besides baking, the Sallies also "darned socks, sewed on buttons, wrote letters, kept money for the men," and sometimes were the bearers of sad news to the soldiers.[8] For this aid by The Salvation Army for the nation's war effort, Evangeline received the Distinguished Service Medal from President Woodrow Wilson in 1919. That same year she capitalized on the Army's zenith of popularity and orchestrated its first national fund-raising campaign, which met its goal of $13,000,000. Evangeline raised money to fund the extension of real-estate holdings and the social programs of The Salvation Army by strategically courting wealthy audiences and by putting on elaborate pageants. These monies supported a wide range of ministries, including homes and hospitals for unwed mothers, industrial homes for job training, parole programs for released convicts, food and shelter for the destitute, and Evangeline Residences—safe and affordable housing for young working women in urban areas.[9]

On Her Evangelistic Method: The Salvation Army

Evangeline was born into The Salvation Army, and it was the only venue she knew for evangelism and social outreach. In this excerpt from her famous speech, "The World's Greatest Romance," she detailed the work of The Salvation Army.

The World's Greatest Romance

The work of The Salvation Army I often describe as the world's greatest romance. This is a bold and startling statement, and may savor of presumption, yet I think as I proceed you will agree that the title is well supported by the story. For, looking through the historic vista of over half a century, we find The Salvation Army a wondrous, chivalrous, adventurous and mysterious tale peculiarly fitting to the term, "romance." But our dictionaries define "romance" as "a most exalted achievement of a most exalted genius." This is just what The Salvation Army is. It is the extremity of an extraordinary imagination made history. The wildest dream of the wildest dreamer materialized. It is the offspring of the greatest love and passion, human and divine, known to the heart of man. Into the fabric of its history is woven heroism of the highest order; miracles of the most convincing character; martyrdom of the truest nature. It is a story throwing into confusion all human probabilities; a story of how God has brought a great thing out of nothing; a story in which He made things which are not to bring to naught things which are,[10] and with His own hand placed the little candle flickering in the darkest places of the earth, high upon a hill, where all the world can see its light.[11]

The Salvation Army is a romance geographically. A ring round a London lamppost expands until it encircles the world.

It is a romance numerically. William and Catherine Booth, my father and mother, sacrificing the promise of a most successful church ministry, start a procession of two along a road in East London with a story to tell, a faith to proclaim. And the procession increases until its train numbers tens of hundreds of thousands.

It is a romance financially. A poverty-stricken mission, begging its bread from door to door to keep its disciples alive, grows into an organization which can appeal to the financial world for the millions necessary to do the work the world is asking it to do.

But, above all, it is a romance spiritually. A young man, our Founder, standing on a slum curb telling the wretched, desolate, churchless masses as they shuffled by in an endless procession, of Jesus Christ, the sinner's Friend, becomes a leader of an army of hosts of men and women who cry in all the languages of the earth, "Behold the Lamb of God who taketh away the sins of the world."[12]

So, perhaps it is not too much to say that The Salvation Army is the world's greatest romance.

The birth of The Salvation Army was a romance. This organization was not born amidst hushed and sacred influences. This organization was born amid the roaring thunder of the darkest neighborhood of the great metropolis— London—under a murky sky in choking fog and spattering rain—the shrill call of the street hawker—the cries of pitiful little children—the coarse laughter of the girl of the street—the curses and oaths of drunken brawlers. It was born in lodging houses, damp cellars, blind alleyways, fever stricken courtyards, the deep recesses of the great bridge, where ragged forms staggered into darkness and fair faces vanished for the last time. It was born where wickedness is without restraint and poverty reaches the lowest stratum of human want. Born amid indescribable horrors, the unmasterful miseries, the inestimable sorrows, sins and tragedies of the underworld. It was like our Lord and Savior, an outcast by the wayside. It was born like Bethlehem's meteor, a flash, a star in the midnight sky.[13] . . .

The Salvation Army's ministry of the streets is a romance. I sometimes think that even those who know us best overlook the service we render the nations in our ceaseless warfare against all that is evil and our maintained advocacy of all that is good in the open street. With unflinching courage we denounce any and every influence that is opposed to the nation's good. We seek to inspire the poor and the ignorant—the highest form of patriotism. I say the highest because we are ever preaching righteousness and it is righteousness that exalteth a nation.[14] It is the principle of righteousness upon which, alone, just and correct government can stand. A nation is great and will increase in greatness only in proportion to the way her people, in precept and in practice, individually and nationally, adhere to the God-inspired principles of truth. Does not the writing upon the wall of our suffering world today tell us that a nation's forces are not alone in the strength of its fleets, the size of its armies, the wealth of its treasury, the extent of its territories, the power of its air force, or even the wisdom of its politics? A nation's power is rather to be found in its world influences. Its ascendancy is righteousness, in the authority of its enlightened teaching—these are the forces which give to a people predominance among the nations of the earth. And so, the officers of The Salvation Army stand in the street—in the frost, in the fog, in the rain and in the sun—and, in the simple language of the common people, tell of God's wondrous love to man. . . .

The story of Salvation Army bands is a romance. I think I can speak of Salvation Army bands as one having authority. On many occasions, I have been called to lead the battle for the right to play brass instruments on the streets, when sorely oppressed by local authorities and the populace. Now, we who have thought about music have discovered that the secret of its marvelous influence is its quick appeal to the human heart. The relation of music is not to ideas, but to the emotions. Music does not first sound the depth of knowledge, it first sounds the depth of feeling. It does not excite to argument or criticism. It awakens a yearning to listen, to receive and to follow. The strains of a country's national hymn do not offer an elaborate definition of patriotism, but they quicken the heartbeat of every patriot to deeds of desperate daring in defense of his country's liberty. It did not take my father long to discover that even beneath tattered garments there is love of harmony; that music appeals to the lowly and uneducated as readily as to the high and tutored.

The coronet and the drum are among the earliest vehicles to attract the masses. At first, they met with bitter opposition and our people were beaten with sticks and stones. Many of them were imprisoned for more than a month at a time. Yet, the progress of our musical forces was so rapid that now there is not an instrument of wind, of key, of pipe, of reed, of string, of parchment, of brass, of wood, of steel or of bone that has not been marshalled into the ministry of The Salvation Army. We have carried spiritual and patriotic music to the congested byways, to the prison cells and to the places of congregated vice and misery.

Attracted by the shining brass, the quick march and the well-known hymn, drunkards have left their drink, girls have come out of their haunts of iniquity, mothers have forsaken their places of toil and little children have turned from their play. The ne'er-do-wells, the loafers, the dull of conscience and the broken of spirit, indeed, the well dressed, who have pursued evil and forgotten good, have followed on the sidewalks to keep within hearing of the strains lifted by over 130,000 senior and junior Salvation Army musicians in every part of the world—some marching under scorching suns of tropical countries and some under arctic skies of northern lands—who give their musically trained service without payment of any kind.

Also, our musicians have taken the inspiring influences of sacred song to the desolate and the cheerless. Many of the bedridden poor, languishing in tenement basements, have caught the strains of the old hymn, "Abide with me from morn till eve, for without Thee, I cannot live. Abide with me when night is nigh, for without Thee, without Thee, I dare not die."

The history of Salvation Army literature is a romance. Theodore Roosevelt said, "Who can estimate The Salvation Army's contribution to the world's good in the output of its evangelistic printing presses?"

We started with *The War Cry*. Small—700 a week. But now, 131 different periodicals printed in over 73 languages, not including many dialects, confronting four-fifths of the human race in their own tongue, with an aggregate circulation of four million per issue, have, as white winged messages of happiness, help and hope, enriched the world. Not one inch of our *War Cry* is given to commercial advertisement. Its every word is concentrated upon and consecrated to the uplift and salvation of men. . . .

You will find this *War Cry* everywhere. In the palaces of the rulers of nations and thrown on the bunks of lumbermen's shanties. You will find it in the rich man's mansion and in the toiler's home. You will find it in the business office of large affairs and tucked under the fruit of the pushcart. You will find it laid under picturesque droplights in fashionable libraries and held up to poor eyesight by trembling hands in the almshouse. You will find it wet with the salty spray on the whaling smack off Labrador. You will find it thumbed by black fingers in the Hottentot's hut and the Zulu's kraal. You will find it spelled over by the leper's dimmed eyes amid the exotic fragrance of southern isles. You will find it dispelling the weariness of the bullock-cart traveler as he journeys over India's scorched sands. You will find it gladdening the heart of the lonely flax-gatherer in the desolate island of St. Helena. You will find it the only piece of literature in the city slum. You will find it held up by condemned hands to catch the sunshine that filters through prison bars. You will find it sounding the same note, singing the same song, carrying the same hope, telling the same story that has echoed the ages, imperishable in its truth, unalterable in its efficacy, everlasting in its glory, the Gospel of Jesus Christ, the power of God unto salvation.[15]

Evangeline exploited and perfected the Army's dramatic pursuits, often filling the 6,000-seat Hippodrome Theater in New York City, where she starred in Salvationist productions. Her well-known dramatic presentation, "The Commander in Rags," featured her early work among the poor in London's East End. The performance required "fifty gingham-dressed slum sisters," "bands, songsters, and soloists," and "live lambs, sheep and, on at least one occasion, a horse."[16] She was also an accomplished harpist, and a collection of her hymns was published in 1927 as *Songs of the Evangel.*

For the last five years of her active service, from 1934 to 1939, she oversaw the Army's work around the world as General of The Salvation Army at its international headquarters in London. She was the first woman and the last member of the Booth family to serve in this position. Upon her retirement, she settled in her sprawling estate, "Arcadia," in Hartsdale, New York, where she died at the age of eighty-five.

On Women

William and Catherine Booth modeled for their children the equality of women and men. They also believed that women have the right to preach, and in 1859, Catherine published her views in a pamphlet titled, *Female Ministry; or Women's Right to Preach the Gospel*. She wrote the pamphlet in response to a minister's critical remarks about Phoebe Palmer,[17] who was holding revival services, along with her husband, Walter, in Great Britain. Catherine preached her first sermon in 1860 when William was ill and unable to hold services in his churches, and she continued preaching for the next thirty years to overflowing crowds. Evangeline recounted her familial heritage and The Salvation Army's stance on women's roles in this written response to a letter from the magazine, *McCall's*.

February 14, 1946
General Evangeline C. Booth
120 West 14th Street
New York, N.Y.

Dear General Booth:

I am making a comprehensive study on women for publication in McCall's Magazine (3,400,000 circulation). We are attempting to evaluate woman's place in our society.

Through research, and by asking the opinions of outstanding leaders, we shall try to determine what is the present status of women's relationship to the desired ideal in democratic society. Based on this evaluation, we shall then make public relations recommendations, looking toward better integration of women into society.

You, as a leader, may care to make some comments on the ideal relationship of a woman in a democracy to voluntary organizations—those devoted to social service; to providing committee leadership; to advocating social action for peace, for progress, for reaction.

For instance, we would like to know what you think is the ideal relationship between a woman and such organizations in terms of membership, active participation, leadership—with particular reference to the conflict (or lack of conflict) between the responsibility as a wife, mother, employee or employer. In this connection, we would also appreciate your indicating any regional (North, South, Middle West, West) and economic-group deviations from the norms which you project; in other words, do your norms refer to the American woman as a whole, or are they subject to variation because of geographic, economic or other conditions?

If you agree that this project merits your cooperation in the public interest, please let us have your point of view. It goes without saying, of course, that an entire book could be written on this one phase of the topic—but a comment from you, of any length from ten sentences to ten pages, will be most welcome. In supplying it, you will be aiding, as I hope to, in helping provide a blueprint of action for millions of American women looking for orientation, in these difficult days of crisis, in psychological and economic security.

Unless you advise us to the contrary, it is our intention to use your name in our symposium, which should receive nationwide radio and press attention, additional to its *McCall's* publication. We shall, of course, be happy to send you, in advance of publication, a copy of our study.

Sincerely Yours,

EDWARD L. BERNAYS

March 3, 1946

Mr. Edward L. Bernays
26 East 64th Street
New York 21
New York

Dear Mr. Bernays:

I do hope the enclosed manuscript will be of service to you. I have had so much of this kind of thing to do in the last year that I find it difficult to produce anything of an attractive nature. However, I sincerely trust the data will prove of some service along the lines that you desire.

Yours sincerely

GENERAL

Women's Place—World

The Salvation Army has been handling the problem of woman's place in society for eighty years, and it is now no problem to us any longer, only an insistent call to service. Indeed, some of your questions sound to me a little elementary. For instance, the allusion in your letter to "economic—deviation from norms," differentiating between special circumstances "North, South, Middle West, West" suggests a certain lack of acquaintance with our principles, experience and service to the community.

For us, both women and men are everywhere those whose life values are lost unless they are saved by an intelligent faith in God. The question is not whether a person lives in Texas or China, but what he is himself. Abilities and training are, of course, important. They should be assets to mankind. Too often they are liabilities and even perils to the community. Everything depends, not on the number of talents, but what we do with them, and this lifts the issue above the educational plane to the upmost level of duty. Education, as we are seeing, often results in great harm instead of great good. "The ideal relationship between a woman" and her organization is the same as a man's, and it means giving all they possess to the purpose of the organization, which, in our case, is the uplift of mankind. If that ultimate relation be truly "ideal," all will be well.

There is no "conflict" in the Salvation Army between "wife, mother, employee or employer." Such an idea is meaningless in our ranks. My own case shows that any officer's commission held by a man may be held by a woman. I served as the fourth General of the Army. Where an officer holds a commission, his wife shares his rank, his responsibilities and his mission. It is thus a rule that the wife of an officer must belong to the Army as a graduate of a training college. Our recognition of woman's full and equal status in the realm of religion did not originate with the Salvation Army. For two centuries before the Army was started, it had been the basis of membership in the Society of Friends.[18]

My father, William Booth, the Founder of the Salvation Army, married Catherine Booth, who is honored and beloved throughout the world as "the Mother of the Army". Husband and wife were mutual in counsel and action, so establishing a precedent that has been followed ever since. There could be no "conflict" with an "employer," for their "employer" was God. Catherine Booth was mother, also, of her own children, eight of them, whom she brought up, instructed in the faith and trained to service—this despite her frail health and the demands made on her as speaker and administrator. She had no time or strength to waste on academic discussions. The need of the world and a divine way of meeting the need were the constraining and com-pelling factors in her whole life. She led the way for the host of women who have followed her into the pulpit.

The Salvation Army honors women. The worst of women are the care of those who may fairly be described as the best of women, and in countless instances a worthless woman has become a worthy example of Christian cit-izenship. In our organization the opportunity to fulfill every kind of task, executive, financial and spiritual, is open equally to women as men. All are united in the supreme objective, which is to bring hope to the despairing, decency to the degraded and justice to the oppressed.

Our training colleges for officers are coeducational. Marriage is permitted, but only after both parties have been granted their commissions—correspond-ing to graduation in other colleges. A third and fourth generation of Salvationists are thus arising, and while in very rare instances there are difficulties over emo-tion and temperament, divorce is unknown in the Army. Our homes are filled with the sweet harmony of true romance, the romance which abides despite the unbroken concentration of every energy on the salvation of men.

Nowhere in the Salvation Army is there any vow of celibacy. In my own case, marriage was laid aside by my own decision. We are a homeloving, homebuilding people.

I was aked [*sic*] only yesterday if, in my opinion, woman was doing her part to meet the demands of present conditions. I replied, I am afraid you have asked the wrong one. In my opinion, woman is really the big thing in the world. When all other anchorage has failed, she has amazed every nation and all races by the way the links of her chain—understanding, confidence and love—have held.

When you ask me to help provide a blueprint for "millions of American women looking for orientation," I cannot do other than recommend the Bible with its unsurpassed teaching of personal rectitude and service to oth-ers. It is in the Cross of Christ that the Salvation Army gets its "orientation," and not only for the time of crisis—after all, every life at all times faces crisis—but for all circumstances, whatever they may be or however they may vary. I might say there is plenty of room in the ranks of the Salvation Army!

To be candid about it, I don't want my life blueprinted. I want it to be growing in abundance and rich memory.[19]

Notes

1. Diane Winston, *Red-Hot and Righteous: The Urban Religion of The Salvation Army* (Cambridge, MA: Harvard, 1999), 146.
2. Even those who married into the family were marked by the Booth imprimatur in very direct ways. All three sons-in-law hyphenated their last names with the addition of Booth as a prefix.
3. Gustave Doré (1832–1883) was a painter and well-known illustrator of over one hundred books. His work was particularly well received in Great Britain, and he opened a gallery in London in 1868 to exhibit his work.
4. Matthew 5:6.
5. Evangeline Booth, "The Picture," The Salvation Army National Archives and Research Center, Alexandria, Virginia.
6. Evangeline's years in Canada overlapped with Minnie Kennedy, mother of Aimee Semple McPherson (see chapter 15), who was deeply involved with The Salvation Army in Ontario, Canada. Aimee was raised in The Salvation Army, and its influence on her was particularly evident in her incorporation of music and drama.
7. Winston, *Red-Hot and Righteous*, 183.
8. Edward H. McKinley, *Marching to Glory: The History of the Salvation Army in the United States of America, 1880–1992*, 2nd edn. (Grand Rapids: Eerdmans, 1995), 156.
9. During her years as Commander of The Salvation Army in the United States, Evangeline increased the real-estate holdings from $1.5 million to 48 million "plus a capital account of $35 million." [Winston, *Red-Hot and Righteous*, 150.] The Army's relief institutions increased in number from 195 to 413 during the first nine years of her tenure, an increase which necessitated greater funding. Lauren F. Winner, "From Drum-Bangers to Doughnut-Fryers: Material Culture, Consumerism, and the Transformation of the Salvation Army" *Books & Culture* (September/October 1999): 47.
10. 1 Corinthians 1:28.
11. Matthew 5:14.
12. John 1:29.
13. Matthew 2:1–2, 9–10.
14. Proverbs 14:34.
15. Romans 1:16. John D. Waldron, ed., *The Harp and the Sword: Writings and Speeches of Evangeline Cory Booth, vol. 1* (New York: The Salvation Army, 1992), 160–68. The speech continues for several more pages.
16. Winston, *Red-Hot and Righteous*, 143.
17. See chapter 4.
18. See n. 1, chapter 9.
19. Evangeline Booth, "Women's Place—World," The Salvation Army National Archives and Research Center, Alexandria, Virginia.

Presbyterian evangelist, wife of evangelist, Billy Sunday and business manager for his evangelistic campaigns

Courtesy of the Archives of the Billy Graham Center.

CHAPTER 13

HELEN SUNDAY (1868–1957)

Helen Amelia Thompson was born into a prosperous Chicago family. Her father, William Thompson, was one of the city's foremost ice-cream manufacturers and distributors. The Thompsons were stalwart members of Jefferson Park Presbyterian Church. Helen, whose nickname was Nell, was converted at the age of fourteen. She attended a business college and worked in the family business. She met Billy Sunday at a social event sponsored by her church. At the time, Billy was playing professional baseball with the Chicago White Stockings. Billy was immediately smitten with Helen, and eventually she returned his interest, despite her father's objections. "To his [her father's] mind ball players were late adolescents—men who refused to work for a living and spent their time playing and drinking beer."[1] Nevertheless, Helen and Billy were married on September 5, 1888.

Shortly after they were married, Billy quit baseball and began working full time in evangelism. His evangelistic campaigns increased in size and frequency, and in due course, he was constantly on the road and lonely without Helen. Even though Helen remained home with their four children, she was constantly giving personal encouragement to Billy and administrative help to his campaigns. The strain on both of them increased until, in 1907, with Helen near exhaustion and suffering from hives, they decided that she would travel with Billy and manage his campaigns. A beloved nanny cared for the youngest two children; the older two were already away at school. During the summers, the family traveled the campaign circuit together. Helen's importance to Billy's success was immeasurable.

By 1907 the Sundays could have settled for a continuation of life and ministry as they were, or perhaps sought a few adjustments to make for more time together. Indeed, if they had decided that Nell would make the children and home her supreme responsibility while Billy took care of the ministry, the next thirteen years would have been markedly different. There is no way that he could have vaulted himself and his infant organization to national fame, material wealth, and numerical success without Nell's administrative skills. An inherently able woman who had picked up some of her father's business acumen, Nell was one of the few people in America who could have kept Billy calm and happy and at the same time reshaped his ministerial team into a nationally renowned phenomenon.[2]

On Her Evangelistic Method: Managing a City-wide Evangelistic Campaign

Helen's responsibilities as administrator of Billy's city-wide evangelistic campaigns required monumental tasks and decisions, such as choosing the building site for the tabernacle,[3] overseeing publicity, managing finances, supervising the staff that numbered as high as twenty-six, and meeting with each city's committee of leading churchmen. In an interview before Billy's New York City campaign in 1917 at the zenith of his career, Helen explained the different strengths that she and Billy brought to the ministry. "You know, we have thought of coming [to New York] many times before this, but I never would consent until I was sure everything would be done properly. It wasn't enough to have a committee of one hundred. It wasn't enough to have the influential men in New York give us their money or even their sympathy. They had to be willing to work. I knew what it meant to tackle New York. Mr. Sunday didn't. He is always so wrapped up in the campaign of the moment that he can't make any plans for the future. I'm the one that has to look ahead."[4]

In this excerpt, Helen detailed the laborious assignment of finding a place and a date to hold Billy's ten-week-long New York City campaign, which would be attended by 1,443,000 people.[5]

It was an exceedingly difficult task to find a suitable location to erect the tabernacle in New York City,[6] it seemed almost hopeless. One site the New York Committee selected was near the polo grounds. I was sent to go to New York to see if it would do. I said, Mr. Sunday preaches in the afternoons on week days, except Mondays, and holds some of his special meetings on Sunday afternoons—all his meetings to men only are on Sunday afternoons. When the baseball season opens and someone makes a home run there will be a burst of applause or yells and it would be ruinous to Mr. Sunday's meeting. Then I noticed the long viaduct and heard the noise of traffic and shook my head, and said—"Gentlemen I'm sorry, but this location won't do." They yielded to my experienced judgment, but nevertheless were quite disheartened for they had worked hard to find that vacant property. I went away and they wrote Mr. Sunday they had found another location. I was sent by Mr. Sunday to decide if it would do. This time it was in the midst of the negro section and the auto parking spaces were inadequate. I said— this won't do—some one asked, why won't it do? I said because we couldn't expect the people to drive their fine limosines [*sic*] and leave them in this neighborhood; besides the transportation and parking facilities are not sufficient to take care of the throngs that will attend. They were more disheartened than before. I tried to encourage them and we had prayer together asking for definite guidance in finding the right spot on which to hold the revival campaign. Later I returned to see the third site the Committee had located; it had some good features, such as plenty of room and the subway had a station at Broadway and 168th Street at the corner of the property. I found out that the City Council would vote to extend the Charter to the Fifth Avenue bus line company if we decided on that location.

I was not entirely satisfied, as I felt it was entirely too far from the center—it was ten miles from Brooklyn and most all the towns surrounding New York City where people who work and have business in New York live. Brooklyn used to be called the bedroom of New York forty years ago. However, I acquiesced and put my approval on it amid great rejoicing on the part of all present.

Chicago had made a request of Mr. Sunday to hold a campaign and he had accepted their invitation, and the time had been set for the spring of 1917. I do not remember the Chicago date of request, but it was made a year or two before we could be free to grant it and give them the promise of the time, probably ten weeks, in the spring of 1917. Then New York City woke to the fact that they just had to have a Sunday campaign. We had been near New York in several campaigns—Patterson, N.J., Philadelphia, Penna., Trenton, N.J., Boston, Mass., Baltimore, Md. and no doubt the news of the phenomenal results were heard with telling effect in New York, so they came to secure time. We were always busy working and could only see the Committee between meetings. We told them the first open date we could give them would be in 1918, as every bit of our time was definitely taken. We had Kansas City, Detroit, Boston, Buffalo and Chicago for our next year's work. The New York Committee argued and insisted on time and declared it would simply be impossible to wait until 1918, said the City Council was favorable to a campaign now, but there was to be an election and all would be changed and we wouldn't be able to secure a permit to have the tabernacle built, and they would not go away. Finally someone suggested, why not try to get Chicago to wait until 1918 and then give New York their ten weeks of time in April, May and June of 1917. It was an unprecedented request, carrying a lot of nerve on New York's part in suggesting it. Then there was a long discussion on how best to go about it to secure the result for New York. They were afraid of telegrams, or even letters, so it was decided to send a representative who could go and present New York's side in such a convincing way to the Chicago Committee that they would step aside and wait a whole year longer in order to allow New York to have the campaign. That sounded sensible—next step, who was qualified to go, not one of the New York Committee felt able to go and "bring home the bacon." Finally Mr. Sunday said—"Ma[7] is the only one for that job. She may not be able to convince Chicago that it would be their duty to give way to New York, but if it is at all possible I'm sure she can do it." I looked at him aghast, the very idea of me having to ask my own home town to give way to New York. I knew how every Chicagoan felt about New York, but the job was finally saddled upon me and letters sent to Chicago stating that Mr. Sunday was sending me on an important mission, and he requested them to notify all the Committees and Preachers of Chicago to meet me at a certain hour on a certain day. I really was overwhelmed with the terrible responsibility and I slept very little, and I had a deep burden of prayer for guidance and help to put it over if it was God's will for us to go to New York.

I reached Chicago—I can't remember what time of the year it was, or what year it was, but I was met by the Chairman and taken to some church or Y.M.C.A.[8] auditorium (I have no recollection of where it was) to address the Chicago ministers and Christian laymen interested in having a Sunday campaign. I laid the situation before them as best I could. There was indignation seen on every hand; finally they began to ask questions and I answered to the best of my ability, telling them that we had no personal desire in the matter—one city was a [sic] good as another to work in; our interest lay in finding out God's will in the matter where He knew the greater good could be done at the particular time. I told them it was not an easy thing for me—a Chicago woman, to come and plead for New York City. Finally a vote was taken and the verdict went almost unanimously to New York; those holding out gave in and they sent New York a unanimous vote exchanging the spring of 1917 to the spring of 1918. I took the night train back east.[9]

Helen managed Billy's campaigns during the height of his popularity. After 1917, the schedule slowed, and the size of the hosting cities decreased, as did the number of staff. Although Helen continued to travel with Billy, their slackened pace enabled Helen to shift more attention to their adult children, who were struggling with financial, marital, emotional, or physical difficulties. She lived long enough to bury her husband and all four children.

On Women

Helen exemplified the roles expected of women in the Fundamentalist wing of Christianity;[10] yet at the same time, she defied them with Billy's blessing. On the one hand, Helen was devoted to her husband and children. Even her so-called autobiography, *"Ma" Sunday Still Speaks*, centered mostly on Billy's evangelism because that was her life.[11] On the other hand, she simultaneously moved beyond familial expectations when she left home to work full time on Billy's campaigns. This decision reflected the priority that the Sundays and other leading Fundamentalists accorded to full-time Christian service, even before marriage and family. As one historian explains, "The Fundamentalist imperative to service always implied that, beyond earning a livelihood and attending to family responsibilities, more was required of both women and men."[12]

In the same way, her views on women's roles cannot be easily categorized, as is evident in a range of newspaper articles published in 1917–1918 as *"Ma Sunday's Column."* In her articles, Helen, as did Billy, denounced what they considered as sinful practices, such as birth control and dancing, and she uplifted values associated with home and family. The closing lines of an article titled, "The Woman who didn't like to Cook," illustrated well these views. "It seems to me that it is as important for a woman to cook well for a man as it is to pray well for him."[13] At the same time, however, she supported women working outside the home. She answered affirmatively the question posed in an article's title, "Should A Woman Work For A Living?" In the article, she stated emphatically, "No, I do *not* think that the story of my correspondent is proof that a wife should not work for herself, if she has been accustomed to work, and wants to work after she is married."[14] Even more telling was her "call to womanhood," a call linked to increased opportunities for women in the wake of World War I. "The great, historic opportunity has been offered to them [women]. The gates have been flung wide for them. At last, the doors of the Doll House have been opened, and they have been invited to come into the great world outside. The rest is in their own hands."[15]

In this excerpt, she encouraged women to believe in themselves and in womanhood in general.

Having Faith in Women

Most men have faith in women, few women have faith in women. I have been astonished at the number of women who have come to me for advice whose only trouble was that they had no faith in womanhood, and consequently, none in themselves.

These women, if one of them was the daughter of a Duke or an Earl, would be so set up about it that she wouldn't notice anybody. But, though she is a daughter of God, I seldom hear her boasting about it.

The world's ideas about women are changing rapidly. The old question used to be: "What does the man want the woman to be?" The present question seems to be worded: "What does a woman want herself to be?" But, in the future, we shall come to asking the right question: "What does God want a woman to be?"

The first question was easily answered. If a woman was a pretty toy, a plaything, who would come to kiss and be kissed whenever she was told, if she could bear a man children and run his house, he was quite satisfied. He married in order to get the work of a mother, a nurse, a cook and a companion out of one woman, and he was peevish when he failed to secure all four.

The question of today is only half-answered as yet. Women do not know what they want to be, because they do not yet know what they are. Only one thing they have learned and that is that they are no longer merely the chattels of the man. St. Paul, indeed, told the women to keep silence in the churches, but he was writing to a congregation at Corinth where the women were behaving outrageously.[16] Far more full of love was the saying of the beloved disciple John, "If the Son make [sic] you free, then are you free indeed."[17]

For the question of the future, which is also the question of the present and the past—What does God want a woman to be?—the answers are quite easy.

God does not want women to be old maids, they were sent to be wives and mothers. To refuse to marry a good man is flinging God's gifts in his face. To refuse to bear children is sinning against the Holy Ghost and dishonoring creation.

God does not want a woman to resemble a man or try to imitate one. If He wanted her to be a man He would have made her one.

God does not want a lazy woman. Id [sic] she will not work, neither shall she eat, and if she will not work for the Bread of Life,[18] she will not eat of that, either.

God does not want a disloyal woman. If she cannot have and hold faith in her sisters, how can she be entrusted with letting her light shine so that people may see her good works.[19] A 'catty' woman cannot be a standard-bearer.

God does not want any kind of woman except the woman who rejoices in this world and rejoices in the hope of the life to come. Joy is one of the fruits of the Holy Ghost[20] and a woman who has faith in womankind is the bearer of perfect joy.[21]

On Her Call to Preach

Helen not only managed Billy's campaigns, but she also spoke at the campaign's meetings for women only.[22] She was therefore not a newcomer to public speaking; yet at Billy's death bed, Helen experienced a distinct call to preach when at age sixty-eight, she begged God for direction for her life's remaining work.

You know, as soon as he [the doctor] left the house, the first thing I did when he was gone was to go in the bedroom, close the door very gently— I even turned the key in the lock of the door on the inside—and I went and knelt down in front of the bed. I put my head on Billy's forearm as he lay there dead, and I said, "Lord, if there's anything left in the world for me to do, if you'll let me know about it, I want to promise you that I'll try to do it the best I know how." I want to admit to you that I didn't see one single thing left for me to do! Billy was my job. We had lived together for forty-seven years—we had traveled together for thirty-nine years in the work—and he was *gone!* There just didn't seem to be anything left for me to do! So I prayed that prayer to God, and just as I finished, my brother called me. He said there was a very urgent call for me, and asked if I could come down, and I said, "Yes, I guess so."

I went to the door, unlocked it, and went downstairs. From then on for the next two days I completely forgot my prayer in the multitude of telegrams and cablegrams and messages sent out to our friends and children, back and forth. Then Friday afternoon two men who had come to attend Billy's funeral told me they would like to have a memorial service in each of their towns—they were from New York State—and they wanted to know if I would come and lead these services as speaker. Well, you know, my first reaction was to scream at them and say, "No! You've no business asking me now. This isn't the time for it, or for me to promise to go! Billy isn't even buried yet!" He was to be buried the next day, Saturday.

But, you know, something happened—before I could speak—just that quickly—the message flashed across my eyes, just like an electric sign: My prayer! "Lord, if there's anything left in the world for me to do, if you'll let me know about it, why, I want to promise you I'll do it." So, I just stood there and shut my eyes, and I said, "Lord, is this You speaking to me through these two men from New York State? Do You want me to go speak in those memorial services? Do I *have* to go?" And I listened and waited a second or two, and it just seemed as though I heard Him say, "Why, certainly! Why not? Of course!" So I opened my eyes, and I said to one of the men, "When do you want me?" And he said, "I'd like to have you come a week from Tuesday night." I hurriedly counted the days and the dates, and I said, "Why that's dad's birthday! That would make it the nineteenth of November." He said, "I know it would. That's why I want you to come to Buffalo then." And so I told him I'd be there.[23]

Helen embarked on her own twenty-two-year preaching ministry. Her preaching engagements mostly consisted of one or two-day evangelistic meetings. The Presbyterian Church gave her an official document in 1935, which granted her permission to work as an evangelist. The document recognized that Helen "assisted her husband in his evangelistic meetings in all parts of the United States, organizing the committees and directing the business, and preaching whenever Mr. Sunday was unable to do so."[24] She was also certified as an evangelist by the Interdenominational Evangelistic Association and was a member of its Board of Directors.

Throughout the last two decades of her life, she shared the platform with a new generation of evangelists, including Billy Graham, who was converted at a Billy Sunday campaign. Before she died in 1957, Helen rejoiced that she was able to "do my little part" for evangelism in America. "I'm so glad that the young men, like Billy Graham, Merv Rosell, Jack Shuler, Jimmy Johnson, and on, a whole lot of others that I can't mention right now, are on the job night and day, out preaching God's blessed Word and giving out the invitation to come and accept Him. And I'm so glad that God has let me do my little part here and there . . ."[25]

Notes

1. Lyle W. Dorsett, *Billy Sunday and the Redemption of Urban America*, Library of Religious Biography (Grand Rapids: Eerdmans, 1991), 34.
2. Dorsett, *Billy Sunday*, 86.

3. The tabernacle was a temporary wooden structure that housed Billy's campaigns, and each city that hosted a Billy Sunday campaign built one.

4. Dorsett, *Billy Sunday*, 106–07.

5. William G. McLoughlin, *Billy Sunday Was His Real Name* (Chicago: University of Chicago, 1955), xxviii.

6. The 1917 New York City campaign tabernacle was " 'the largest structure for public meetings ever erected in New York.' It could comfortably seat 16,000, with standing room for 4,000 more, and it had cost over $65,000." McLoughlin, *Billy Sunday*, xvii.

7. This was Billy's nickname for Helen.

8. The Young Men's Christian Association (Y.M.C.A.) is an interdenominational Christian organization whose original mission was to minister to the whole man in body and soul.

9. William A. Sunday and Helen T. Sunday, *The Papers of William and Helen Sunday (1882–1974)*, ed. Robert Shuster, Archives of the Billy Graham Center, Wheaton College, Wheaton, Illinois.

10. The Fundamentalist wing of Christianity is a conservative movement that emerged in the early years of the twentieth century in reaction to what they considered to be liberalizing trends in Protestantism. The movement gets its name from the "fundamentals," which are these five non-negotiable truths about Christianity: virgin birth of Christ, substitutionary atonement (the doctrine that Jesus' death paid the debt for humanity's sin), bodily resurrection of Christ, veracity and supernatural quality of miracles, and inerrancy of the Bible. Margaret Lamberts Bendroth, *Fundamentalism and Gender, 1875 to the Present* (New Haven, CT: Yale University, 1993), 4.

11. The comment has been made that in her own evangelism she spoke of two subjects—Billy Sunday and Jesus Christ. Dorsett, *Billy Sunday*, 160.

12. Michael S. Hamilton, "Women, Public Ministry, and American Fundamentalism," *Religion and American Culture* 3 (Summer 1993), 174–75. This primary commitment to service was particularly true in Fundamentalism prior to 1950, according to Hamilton.

13. Helen Sunday, "The Woman who didn't like to Cook," *The Papers of William and Helen Sunday*.

14. Helen Sunday, "Should A Woman Work For a Living?" *The Papers of William and Helen Sunday*.

15. Helen Sunday, "The Call to Womanhood," *The Papers of William and Helen Sunday*.

16. 1 Corinthians 14:33–34.

17. John 8:36.

18. The Bread of Life is Jesus. See John 6:35, 48–51.

19. Matthew 5:16.

20. Galatians 5:22.

21. Helen Sunday, "Having Faith in Women," *The Papers of William and Helen Sunday*.

22. The women's meetings were led by one of Billy's assistants, Virginia Asher. After Virginia left Billy's employment, she founded a national organization, the Virginia Asher Businesswomen's Council, which ministered to the spiritual and emotional needs of working women. [Bendroth, *Fundamentalism and Gender*, 85.] Billy employed a number of women assistants. "Of Sunday's

50 various assistants, 15 were female." Bendroth, *Fundamentalism and Gender*, 133, n. 52.

23. Helen Sunday, *"Ma" Sunday Still Speaks* (Winona Lake, IN: Winona Lake Christian Assembly, 1957), 39–40.

24. Helen Sunday, General Correspondence, *The Papers of William and Helen Sunday*. I am grateful to James G. Mentzer for this reference.

25. Sunday, *"Ma" Sunday Still Speaks*, 25.

Methodist holiness evangelist, Methodist deaconess, founder and principal of Epworth Evangelistic Institute and Chicago Evangelistic Institute, author of *Revelation, Heart Purity*, and *Upper Room Messages*, recipient of an honorary Doctor of Divinity degree from Taylor University

Courtesy of Vennard College Archives.

Chapter 14

Iva Durham Vennard (1871–1945)

I va May Durham was born near Normal, Illinois, the youngest child of Jacob and Susan Durham. When she was five years old, her father died from tuberculosis, which he had contracted while enlisted in the Union Army during the Civil War. Her mother subsequently supported the family through various innovative business ventures including a dressmaking and hat shop, a photograph gallery, and a farm on government land claims in South Dakota. At the age of twelve, Iva was converted and joined the Methodist church. Six years later, after attending a holiness camp meeting where the Rev. Joseph H. Smith[1] was the preacher, Iva experienced sanctification. Along with her religious interests, she was committed to education. She was graduated from Illinois State Normal University, and then for several years, she taught school before attending Wellesley College for a year in 1892. Her plan was to finish her senior year of college at Swarthmore College where she had a full scholarship. The summer before she was to leave for Swarthmore, she encountered Joseph Smith again at the camp meeting. Her biographer recorded that Smith expressed disappointment in her educational plans. "When I knew you a few years ago, I thought you were one young woman who was going to be spiritual; and more than that—a spiritual leader. But I see you seem to have gone mostly 'to top.'"[2] In this excerpt, Iva described the anguish of a night "praying through" her educational ambitions while seeking to discern God's will.

On Her Calling to Ministry

When I was twenty-two years of age, that is a long time ago, how I do thank God, young people, that at that time in my life I really went through that experience of dying out to my own self will. I do not mean that God broke my will and that I have not had any will since, but God did subjugate my will to His will as far as I could understand it... That summer when I got that settled, that question settled, I had been praying through one whole night of distress and pressure, and as morning came I realized that I had really let go and I had expected because I had been in camp meetings and had heard people shout, that I perhaps would shout. I wanted to shout, and I was disappointed not to shout. But instead of shouting the emotion which came to me was a sense of emptiness. Do you understand that? I was emptied out of my own self. That sense of emptiness and I remember kneeling beside my bed with a Bible open before me and I said, O Lord, give me something now that I can tie to. It seemed as if everything was swept away and the biggest thing I had to give up was my air castles. Not so much in hand, but I had many dreams and ambitions and they were air castles, and they were more precious to me than anything else I had, but I had to lay them aside, and I said, "Lord, you must give me something that I must tie to." And under that sense of pressure, God gave me a verse, a lifetime commission, and that has been my life verse. It was a verse from Isaiah, "Arise, shine; for thy light is come, and the glory of the Lord is risen upon thee."[3] It was like balm to my heart. I felt that He had accepted me, that my consecration was complete and that God had accepted it. The peace of holiness, the sense of purity took possession of my soul and with that experience of that life verse being given to me . . . It has been more real and more sacred to me than any of those that I have had. It is a commission, a lifetime commission.[4]

Opportunities immediately came her way to participate in evangelistic meetings, first as a singer then as a preacher. One request came from a couple in Lodge, Illinois, where "there was no pastor and no regular church service. This one Christian man rented an abandoned saloon building, and someone loaned an organ. Miss Durham had to be the entire evangelistic party. She led the singing, played the organ, preached, and conducted the altar service. But the room was filled night after night." Her biography recalls her feelings about that revival, "It was a far cry from Wellesley and the New England Conservatory, but my heart was at rest through it all."[5] In 1895, Iva entered the Methodist Deaconess Home in Buffalo, NY.[6] She was assigned to be a deaconess evangelist, and in that capacity she held evangelistic meetings in churches throughout the state of New York. After several years, she left this work to concentrate on training workers in evangelism.

On Her Evangelistic Method: Training Schools

Iva founded two schools—Epworth Evangelistic Institute and Chicago Evangelistic Institute—for the purpose of training students in evangelism. In 1901, Iva began Epworth Evangelistic Institute, a Methodist deaconess training school in St. Louis, Missouri. From the outset, she encountered opposition from leading Methodist clergymen and laymen in that city. They objected to women teaching theology and Bible rather than clergymen and to women being trained in evangelism rather than religious education. Their opposition came to a crisis point when Iva was on maternity leave. She had married Thomas Vennard, a British architect, in 1904, and their son, William Durham Vennard, was born five years later. While she was recuperating from the birth, her opponents took matters into their own hands and revised the school charter, removed evangelism courses from the curriculum, and replaced Epworth's female faculty with clergymen. Iva resigned as Principal of Epworth Evangelistic Institute scarcely eight years after she founded the school.

The next fall she opened Chicago Evangelistic Institute (CEI), an interdenominational, coeducational, holiness training school, devoted to training men and women as evangelists, missionaries, pastors, and other Christian workers. In this excerpt from CEI's first bulletin, *Heart and Life*, Iva explained her rationale for the school.

Thou Art Come To The Kingdom For Such A Time As This

. . . has the holiness movement[7] any right, in its legitimate province, to under-take educational work? We need to bear in mind that the word **movement** does not mean **church**. In these forty or fifty years, in which the holiness movement has been making history, it has never been the aim to mold it into ecclesiastical form, but rather to culture the life and feed the fire of holiness and let it run into the ecclesiastical molds already made, bringing this blessed scriptural truth to all denominations of Christian people and seeking to bring it in the form best adapted to their thinking.

Let us be frank enough to say that the history of this work proves that the spreading of holiness is more often hindered than helped by ecclesiastical authority and that this full salvation[8] ministry cannot be bridled and held by any one humanly organized company. It must find the hungry soul in any church regardless of church form.

The truth of holiness, the baptism with Holy Ghost which cleanses the heart from inbred sin, is bigger than any one church and every church needs it and every child of God longs to know its reality. The legitimate work then of this **movement** is, of course, an evangelism which will sink sectarian and ecclesiastical considerations into their proper secondary place and exalt this scriptural standard of holy living to its rightful place of primary importance. Thus far we are all agreed: full salvation evangelism is certainly within our legitimate province.

But how shall we build up an evangelistic force, trained doctrinally and thoroughly furnished with the scriptural authority, if we do not have training schools for this purpose? There is much to be said for the necessity of colleges and universities in this movement, where our young people may be equipped for all the avenues of life without making shipwreck of their faith, but the limitations of this article confine us to the consideration of training schools in particular. All that could be said in defense of holiness colleges applied with added emphasis to a holiness training school. If churches standing for their own denominational creeds and methods of work have found it necessary to have denominational training schools, the same necessity compels the interdenominational holiness movement to have an interdenominational holiness training school. It is a principle granted by all thinking people that education, the training of our young people in doctrine and the culturing of their soul life in holy vision and service, is the sane and sure way of conserving the results of our holiness evangelism. Therefore, as a holiness movement we not only have a right to develop educational work but it is our necessity. If we believe the definite truth of scriptural holiness is worth preserving, in the face of modern skepticism and human religion then the conclusion is inevitable, we must devote ourselves to special training schools where our young people will be reinforced and equipped to stem the untoward tide....

We have already touched upon the interdenominational feature which lies at the very foundation in our conception of this work. The time is surely passing when church people think that loyalty to one's own denomination demands an intolerance of all other denominations.... Spiritual people in all the churches are discerning between sectarianism and true denominationalism and are coming to see that true Christian unity is not the gathering of all Christians into one particular ecclesiastical organization where we will have a monopoly of full salvation while all other bodies go to wreck and ruin, but the unity of the Spirit will bind the children of God together in holy living in all denominations. If the conception of the work of the holiness movement is sound, then the need of an interdenominational holiness training school is imperative for the **equipment of young people to stand as leaders** in all the churches for the pressing of this glorious warfare.

A training school which will meet the full need of our present situation must not only be interdenominational in its relation to the churches, it must be **intersectional** in its relation to all branches of the holiness movement. This is exactly the aim of Chicago Evangelistic Institute. Its foundations are laid for the training of young people East and West, North and South. We are not giving ourselves to the building of any organization but to the strengthening and serving of them all through our young people who are being trained to push the battle of scriptural holiness through all the channels as God opens their way.[9]

On Women

Through her schools, Iva trained and equipped women to be evangelists, pastors, missionaries, or other Christian workers. The curriculum for every degree program at CEI was the same for all students, male and female. Every student took courses in Bible, theology, church history, evangelism, philosophy, sociology, and missions. Men and women vied for awards in preaching and exposition, and often a woman won first place. For their practical work in evangelism, men and women participated in CEI's radio ministry, preached from the school's gospel automobile, and worked as preachers and evangelists in Chicago city missions. CEI's female graduates, as did Epworth's graduates, served in every possible position in the church, including senior pastor.

While Iva was Principal at Epworth, she addressed women's issues more frequently and directly than at any other time in her life. Perhaps the looming hostile takeover of Epworth by her male detractors compelled her to be more outspoken on behalf of women in a public venue. As editor of Epworth's bulletin, *Inasmuch*, she included a regular column titled, "Chiefly About Women," that reported news from Epworth's alums as well as news about women's issues around the world. In one issue, Iva used the column to celebrate the successful passage of women's suffrage in New Zealand. In addition, Iva wrote a series of articles defending women's ministry in past generations as well as presently. In this article from that series, Iva urged Methodist women to devote themselves to Christian service, now that they were no longer "cramped by the old time notions of a woman's very narrow sphere . . ."

An Appeal to Young Women
The harvest is plenteous, but the laborers are few[10]

The nineteenth century will stand out in history as "the discoverer of woman" and it is for the womanhood of this twentieth century to prove what this discovery shall mean. No longer cramped by the old time notions of a woman's very narrow sphere, our girls today find wide open doors for culture and education and travel. They may enter business if they choose, and the professions are inviting them. But in no realm of activity does the door swing wider than to Christian service.

The Church is recognizing the necessity of the labor of trained, capable, spiritual women, and today she offers a magnificent opening for her consecrated daughters.

When Methodism first came into existence, its peculiar stamp moulded in Pentecostal fire was that the gospel was preached to the poor. In those days the Methodists were a "by-word and a hissing" but the common people heard the gospel and multitudes gladly accepted it.

God has greatly blessed this branch of His church. We have grown in intellectual power and today have our splendid educational system and institutions of learning. We have grown in wealth and influence, but God has never excused us from our original call.

The genius of Methodism is this ministry to the common people. But we have fallen upon times, especially in our great cities, when those whom we would serve are estranged from us. The poor, the small wage-earners, do not seek us. It is not sufficient for us to have a handshaking committee at the church. These perishing multitudes whom we must reach will not come to be shaken hands with. We must go out into the byways and hedges.[11] We must find the way into their homes, and hearts. We must win their confidence and become their friends. We must bring them to our Christ. Has not the Deaconess Movement been restored by God to the modern church for just this necessity? Has not our Queen come to the Kingdom for just such a time as this?

The demand for women's service was never so urgent. Deaconesses are needed in all our large cities, in our factory centers, our mining districts, and among our ever increasing foreign population. They are needed in our gospel settlements and missions, in our hospitals and schools, and orphanages and homes for the aged. They are needed in our large churches. They are needed for all sorts and conditions of men. They are needed as evangelists, teachers and nurses. And not only are they needed in the home land but the piteous cry of suffering which has gone up to the Throne of God from foreign lands has come in its echo to us. The wail of this "winsome erring child"—Humanity, has reached us.

The consecrated womanhood of Methodism is responding. That mother love in every good woman's heart broods over the misery of neglected childhood and down-trodden womanhood, and yearns to be a messenger of good tidings to those who sit in darkness.

We believe that our noble young women are being stirred by the Holy Ghost to give themselves to this blessed life of service.

The call must be heard by the very cream of our Methodist young womanhood. The work needs women with developed and trained powers, with breadth of vision, and soul capacity for loving.

The call must be heard in our sheltered homes and colleges and among our women of talent and ability.

The call is heard. God attends to that. But our girls are hesitating, not that they do not long to obey the Heavenly vision, but they do not know how to sever the home ties and enter the field of labor.

Women lack aggressiveness. Men know how to forge ahead and make a place for themselves and it is expected of them. Parents count on it from the cradle that when the son is grown he must take a post of responsibility in the world but they cannot spare their daughters.

Girls have a battle on hand when they begin to make it known that God hath put his hand upon them for service. Their parents would be willing for them to be married and go to the ends of the earth with a good man, but they cannot trust the kindness and wisdom of God when He chooses their daughters as colaborers with Jesus Christ. May God bring our Methodist fathers and mothers to a deep consecration where they come to see that it is as much a dignity to have a daughter giving her life to Christian service as to have a son in the ministry.

Perhaps the easiest and most natural way for a young woman to enter Christian service is to come to some one of our training schools and take the course of Bible study.

Those in authority have opportunity to study her fitness for the various lines of work and when she is graduated she is ready for the recognition of the church and goes out under appointment to take up the kind of work she can do best. . . .

May God grant that scores of young women who read this article may open their hearts to the leading of The Holy Spirit and find their way as reapers into the Harvest.[12]

"Perishing, perishing. Harvest is passing
    Reapers are few and the night draweth near.
Jesus is calling thee. Haste to the reaping,
    Thou shalt have souls, precious souls for thy hire."[13]

Along with her educational endeavors in evangelism, Iva was committed to foreign missions. She helped to found the National Holiness Missionary Society (later World Gospel Mission), and served on its board and as treasurer. In 1920, Iva and Thomas, her husband, took a year-long world missionary tour. Before she left, her Methodist pastor presented her with a local preacher's license. Thomas' unexpected death in 1930 was a grievous loss to Iva as well as to CEI. His expertise as an architect had proved invaluable with the repairs and renovations of CEI's aging buildings.

Iva was Principal of CEI until her death in 1945, a tenure of thirty-five years. Several years later, CEI was relocated from Chicago, a move that Iva always resisted, despite persistent financial hardship, because of her commitment to urban ministry. However, with CEI's original buildings in desperate need of repair coupled with an unsuccessful capital campaign, the financial crisis was inescapable. In the meantime, a holiness school in rural Iowa—Kletzing College—was going bankrupt, and the campus was offered to CEI. With no alternative in sight, CEI administrators and faculty made the difficult decision to move to Iowa. Eight years later the school was renamed Vennard College to honor its founder, Iva Durham Vennard.

Notes

1. Joseph H. Smith (1855–1946) was a Methodist minister, evangelist, and leading figure in the holiness movement (see n. 7 below).
2. Mary Ella Bowie, *Alabaster and Spikenard: The Life of Iva Durham Vennard, D.D., Founder of Chicago Evangelistic Institute* (Chicago: Chicago Evangelistic Institute, 1947), 46.
3. Isaiah 60:1.
4. Iva Durham Vennard, Chapel Message at Chicago Evangelistic Institute, February 18 (no year given), Vennard College Archives, University Park, Iowa.
5. Bowie, *Alabaster*, 52.
6. The modern-day deaconess movement emerged in the late nineteenth century in America as an avenue for full-time Christian service for women. Its roots go back to the early Christian church, where deacons and deaconesses were set apart for service (the Greek word for service is *diakonia*); see Acts 6:3–4; Romans 16:1–2; 1 Timothy 3:8–12. Deaconesses worked as nurses, teachers, visitors, and evangelists, particularly in poor, urban areas. For more on the deaconess movement in several denominations, see Susan Hill Lindley, *"You Have Stept Out of Your Place": A History of Women and Religion in America* (Louisville, KY: Westminster John Knox, 1996), 128–34. For more on the deaconess movement in Methodism, see Mary Agnes Dougherty, "The Methodist Deaconess, 1885–1919: A Study in Religious Feminism," Ph.D. Dissertation (University of California, Davis, 1979) and Jean Miller Schmidt, *Grace Sufficient: A History of Women in American Methodism, 1760–1939* (Nashville, TN: Abingdon, 1999), 197–212.
7. The holiness movement coalesced in America in the mid-1800's around John Wesley's notion of sanctification or holiness (also known as Christian perfection, or full salvation). It was fostered early on mostly by Methodists who had experienced sanctification, such as Phoebe Palmer (see chapter 5). As the movement matured and faced increasing antagonism from Methodist leaders and laity, an increasing number of separate holiness denominations were founded (The Church of the Nazarene, The Salvation Army, The Pillar of Fire) as well as holiness schools, such as Vennard's CEI. For more on the development of the holiness movement, see Melvin E. Dieter, *The Holiness Revival of the Nineteenth Century*, 2nd. edn. (Lanham, MD: Scarecrow, 1996).
8. This term is synonymous with sanctification, holiness, or Christian perfection.
9. Iva Durham Vennard, "Thou Art Come To The Kingdom For Such A Time As This" *Heart and Life* 1 (October and November 1911): 6, 8, B.L. Fisher Library, Asbury Theological Seminary, Wilmore, Kentucky.
10. Matthew 9:37.
11. Luke 14:23.
12. John 4:35–37.
13. Iva Durham Vennard, "An Appeal to Young Women," *Inasmuch* 2 (November 1906): 8–9, Vennard College Archives, University Park, Iowa.

Faith-healing Pentecostal evangelist, founder of The International Church of the Foursquare Gospel, author of *This Is That: Personal Experiences, Sermons and Writings, Give Me My Own God, In the Service of the King,* and *Divine Healing Sermons*, an early pioneer of radio evangelism

Used by permission, ICFG Heritage Department.

CHAPTER 15

AIMEE SEMPLE MCPHERSON
(1890–1944)

Aimee Elizabeth Kennedy's life was a study in profound contrasts, ranging from a rural Canadian farm to Los Angeles stardom. These contrasts provided ample fodder for her many supporters and critics who regarded her either as a fervent Christian or a fevered charlatan. Generally regarded as one of the most successful women evangelists of all time, her first eighteen years were quite unspectacular. She was the only child of James Morgan Kennedy, a farmer and devout Methodist, and Minnie Pearce Kennedy, an orphan who was raised in a Salvation Army home. From a young age, her mother encouraged Aimee's participation in The Salvation Army, whose music and pageantry fueled Aimee's dramatic tendencies.[1] In her adolescent and teen years, she chose a Methodist Church over The Salvation Army due to the distance of the latter and the greater popularity of the former. With the encouragement of the Methodists, she saw her first movie and read her first novel. Then, on a wintry, December day in 1907, while en route to a play rehearsal, Aimee implored her father to stop for a moment at a storefront Pentecostal church. Her curiosity led not only to her conversion and calling to evangelistic work, but also a crush on the preacher, Robert Semple.

On Her Conversion

It was at the close of a series of revival meetings in our town that my dear mother urged me to join some church, but I thank God I was not a hypocrite to join a church. I had no confidence in, and knew the lives of its members were full of worldliness and insincerity. One night, in desperation at her urging and wanting to settle the question once and for all in my mind, I kneeled down by my open bedroom window, and somehow as I looked out upon the white night, clad in the soft mantle of snow, the whole floor of heaven seemed ablaze with stars, and somehow they looked too wonderful to have been placed there accidentally by the whirling motion of the sun which had thrown them off from itself as our Darwinian[2] books declared. It seemed there must have been the mighty hand of a Creator behind them somewhere.

Suddenly I flung out my arms towards the resplendent heavens, and I cried out, "O, God, if there be a God, reveal yourself to me." When an unbeliever prays the above prayer in sincerity, God always answers that prayer.

It was just a few days later when, as my father and I were driving down Main St., in the carriage, I saw a peculiar sign on a window reading "PENTECOSTAL MISSION." This was something new I had not heard of before, and I determined to go in and investigate. The following evening I attended the service, and heard a tall young man evangelist preach from the second chapter of Acts. "Repent and be baptized, every one of you, for the remission of your sins, and ye shall receive the gift of the Holy Ghost; for the promise is unto you and to your children and to all that are afar off, even as many as the Lord our God shall call."[3] He really talked as though he believed the whole word of God, that Jesus was the same yesterday, to-day and forever,[4] that He healed the sick and still performed miracles.

As he was speaking he suddenly raised his hand and broke out speaking in other tongues, and sinner as I was, I had the interpretation within myself: "You are a lost, miserable, Hell-deserving sinner." The word of God says in I Cor. 14, "Tongues are a sign to them that believe not." This certainly was true in my case, for although I did not understand the significance of speaking in tongues, I never from that moment doubted that there was a God. I had entered the mission a proud, haughty girl dressed in fashionable, worldly attire, my hat laden down with flowers, with high-heeled shoes, etc., and as I look at myself today stripped of all the gaudy attire of this world I hardly recognize that creature of eight years ago. As he continued to preach I became conscious of the awful presence of an angry God in whose presence I stood laden down with sin.

I rushed from that mission seized with an unrelenting conviction for sin with which I battled for twenty-four hours. I argued with myself that I could not give up my elocution work, as Christmas was at hand, and I was billed for all the church concerts and other amusements for miles around. It was a desperate struggle while it lasted, but the Spirit was victorious, and the following evening while driving home in the carriage (we lived five miles in the country) I suddenly threw up my hands and screamed aloud, "Oh God! be merciful to me a sinner." Immediately my burden was gone, the glory of God shone round about the carriage, and I was a new creature in Christ Jesus. I had a new heart—a heart from sin set free for which to praise my God. . . .

As I continued to attend the mission services I learned that there was more, yes, oceans more, ahead of me, that the Latter Rain[5] was falling on the earth. Also that the Lord was baptizing His saints with the Holy Ghost and fire just as He did on the Day of Pentecost,[6] and I became a diligent seeker for this gift. With eyes filled wide with wonderment, I beheld people shaking under the mighty power of God, heard them speaking with tongues as they did throughout the word of God when receiving the Holy Ghost. I saw the sick healed and many prostrated under power of the Holy Ghost, as Paul was on the road to Damascus,[7] and as John when he said, "I fell at his feet as one dead."[8] . . .

The following two days I made a business of seeking the Lord, only stopping long enough to catch a little food and sleep. Friday night I waited before the Lord till midnight, Saturday morning I got up at break of day, and going into the parlor of the lady's home where I was staying, I kneeled down at a large morris chair in the corner with a real determination in my heart. You ask if I was not afraid of getting a wrong spirit, or being hypnotized as my parents feared. There was no such fear in my heart; I trusted my heavenly Father implicitly according to Luke 11. I opened my Bible to this passage, and clung to it. You remember it tells us that we are to "ASK AND YE SHALL RECEIVE, SEEK AND YE SHALL FIND," and assured me that "EVERY ONE THAT ASKETH RECEIVETH," also that if I ASK FOR BREAD HE WILL NOT GIVE A STONE.[9] I was assured that the Lord was not bestowing serpents or scorpions on His blood-washed children when they asked for food. Had He not said IF your earthly fathers know how to bestow good gifts upon His children, how much more would my Heavenly Father give the Holy Spirit to them that ask Him?[10] So having all confidence that God would be true if every man was a liar, I began to seek in desperate earnest. He said because of my importunity he would rise and give. I remember saying, "O Lord, I will stay right here till you pour out on me the promise you commanded me to tarry for, if I die of starvation. I am so hungry I can't wait another day. I'll not eat another meal until you baptize me."

After a time I ceased to beg the Lord for it, and realized I was not waiting for Him but that He was waiting for me, so I began to praise Him, and the deep "Glory, Glory, Glory to Jesus" rolled from my heart.

All at once my arms began to shake, gently at first, then violently, till my whole body was quaking under the power of the Holy Spirit. I did not consider this at all strange, as I knew how the batteries we experimented with in the laboratory at college hummed and shook and trembled under the power of the electricity, and here was the third person of the Trinity, coming into my body, in all His fulness [sic]. O, Glory! that sacred hour is so sweet to me, the remembrance of its sacredness thrills me as I write. I seemed to be lost in God. My body had sunk to the floor, but I felt as though I was caught up into clouds of glory. My lungs began to fill and heave under the power, my throat began to twitch, my chin to quiver and then to shake violently. My tongue began to move up and down and sideways in my mouth. Unintelligible sounds as of a stammering lip and another tongue spoken of by Isaiah 28:11[11] were heard. My whole soul longed to praise Jesus: then suddenly out of my innermost being flowed rivers of praise in other tongues, as the Spirit gave utterance. Acts 2:4. I, even I, away down here in 1908, was speaking in an unknown tongue. I shouted, "O, glory! the word of God is true, the promise is really to them that are afar off, even as many as the Lord our God shall call."[12]

Ignoring parental objections and high school graduation requirements, Aimee energetically gave her whole attention to the Pentecostal revival as well as to the evangelist, Robert Semple. Within two months of her conversion, seventeen-year-old Aimee was engaged to Robert who was nine years her senior. On August 12, 1908, they were married. They soon relocated to Chicago, where they assisted the Pentecostal movement in that city. Then in 1910, Aimee and Robert left for China to stir up the Pentecostal revival in that country. Several months into their stay, they contracted malaria after ignoring safeguards concerning food preparation, believing that God would keep them from sickness. While they were both in the hospital, they celebrated their second wedding anniversary by sending love notes via nurses between the men's and women's wards. Robert died leaving Aimee inconsolable and eight months pregnant. She named their daughter, Roberta, after her deceased husband, and gave her the middle name, Star, because the child was the only bright spot in the darkness.

The next years were desperate ones for Aimee. Upon her return to the States, she tried alternately to fit in with Robert's Pentecostal friends in Chicago and her mother's Salvation Army work in New York, all the while caring for Roberta. Neither work was satisfying. In 1912, while mired in loneliness and disappointment, she met and married Harold Stewart McPherson. Shortly after the birth of their son, Rolf Kennedy McPherson, Aimee went through two surgeries that left her quite debilitated. While in this weakened condition, she believed that God's call to evangelism came again, as it had when she was a teenager,[13] along with God's promise to heal her if she would comply.

On Her Calling to Evangelistic Work

It was just at the time of my greatest perplexity, when I had begun to lose out spiritually and wander away from the Lord, and was longing to make a home for the baby, that I married again. Before the marriage took place, however, I made one stipulation wherein I told my husband that all my heart and soul was really in the work of the Lord and that if, at any time in my life, He should call me to go to Africa or India, or to the Islands of the Sea, no matter where or when, I must obey God first of all. To this he agreed and we were married under these conditions, and settled down in a furnished apartment. . . .

When my husband received an invitation from his mother to come to her home in Rhode Island I was willing to consent to board the boat in my endeavor to "flee unto Tarshish from the presence of the Lord."[14]

But Oh, dear reader, what a great wind the Lord sent out into the sea! Such a mighty tempest was there in the deep that our frail domestic craft was rocked to and fro, so that the ship was like to be broken.

Day by day matters grew worse instead of better; I grieved and mourned and wept for my Jesus and the old-time place in Him. I was a mystery and a constant source of discomfort to those round about me.

Earthly things—home—comfort—Oh, what did these matter? I was out of His dear will, and my soul refused to be comforted.

Shutting myself away in my room I would sit on the floor in the corner behind the bed, and cry over and over the one word that I could say when I tried to pray:

"Oh—Oh—Jesus! Jesus! Jesus!! JESUS!"

Seeing my unhappy, melancholy state, my mother-in-law advised us to rent and furnish a home of our own, saying that the work would occupy my mind and keep me from thinking so much about myself. This was done. With the help of our parents and our own earnings, a well-furnished home was made, containing all that heart could wish—B-U-T J-E-S-U-S, and Oh, without Him nothing matters!

"Why can't you be happy and act like other folks, and forget your troubles?" I was asked again and again. Time after time I tried to shake myself from my lethargy and depression and busy myself with household duties. Such a fever of restlessness came upon me that it seemed as though I must wear the polish off the furniture and the floors by dusting them so often. A dozen times a day I would take myself to task as I would catch sight of my tearful face in the looking-glass, saying:

"Now, see here, my lady, this will never do! What right have you to fret and pine like this? Just see those shining, polished floors, covered with soft Axminster and Wilton rugs. Just look at that mahogany parlor furniture and the big brass beds in yonder, the fine bathroom done in blue and white, the steam heat, the softly-shaded electric lights, the pretty baby's crib with its fluff and ribbons, the high-chair and the rocking-horse. Why aren't you glad to have a home like this for the babies, as any other mother would be?"

"Why, it's perfectly ridiculous for you to think of going out into the world again, and—remember—if you found it hard with one baby before, what do you suppose you would do now with two?"

Having had it thus out with myself, I would return to my work, half satisfied for a few minutes saying:

"Well, yes, that's so. I had better give up all thoughts of such things, settle down and get used to my present life."

But, Oh, the *Call of God* was on my soul and I could not get away from it. For this cause I had been brought into the world. With each throb of my heart I could hear a voice saying:

"Preach the Word! Preach the Word! Will you go? Will you go?" and I would throw myself on my knees, tearfully sobbing:

"Oh, Lord, You know that I cannot go. Here are the two babies and here is the home, and here is husband, who has not the baptism and is not even seeking it.[15] I will work here in the local mission, and that will do." But no, the answer still came back, clear from heaven:

"Go! DO THE WORK OF AN EVANGELIST; Preach the Word! The time is short; I am coming soon."

"Oh, Lord, I am in a pretty state to preach the Gospel, I am. Why, I feel so miserable and down and crushed. I need some one to help me instead of me helping others." At times, lifting my eyes quickly after prayer, I could almost see the devil rubbing his hands and leering at me, saying:

"There's no hope. You might just as well give up. Everyone knows you've backslidden,[16] and would have no confidence in you." Then would ensue another spell of bitter weeping.

My husband and his mother would often say:

"Well, Aimee—I don't see what more you want. I don't believe anything could make you happy. It must be your disposition." (Why, bless the Lord, when in His will I am so happy and full of gladness, my feet and my heart are so light, that they cannot keep from dancing. It seems that no one on earth could possibly be so happy as I.)

My nerves became so seriously affected that the singing of the teakettle upon the stove or the sound of voices was unbearable. I implored the little one to speak in whispers. I hated the sunshine and wanted to keep the shutters closed and the window-shades drawn tightly. The doctors said I would lose my reason if something was not done. I became very ill in body and inside of one year two serious operations were performed. Each time, before going under the surgeon's knife, and during many other times of critical illness, when it seemed as though I were going to die, I would call the saints to pray for me that I might be delivered, but each time they prayed I could plainly hear the voice of the Lord saying:

"Will you go? Will you preach the Word?" I knew that if I said "Yes", He would heal me. But how could I say "Yes?" Difficulties rose like mountains in my path. Oh, now I have learned, that no matter what the obstacles may be, if Jesus says "Go", and I start, by the time the obstacle is reached I will either be lifted over it or it will be gone. God does not ask us to do the impossible. If He tells you to do a thing, no matter how hard it seems, you just start to do it and you will find, like Christian of old, that the lions are fettered and unable to hinder your progress.

After the first operation I was worse instead of better. Complications set in, heart trouble, hemorrhages from my stomach, and intense nervousness among others. The doctors said that another operation would be necessary. . . .

The second operation was put off and put off, with some vague hope of trusting God, but how could I trust Him when out of His will, and when every time in prayer I got the answer which throbbed and pounded through my being with every pulse-beat—

"Will you go? Will you go? Preach the Word! Preach the Word!"

At last, doubling over with a scream with appendicitis, on top of all else, I was rushed again to the hospital. As I was being prepared for the operating table I prayed earnestly from my valley of despair—

"Oh, God, please take me home to be with You. It doesn't seem possible for me to go back and I certainly cannot bear it to go on. I am a misery to myself and to everybody round about me. Please, please take me home to be with You." But Oh, I am so glad that He spared me. Praise His precious name. . . .

About two in the morning the white-robed nurse, who had been stroking my hand, saying: "Poor little girl; poor little girl," seemed to be receding.

The fluttering breaths which I could take were too painful to go deeper than my throat. Everything grew black—someone said:

"She's going." Just before losing consciousness, as I hovered between life and death, came the voice of my Lord, so loud that it startled me:

"NOW—WILL—YOU—GO?" And I knew it was "Go", one way or the other: that if I did not go into the work as a soul-winner and get back into the will of God, Jesus would take me to Himself before He would permit me to go on without Him and be lost.

Oh, don't you ever tell me that a woman cannot be called to preach the Gospel! If any man ever went through one-hundredth part of the hell on earth that I lived in, those months when out of God's will and work, they would never say that again.

With my little remaining strength, I managed to gasp:

"Yes—Lord—I'll—go." And go I did![17]

With her resolve to be an evangelist, her health improved, but Harold's support of her plans did not. Aimee recalled that he repeatedly discouraged her. Finally in the spring of 1915, Aimee secretly boarded a train with her two children and ran away to her parents' farm. Upon her arrival back home, she immediately left the children with her parents in order to attend a Pentecostal camp meeting. While there, she felt accepted and affirmed in her evangelistic endeavors, and she was subsequently invited to hold meetings in other locations. Harold discovered her whereabouts, and for a while, they were reconciled. Harold helped Aimee on her first road trip when, in the summer of 1916, she toured New England holding evangelistic meetings in a tent.[18] These campaigns continued for several years, expanding north to Maine and south to Key West, Florida. Harold and Aimee worked together until in 1918, they quarreled bitterly, went their separate ways, and subsequently divorced in 1921. Harold's place was quickly filled by Aimee's mother who was savvy in business matters and administrative details.

In the fall of 1918, Aimee had her tent shipped to Los Angeles, and she drove the children and her mother on a "transcontinental gospel tour," holding evangelistic meetings from her car along the way. She settled her family in a home in Los Angeles, and then crisscrossed the United States and Canada holding increasingly larger meetings and healing services in city after city. Her magnificent, permanent platform in Los Angeles, Angelus Temple, was opened in dramatic Aimee fashion on January 1, 1923, the same day that her float—a floral model of Angelus Temple—won a prize in the Tournament of Roses competition.

On Her Evangelistic Method: Angelus Temple

Angelus Temple was the center of her million-dollar evangelistic enterprise and the headquarters for the denomination she founded, the International Church of the Foursquare Gospel.[19] In addition to the nightly services and three on Sunday, Angelus Temple sponsored a range of ministries and activities, including a Commissary with food, clothing, blankets, and household items for those in need, a prayer tower where volunteers literally prayed without ceasing, a radio station that broadcast her daily 7:00 A.M. show, "The Sunshine Hour," a Bible College—L.I.F.E. (Lighthouse of International Foursquare Evangelism)—which offered training for students in evangelism and mission work, a publishing house, telephone call-in ministry, and weekly healing service.

In the following excerpt, a typical Sunday evening service was described through the voice of Angelus Temple.

If Angelus Temple Could Speak

High from the streets my mighty walls arise; looming, towering up, up and away—then sweeping inward, in soft graceful curves, upholding the awe-inspiring height and enormity of my magnificent dome—the largest, unsupported concrete dome in the continent of America, I am told....

Wonderingly, admiringly, the passerby, the tourist, the multitudes passing afoot and by car lift their eyes and gaze questioningly upon me. Catching up the sunlight, my newly painted walls seem almost to be living, moving, pulsing things as they flash and glow and flash again,—signalling the message to every soul that looks:

It's true! It's true! The dreams, the hopes, the prayers have all come true. And here I stand—the visible answer from the invisible God who still doth live and move and answer prayer.

And down below, standing on the earth by my mighty foundations, the little Evangelist lady, her mother, and immediate friends clasp their hands, lift up their faces and gaze on me through misty tear-dimmed eyes, and say:

"Dear Temple, child of our dreams, our faith, our labors and our prayers. Are you really true? Let us touch you! Let us prove again that this mighty miracle is really standing in our midst; that you are really up and open with shining doors flung wide unto the hungry and needy sons of men; that by your most miraculous erection, it has been proven again unto the world that Faith and Prayer still triumph; that unto her who believeth there shall still be a performance of those things which were told her by the Lord."

"Mighty Temple, glorious Temple, you are no longer merely a vision, —a fondly cherished dream, a shining hope, a flaming desire, —you are a concrete reality.

With you the realization far exceeds the fondest anticipation. Yet, let me whisper it softly, you great, precious crown of our fourteen years of ministry— you were none-the-less real in our hearts when we saw you only through the eyes of Faith and prayed your first materials down from heaven." ...

Through the doors of my wide set columns and arches a steady stream of humanity flows. Old and young, rich and poor, sinner and saint, sick and well, afoot and by trolley, in purring motor cars and in wheel chairs, with springing, joyous stride and painfully slow on crutches—on, on, they come.

Through my doors they surge, seeking a glimpse of the tender Lord Jesus, Who biddest them all: "Come unto Me."[20]

Within my courts the servants of the most high God[21] minister humbly unto the Lord and to His saints; tending reverently and with all diligence, the revival fires that burn unceasingly upon the sacred altars day and night.

It is Sunday night, —in and in, the great sea of humanity sweeps 'till they fill the ground floor of my auditorium, and not an available inch of space is left. Still in they surge over the shining red floors of my lobbies, up the grand stairways, to pack the first and second half of my great balcony, 'till not another seat is left.

Move over, everybody! Mother, would you mind holding your little girl on your lap to make room for this gentleman? Brother, would you mind taking your overcoat off that seat so that this lady might sit there? Yes, yes, you may have the seats which have been reserved for the ushers. None of them will have a moment to be seated tonight. The streets outside are black with people. I will never be able to hold them all.

There, there, ushers, rope off the stairways leading to the first balcony. Throw open the passages leading up through the social foyer to the third floor. Let them pack the galleries now. This way, brother; this way sister; go clear in as far as you can go. Leave the end seats for the newcomers. That's right. Lady, would you mind bringing your baby down to the nursery? This sister will hold your seat for you until you get back. You'll enjoy the meeting much better, and run no risk of the baby disturbing the speaker. Oh, yes, it's a beautiful nursery with a trained nurse in charge, and many assistants. I knew you would like it. See, it says "Baby Bank—Check Your Baby Here." The Evangelist and her mother spent hours selecting these little tables and chairs, these cribs and soft beds, pink, blue, white, grey, ivory—which will you put your baby in, mother? Leave her bottle. We'll make sure that the milk is just the right temperature. Now your baby is Number 43. Take this slip, will you? And sit right in the mother's section, so that we can call you quietly if you are needed. . . .

And just to think this has been such a busy day, —from seven o'clock this morning when scores of pilgrims could be seen wending their way through my doors and up the steps just as the sun was rising in the East, making their way to the "Hundred and Twenty" or "Upper Room"[22] on this, as on every other morning, for the sunrise Prayer Service and "Tarrying Meeting."[23] Since Sunday School at nine-thirty; preaching services at ten-thirty and again at two-thirty in the afternoon, these multitudes have surged and eddied about my edifice. . . .

At the signal note the great chorus standing now behind the people in the first balcony drenches the audience in a shower of golden-voiced melody:

"Holy, holy, holy,
Lord, God Almighty"

The people are turning in wonder to see from whence this music springs.

"All thy works shall praise thy name
In earth and sky and sea
Only thou art holy, merciful and mighty,
God in three persons, —the Blessed Trinity." . . .

The ministers are on the platform. The Evangelist, Sister McPherson, is in her place. The choir director is standing out on the edge of the platform. With one motion of his hand, the entire sea of people spring to their feet, and almost split my dome with the volume of their song . . .

Hush! The harpist is now running her fingers over the strings. Melody, such as one has dreamed of hearing in heaven, comes floating out in mellow tones and rises to fill the vastness of my dome and shower down upon the people. Now a quartette is singing! Now, the announcements are being made.

The choir is singing during the offering and it is time for the address of the evening. How the people listen—how they sit forward in their seats, drinking in every word! It seems as though the whole world is hungry—hungry to hear the story—the old new story of Jesus and His love. For over an hour, the speaker stands there, pouring out her heart, telling of the Lamb for sinners slain[24]—of His power ever present to comfort, strengthen and guide. It is the "Four-Square Gospel" which is being preached, portraying Jesus Christ the only Saviour, the Baptizer with the Holy Spirit, the Great Physician and the soon Coming King.[25]

Now the altar call[26] is given—standing there with hands out-stretched, the evangelist is giving a simple call for sinners and wanderers to come home to the Saviour and to be washed in the fountain filled with blood.

And how they come! Pouring down from the galleries—streaming down the ramparts—from the balcony—flowing down the aisles of the main auditorium. It seems that they are coming from every direction at the same time.

Hurry, ushers! Hurry altar workers! Hurry ministers! Meet them as they come. Guide them in the way. Some of their eyes are blinded with tears. Deal with them tenderly. Show them where to kneel. Some of them have never confessed Christ before in all their lives, as Saviour and Lord. Some of them have never prayed since Mother died and they learned to lisp "Now, I lay me down to sleep." . . .

Now the glory is coming—the Evangelist has led the people in prayer and they repeat it after her, sentence by sentence—that plea for forgiveness, which brought them step by step into the place of absolute faith and confidence wherein they rejoiced in the Lord for deliverance and cleansing by His blood. . . .

The benediction is pronounced and the river is flowing out again, but they will be back—many of them, just as the sun is rising on the morrow.

O, yes, I am a Temple—a mighty glorious Temple. Builded by faith, and hope, and love. Erected by prayer and trust and courage in the land of the sunset sea. But I doubt that any other building feels, if buildings can feel, quite so happy as I tonight. My altars have been wet with tears. I can show you proudly some of the pools that dripped upon the rose-taupe carpet that lines my chancel space. My frame has trembled 'neath the shouting of thousands of lifted voices, my dome has reverberated with triumphant songs. Already over a thousand souls have been born again into the Kingdom at my altars, and my Evangelist pastor has patted me on the back and told me that I have paid for myself and been worth my weight in gold and made up to her mother and herself every hour of anxiety and prayer and sacrifice that she had put into me by the souls which have already been won in me. And I have yet before me—if the Lord tarries, many years of faithful service.

That is why I wonder if any other building is quite so happy and contented as I, under the silvery beams of a California moon tonight.[27]

On Women

In many practical ways, Aimee supported women in ministry. On Friday evenings, LIFE students, both male and female, preached at the Temple's service. Women graduated from LIFE Bible College and organized Angelus Temple branch churches in other cities, particularly in the western states. In addition, Aimee "ordained women, appointed them to pastorates, sent them as missionaries, put them on her Bible school faculty, and otherwise encouraged them just as she did men."[28] She even amended later her denomination's bylaws to recognize the ministry of women in an official way: ". . . there shall be no discrimination between men and women in relationship to their duties, activities, ecclesiastical and spiritual standings and recognitions in the Foursquare Gospel Organization. All executive offices shall be open to both men and women in good standing in the organization."[29] However, there was another side to Aimee with regard to women in ministry. During her lifetime, the number of women pastors in these branch churches actually declined by 50 percent, with the downward trend beginning around 1927. As far as Angelus Temple offices were concerned, she decreed that women could be deaconesses, but only men could serve the higher office of elder. When Aimee baptized converts at the Temple, she was never accompanied by a woman, only a man.[30]

This sermon illustrated her vacillation about women. She described male and female genders with stereotypical characteristics, such as claiming that men have more "logic and wisdom" than women. Similarly, family roles fell along gender lines; the "rugged" father provided "bread for the larder" as well as "advice and counsel," while the mother "rocks the little ones." Nevertheless, she encouraged women to go out, beyond the family, to preach the gospel. Her rationale for women preaching was connected directly to her belief that the end was coming soon. In these latter days, as she explained, "one of the signals and signs preceding the second coming of Jesus Christ is that of WOMEN PREACHING THE GOSPEL. In fact, the Lord will not come until at least a few of His handmaidens have preached the Word."[31]

Aimee preached this sermon for a baccalaureate service at LIFE Bible College.

The Servants and the Handmaidens

Baccalaureate Sermon

To the Watchmen Class, January 7, 1930

"Upon the servants and upon the handmaids in those days will I pour out my spirit."[32]

WE ARE LIVING on the edge of time, nearing the coming of the Lord Jesus Christ!

Even now He is donning those glorious coronation robes! Even now the orchestras of Heaven are adding the final touches to the wedding march which shall resound throughout the Eternal Heavens as we go Home through the Appian Way[33] of the stars to be with our Lord! On earth, all is coming in readiness! Prophecy is being fulfilled on every hand; signs in Heaven above us, signs in earth beneath! While the love of many is waxing cold and they are falling asleep, thank God, something else is happening! There is a mighty moving unto God among the people today! There is a mighty stirring in the chamber of the Bride! Virgins are filling their lamps with oil preparing for that great day when the Son of man cometh![34] The time is short! Of necessity we must work fast! Whatever we are to do, we are to do it now if ever! If we intend to give our lives to Jesus Christ, we are to do it now! The Lord is calling the handmaidens today as well as the servants; the daughters as well as the sons.

There are some who believe that a woman should never witness for Jesus Christ—that her lips should be sealed. This is not according to the Word of God. "Your sons and your daughters shall prophesy!"[35] In this day, God has a real message for the women as well as the men and He is using them to help gather in the wheat, for the fields are ripe unto harvest[36] and the time grows short. Sometimes we wish we were men, that we might go out into the byways and blaze new trails. How wonderful it would be to get out into the far reaches of the world? Nevertheless, God has a work for the women of today with their sweet voices, their shining faces, their tender hands, and their loving spirit. Just as there is room for a father and a mother in family life, so there is room for both the servant and the handmaiden in the Lord's work. Each have their place. The father surely is needed with his ruggedness, his ability to provide bread for the larder, and his advice and counsel. But who would say we do not need the mother in the home to rock the little ones and teach them the tender things of life? Besides, the mother often can reach the heart of a child when the father has failed. So it is in the Church of Jesus Christ, there is a place for the sons and daughters; the servants and the handmaidens.

How we thank God for the men who have blazed the trail in the years that have passed—the Daniels, the Moses, the Josephs, the Samuels, the Pauls, the Peters, the Wesleys,[37] and the Luthers![38] We bless their memories unceasingly for they were the saints of yesterday who paved the way for those who were to come after them. But I would bring a message to my sisters just now: "Go on with the Word of God!" God has used the womenfolk!

As I look back into those other days, I remember Miriam and the sweet music of her timbre, and how God used her. He used Deborah too, as she went forth with flaming banners, leading her troops, conquering and triumphant. She was a real leader, a statesman, a politician, and a devout follower of Jehovah. Then there were the Rebekahs who were the mothers of their line and race. Rebekah went down to the fountain and filled her pitcher to the brim with clear, sparkling water. I can see her now moving across the stage of life, pausing a moment at the fountain, filling her vessel and emptying the water out to the thirsty. God grant that we may all be Rebekahs, filling our own pitchers with the Living Water[39] so that we may give of it to the thirsty! We may not have all the logic and wisdom of the men but surely we can do this. On down through the years I see the Ruths and the Naomis gleaning in the harvest fields. Sister—there is a place for us! The field is wide. The men have had the harvesting to do for centuries and they have not completed it as yet. They should be willing for us to glean that which they have missed anyway. And we shall glean in the fields until evening and then beat out that which we have gleaned. God grant that it may be an ephah[40] of barley that we may take with us on to the City!

God uses the Marys too. Do you remember the sweet, precious virgin who offered her heart to the Lord, and how she sang those inspired messages of praise? How marvelously she was used of God! There certainly is a place for the madonnas and the mothers in the plan of the Lord for today! I can see the Dorcases down through the years—that dear little Dorcas of the Bible days who sewed, toiled, and labored so faithfully. How they loved her! We have them right here in their faithful ministry to the Lord Jesus Christ, many of them. Through the centuries I seem to see them coming; these witnesses, these precious women of God, telling the story of His redeeming love. There are the Florence Nightingales;[41] those angels of the shell-torn battlefields. I can see them now, those brave women of the old war days, telling the story of the Gospel, starting the blessed ministry of the Red Cross, organizing military hospitals, going among the dying soldiers upon the battlefields, putting the canteen to fevered lips and giving them a drink of cold water in the Master's name. Marching! Marching! Those precious women of yesterday! Tramp! Tramp! Tramp! An unbroken, steady line of heroic womanhood! It was not only yesterday that the Lord used women, He has used them since time began and is still using them, praise the Lord![42]

Aimee's ministry was irreparably altered on May 18, 1926, when she suddenly disappeared for six weeks. She steadfastly maintained, even in the face of contrary evidence, that she was kidnapped on the beach after a swim by a man and woman who asked her to come to their car to pray for their dying baby. The abduction story continued with her being held captive for ransom in a shack in the Mexican desert. Eventually she escaped, and despite her story's inconsistencies, an estimated crowd of 50,000 people welcomed her back to Los Angeles. She was brought to court on charges of obstructing justice but was acquitted. Following the disappearance fiasco, she carried on the ministry of Angelus Temple, held expansive evangelistic meetings in many cities, and solidified the denomination she founded. Nonetheless, her health began to deteriorate as did her close personal relationships. Aimee and her third husband, David Hutton, were divorced shortly after they were married. She quarreled bitterly with her mother, her daughter, and several close associates, and those relationships were damaged beyond repair. Only her son, Rolf, was in her good graces when, on September 27, 1944, she died from an overdose of sleeping pills in a hotel room in Oakland, California. The autopsy report declared her death accidental. As throngs of her followers had surrounded her for several decades, no matter what her personal trials, so they did at her death as 50,000 people filed past her casket in Angelus Temple.

Notes

1. According to Aimee's autobiography, her mother, Minnie, begrudged the monotony of farm life and reveled instead in the pageantry of soul winning with The Salvation Army. Minnie believed that God had called her to preach the Gospel, but since she had somehow missed the opportunity, she prayed for a girl who would go in her stead. Even before the child's birth, Minnie prayed, "Lord, give me a little baby girl; I will give her unreservedly into your service that she may preach the word I should have preached, fill the place I should have filled, and live the life I should have lived in Thy service." [Aimee Semple McPherson, *This Is That: Personal Experiences, Sermons and Writings* (Los Angeles: Bridal Call Publishing House, 1919), 14.] Six weeks after Aimee's birth, Minnie took her in an open carriage five miles to the nearest Salvation Army mission to dedicate her to God's work. Minnie was an integral part of Aimee's evangelistic success until a bitter disagreement between them over Minnie's management of Angelus Temple's business affairs led to an estrangement that was not reconciled by the time of Aimee's death.

2. Charles Darwin (1809–1882) was a British naturalist who became legendary for his theories on natural selection and evolution. Aimee considered these theories to be antithetical to "the mighty hand of a Creator." For more on her view of creation and evolution, see Edith Blumhofer, *Aimee Semple McPherson: Everybody's Sister*, Library of Religious Biography (Grand Rapids: Eerdmans, 1993), 56–57.

3. Acts 2:38.

4. Hebrews 13:8.

5. The latter rain metaphor came from three biblical texts: Deuteronomy 11:14; Joel 2:23; James 5:7. Joel 2:23 reads: "O children of Zion, be glad and rejoice in the Lord your God; for he has given the early rain for your vindication, he has poured down for you abundant rain, the early and the later rain, as before." The extraordinary occurrences on the Day of Pentecost (Acts 2:1–4) were interpreted as the early rain; latter rain referred to the similar, miraculous events taking place right then in their own day. For more on the latter rain, see Grant Wacker, *Heaven Below: Early Pentecostals and American Culture* (Cambridge, MA: Harvard University, 2001), 254 and "Playing for Keeps: The Primitivist Impulse in Early Pentecostalism," in *The American Quest*

for the Primitive Church, ed. Richard T. Hughes (Chicago: University of Illinois, 1988), 203–07; see also Donald Dayton, *Theological Roots of Pentecostalism*, Studies in Evangelicalism, No. 5 (Metuchen, NJ: Scarecrow, 1987), 26–28.

6. Acts 2:1–4.
7. Acts 9:1–9.
8. Revelation 1:17.
9. Matthew 7:7–11.
10. Luke 11:13.
11. "Truly, with stammering lip and with alien tongue he will speak to this people . . ."
12. Acts 2:39. Aimee Semple McPherson, *The Personal Testimony and Life of Aimee Semple McPherson* (Chicago: Pentecostal Herald, 1915), 5–11. I am grateful to Matt Sutton for this excerpt.
13. Shortly after her conversion, Aimee felt that God had called her to evangelistic work. She had an "intense, heaven-sent longing to be a soul winner," and she pledged, at that moment, that she "would be willing to crawl upon my hands and knees from the Atlantic to the Pacific just to say to one poor, lost soul—'Dear sinner, Jesus loves you.' " Aimee Semple McPherson, *This Is That: Personal Experiences, Sermons and Writings of Aimee Semple McPherson, Evangelist* (Los Angeles: Echo Park Evangelistic Association, 1923), 50–51.
14. Jonah 1:1–3. See also n. 33, chapter 7.
15. Her reference is to the baptism of the Holy Spirit, which often manifested itself, as in her case, in the speaking in tongues. For more on the baptism of the Holy Spirit and speaking in tongues, see Wacker, *Heaven Below*, 5–6, 40–44.
16. See n. 15, chapter 2.
17. McPherson, *This Is That* (1923 edn.), 71–76.
18. Large tents for housing evangelistic meetings began to be used as early as 1842 by the Millerites, a group who encouraged women to preach as evidence of the soon return of Jesus Christ [see Brekus, *Strangers & Pilgrims*, 321–22]. Several decades later, Maria Woodworth-Etter (see chapter 7) traveled with her own tent. In order to hold the increasingly large crowds that attended her 1890 Oakland, California meetings, she spent $1,325 for a tent spacious enough to accommodate 8,000 people. A generation later, Aimee began her full-time evangelistic work in a 40 by 80 foot tent. She recalled the first time she pitched this tent in vivid detail. "Knowing little of the winds and power of the elements which have to be taken into consideration when picking out a location for a tent meeting, we, in our ignorance, selected a fine, high hill, on the bluff of the bay where those who came to meeting could enjoy the breeze and the water. The series of meetings was almost over when one forenoon the last wind storm came, and in spite of all our efforts, down went the big tent with many tears in its rotten old seams which we had worked for hours to sew up, just a short time ago." Her commitment to her evangelistic work was matched by her spirit of resourcefulness; she and a little boy managed to ready the tent for the evening service. McPherson, *This Is That* (1923 edn.), 87.
19. The Church of the Four Square Gospel reflected the synopsis of her fourfold teaching about Jesus: the Only Savior, the Great Physician, the Baptizer with the Holy Spirit, and the Coming Bridegroom, Lord, and King.

The four-square gospel idea had been developing for several years, but Aimee first explained it during her 1922 Oakland revival to a crowd of 7,000 people, who were gathered in a tent that spanned a half acre, to hear her sermon, "The Four Square Gospel." In another sermon several days later, Aimee connected the four-square gospel with the four faces of God described by the prophet, Ezekiel. "Ezekiel related the faces of a man, a lion, an ox, and an eagle. [Ezekiel 1:10]. The face of the man, Sister explained, typified Christ the Savior; the face of the ox, Christ the burden-bearer and healer; the face of the eagle, Christ the coming King; and the face of the lion, Christ "the mighty baptizer with the Holy Ghost and fire." Later, when the story had taken form, she recalled the "witness of the Spirit" that she had perceived as 'waves, billows, oceans of praise rock[ing] the audience, which was borne aloft on the rushing winds of Holy Ghost revival." [Blumhofer, *Aimee Semple McPherson*, 192]. Others had developed the idea of a fourfold gospel earlier than Aimee's exposition of it. See Dayton, *Theological Roots of Pentecostalism*, 21–22, 106.

20. Matthew 11:28.
21. Daniel 3:26; Acts 16:17.
22. Acts 1:13–15.
23. A tarrying meeting provided an opportunity, outside of the organized worship service, for further instruction and guidance in the Christian life. In Pentecostal circles, the tarrying meeting was often the occasion for spiritual manifestations.
24. John 1:29.
25. See n. 19 above.
26. See n. 14, chapter 5.
27. McPherson, *This Is That* (1923 edn.), 526–37.
28. Blumhofer, *Aimee Semple McPherson*, 362.
29. International Church of the Foursquare Gospel, "Report of the Annual Convention" (1936), 6, International Church of the Foursquare Gospel Archives, Los Angeles, California. I am grateful to Matt Sutton for this reference.
30. Blumhofer, *Aimee Semple McPherson*, 360–63.
31. "Pre-Millennial Signals Towers" Sermon delivered in the Angelus Temple, Sunday afternoon, August 24, 1924, International Church of the Foursquare Gospel Archives, Los Angeles, California.
32. Joel 2:28–29; Acts 2:17–18.
33. The Appian Way was one of ancient Rome's main roads.
34. Matthew 25:1–12. This parable about the ten virgins who were waiting to usher in the bridegroom was a favorite of Aimee's, and it supplied the title of her monthly publication, *The Bridal Call*. Blumhofer, *Aimee Semple McPherson*, 119.
35. Joel 2:28–29; Acts 2:17–18.
36. John 4:35.
37. John (1703–1791) and Charles (1701–1788) Wesley were brothers who led the eighteenth-century Methodist revival in Great Britain. John was an Anglican clergyman, evangelist, prolific writer, and organizational genius; Charles wrote more than 9,000 hymns and poems, many of which contain the theological emphases of the Wesleyan tradition.

38. Martin Luther (1483–1546) was a leader of the Protestant Reformation. In 1517, he posted his infamous 95 Theses, a document which critiqued the practice of granting indulgences by The Roman Catholic Church, on the door of the church in Wittenberg, Germany. Although he was a priest, he was excommunicated from the church for his heretical views. Various Lutheran denominations worldwide have been founded on his teachings.

39. John 4:10–11.

40. An ephah is a dry measure approximately equal to two-thirds of a bushel.

41. Florence Nightingale (1820–1910) rose to fame for her work as a nurse during the Crimean War (1851–1854). After the war, she continued to labor for the improvement of sanitary conditions and health care in hospitals.

42. Aimee Semple McPherson, "To the Servants and the Handmaidens; Baccalaureate Sermon," *Bridal Call* 13 (February, 1930): 5–6, International Church of the Foursquare Gospel Archives, Los Angeles, California.

Pentecostal holiness evangelist, founder and bishop of The Mount Sinai Holy
Church of America

Courtesy of Minerva R. Bell, Mount Sinai Holy Church of America.

CHAPTER 16

IDA ROBINSON (1891–1946)

I da Bell was the seventh of twelve children born to Robert and Annie Bell in Hazelhurst, Georgia. The family relocated to Pensacola, Florida, while she was still young. As a child, Ida did not learn to read and write. While in her teens, she was converted at an evangelistic street meeting. Shortly after, she began to lead prayer services in homes. In 1909, she married Oliver Robinson. They resided in Pensacola for several years until 1917, when Ida's sister invited them to move to Philadelphia for better employment opportunities. She did street evangelism in Philadelphia under the auspices of The United Holy Church of America. In 1919, she was ordained an elder and then appointed to a small mission church, where she was successful in pastoral ministry and itinerant evangelism. In Ida's estimation, however, prospects for women within The United Holy Church were decreasing as male leaders debated issues of ordination and pastoral authority for women. This situation conflicted with a promise from God given to her, "that He would do a great work through the women as time passed on."[1] In January, 1924, she spent ten days in prayer and fasting, and she believed that God was calling her to "Come out on Mount Sinai,"[2] so that "I will use you to loose the women."[3] Immediately she set out to establish a charter for a new denomination, The Mount Sinai Holy Church of America.[4] The charter was accepted while she was preaching in Burgaw, North Carolina, and the first church of the new denomination was established there with Malinda Cousins as the pastor.

On Her Evangelistic Method: Founding and Presiding Over a Denomination

The denomination spread rapidly, largely due to Ida's own evangelistic work,[5] along the eastern seaboard, from New York to Florida. Every year ministers and workers from across the denomination gathered in Philadelphia for a convocation at the mother church, Mount Olive Church.[6] Ida, who was consecrated as bishop in 1925, presided over the convocation, which lasted for several days. This excerpt recounted her responsibilities as the denomination's leader at the ninth annual convocation.

As the Bishop stood at the table [communion table] that was bedecked with silver and pure white linen, surrounded with a host of saints, all dressed in white, it was indeed a beautiful spectacle. Hundreds of saints communed during this service. The Bishop was in immediate charge. . . .

During the third day of the session Bishop called the convocation together to serious thought and consecration as regards divine healing. The Bishop was very forceful in dealing with this subject, and assured that "God is the same yesterday, to-day, and forever more."[7] And, said she, "if a sufficient number of you had absolute faith in God to the extent of performing in this day as during the days of His visibility, great work could be done and would be demonstrated in this age of unbelief and hard-heartedness." After the brief but searching message, she invited those who suffered physical disorders to gather around the altar and depend solely upon God to heal their infirmities. It was a glorious and very impressive service. As the infirmed kneeled at the altar the Bishop proceeded to anoint them with oil[8] after a brief prayer. . . . Many of those who were anointed received complete and immediate divine deliverance. I have never seen God's power more effectively demonstrated than during this divine healing service. It was some time before quietness was resumed, for those who were divinely touched were naturally expressively jubilant. . . .

Bishop Robinson delivered her annual message with such force and clarity, the exceedingly large audience that occupied every available inch of space in the big tabernacle was for two hours thrilled with one of the most forceful messages that was ever delivered in our great church.

It was a splendid day for the occasion. The audience was made up of out-of-town groups as well as those from Philadelphia. Busses, taxis, private cars, street cars and every conceivable kind of vehicle was used to provide transportation for those who were there to enjoy the Bishop's annual sermon on Sunday morning. Some arrived early on Saturday evening while some were later and still others arrived midnight Saturday and early Sunday morning. Those who arrived too late to make reservations for sleeping spent the night out in front of the church and on side streets in their cars and busses and arose early to be the first to occupy seats that were advantageous in preparatory for the sercon [sic]. Those who came late could not gain entrance to the main auditorium. Worse yet, just before the Bishop ascended the rostrum to begin her message, entrance could not be gained either down or upstairs. . . .

After some brief remarks of timely greetings, she selected her text from II. Chronicles 7:14—"If my people which are called by my name shall humble themselves and pray and seek my face, and turn from their wicked ways; then will I hear from heaven and forgive their sin and will heal their land." Many beautiful pictures were portrayed with thoroughly understandable demonstration. A very lovely demonstration was made with one of the ministers in the rostrum. She showed in the demonstration the condition of Lazarus and Divies,[9] two Bible characters who died. One was a Christian, while the other was not. As the demonstration progressed and was harmonized so appropriately with her text, bringing all the facts concealed in the parable as related by Jesus Christ, to plain view of the audience. When her listeners realized the significance of the parable, ebullition prevailed for a period of five minutes during which time the speaker was unable to continue.

Truly, I have never seen the Bishop more forceful and dynamic in the act of preaching. Prayer as used by the Bishop was the substance of the highly interesting sermon. She mentioned many of the patriarchs in both the new and old testament who were unmercifully persecuted by their foes, both on land and sea. They were afflicted because of the testimony they held. But in each case, notwithstanding the expiration of same, many of them were delivered by prayer and prayer only.

As the Bishop emphasized it, prayer penetrated the waters of deep Galilee and aroused a big fish that saved God's preacher,[10] the prayer that stilled vicious lions that could not hurt the pious Daniel,[11] the prayer that cooled the flames in the hot furnace of wicked Babylon,[12] the prayer that closed up heaven for a period of three years to avenge God's prophet;[13] the prayer when the church of God was going through the most distressful period of its history, opened up heaven and God with the outpouring of the Holy Ghost, baptized every believer that was in the church at Jerusalem as recorded in the Acts of the Apostles 2:4.

Nearing the close of her message, Bishop, in graphic deliberation outlined the return of the Lord back to earth, shortly the millenarian city was established, the host of Mt. Sinai with the rest of the saints were ushered in singing a song, "My soul's got a home"; this, of courses [sic], was unbearable. The congregation rose singing and the glory, God filled the big tabernacle. A liberal offering was given the Bishop after the sermon.[14]

Ida was a well-known preacher. "Her preaching became famous both in Philadelphia and New York, with many coming to her evening services after attending their own services earlier in the day."[15] During her sermons, which often lasted several hours, she alternated between preaching and singing. Her preaching style was quite energetic, and as she preached, she would walk through the aisles "often pausing to speak directly to members and worshippers."[16] Central to her preaching was the doctrine of sanctification. In a sermon entitled, "Can These Bones Live?"[17] she called her hearers to renounce sin and to live a holy life.

Have you conquered sin? All unrighteousness is sin. Can you make the straight gate,[18] playing and writing numbers? You are playing to win or lose — high class gambling in a modern way. Fornicating, having a good wife, but you must have your sweetheart, too. Adultery. Two and three living wives. Whoremongers. Cannot be satisfied with one wife, trying to flirt with every woman or man you meet. Liars, preaching the word of God, diluting it to fit your own lives. Such that has been dilapidated with sin. O! you know I am preaching the truth and you might as well say, Amen! because I have opened my mouth unto the Lord and I will not compromise with the world if I don't have a friend.[19]

The emphasis on holiness was also encapsulated in several stanzas of the favorite hymn at Mount Sinai services, "The Standard of Mount Sinai is Good Enough for Me."

> We don't use tobacco over here; don't smoke or drink or chew,
> We don't make Moonshine, don't drink it, and won't sell it to you,
> Mount Sinai's standard reaches so high, no adulterer may abide,
> But woman to one husband, man to one wife, no sweethearts on the side.
>
> *Chorus*
> Oh, it's good enough for me, it's good enough for me,
> The standard of Mount Sinai is good enough for me,
> You may go North or South, East or West, on land or over sea,
> Mount Sinai's standard is the best, and good enough for me.
> On beauty of Mount Sinai is the way the people dress,
> Which is as becometh Holiness, but they always look the best,
> Don't think its people look like bums, as you can plainly see,
> You'll find they're very up-to-date, and it's good enough for me.[20]

These holiness standards were not only for the individual; they also applied to societal issues, such as the draft for military service. The denomination's policy cited that members must submit to the draft, but they could not bear arms: "We believe that the shedding of human blood or the taking of human life is contrary to the word of God. This belief makes us adverse to war in all its forms. In times of war, when laws are passed requiring induction into the Armed Forces, we submit to the provisions thereof because of the teaching of Romans 13:1[21] . . . Our members are instructed to accept induction into the Armed Forces *only as Partial Conscientious Objectors . . . not to submit to the bearing of arms in any manner.*"[22]

On Women

Women in The Mount Sinai Holy Church enjoyed unlimited opportunities for ministry. At its founding, women comprised six of nine members of the Board of Elders as well as the top four officers. Female ministers far outnumbered male ministers; in 1946, the year of Ida's death, 125 of the denomination's 163 ministers were women.[23] Ida's closest associates were always women. She had a personal secretary, also a leader in the denomination, who read to her and transcribed her sermons because she was illiterate. When Ida was holding evangelistic meetings, she traveled in a caravan of large limousines with several female church elders, all of whom wore long, black, ministerial gowns.

Ida emphasized the importance of various women in the Bible. About Mary, Jesus' mother, Ida declared, "If Mary can carry the Word of God[24] in her womb, why can't I carry the Word of God on my lips?"[25] At the Easter Sunday Sunrise Service, Ida would take up her tambourine and lead the congregation in singing about Jesus' female disciples, who first announced the good news of his resurrection:

> Didn't those women run,
> Didn't those women run,
> They ran the good news to spread.
> The angel told them to go
> For Jesus had gone on before.
> 'He is risen just as He said.'[26]

One of Ida's sermons on women's rights was put in verse form after she preached it, and the poem was then published in the denomination's newspaper.

"Woman's Rights"
        By
Lillia M. Sparks
St. Matt. Holy Church, Pensacola, Fla.
Composed from our Bishop's Sermon

There's neither Jew nor Gentile,
To those Who've paid the price;
'Tis neither Male nor Female,
But one in Jesus Christ.[27]

I am going to tell you friends
Without the slightest doubt,
A day is coming very soon,
When your sins will find you out.

A day is coming very soon,
When sin you cannot hide;
Then you will wish you'd taken,
The Bible for your guide.

You'll wish you had let women alone
When they were trying to teach.
You'll be sorry you tried to hold them down,
When God told them to preach.

Come, dear brothers, let us journey,
Side by side and hand in hand;
Does not the Bible plainly tell you
Woman shall co-ordinate the man?

The hand that rocks the craddle [sic],
Will rule the world, you know;
So lift the standard high for God,
Wherever you may go.

Some women have the right to sing,
And some the right to teach;
But women, called by Jesus Christ,
Surely have the right to preach.

Some men will call you anti-Christ,
And some would rather die;
Than have the Spirit poured out,
When women prophesy.[28]

To prophesy is to speak for God,
Wherever man is found;
Although lots of hypocrites,
Still try to hold them down.

So be steadfast in the Word of God,
Though fiery darts be hurled;
If Jesus Christ is on your side,
He is more than all the world.[29]

By the time of her death at the age of fifty-four, the denomination she founded consisted of eighty-four churches, more than 160 ordained ministers, an accredited school in Philadelphia, mission work in Cuba and Guyana, and a farm in South Jersey, which provided a safe haven for members to escape the city slums for a short vacation.[30]

Notes

1. "Brief History of Mount Sinai," Pamphlet prepared for the Sixty-Fifth Anniversary, 3; given to the author by Elder Minerva Bell, Historian, Mount Sinai Holy Church of America.

2. Mount Sinai is the mountain on which Moses received the law; see Exodus 31:18; 34:29, 32.

3. "Brief History of Mount Sinai," 3.

4. This denomination was incorrectly included in a book on African American religious cults. The phenomena cited as examples of cult-like behavior are simply characteristics of a holiness Pentecostal denomination, such as "Tongues and other evidences of possession," "Testimonies during ordinary services," and "Insistence on sanctification and unusual experience." Arthur Huff Fauset, *Black Gods of the Metropolis: Negro Religious Cults of the Urban North*, vol. III, Publications of the Philadelphia Anthropological Society (New York: Octagon, 1974), 69.

5. "Minerva Bell estimates that between 1924 and 1932 every new church started by Mount Sinai was started by Bishop Robinson herself." Harold Dean Trulear, "Reshaping Black Pastoral Theology: The Vision of Bishop Ida B. Robinson," *Journal of Religious Thought* 46 (1989): 25.

6. Mount Olive is a mile-long hill near Jerusalem, which served as the city's watch-tower. Jesus often prayed in a place called Gethsemane, which is located on Mount Olive. The writer of the gospel of Luke indicated that it was Jesus' custom to go there; see Luke 22:39. On the night of Jesus' arrest, Jesus was praying at Gethsemane; see Matthew 26:30, 36; Mark 14:32; Luke 22:39.

7. Hebrews 13:8.

8. James 5:14–15.

9. The reference here is to Jesus' parable about the rich man and Lazarus (Luke 16:19–31). The rich man is not given a name in the biblical story, but he has been referred to as Dives because *dives* in the Vulgate, the Latin translation of the Bible, is the word for "rich man."

10. Jonah 1:17.
11. Daniel 6:16–28.
12. Daniel 3:19–30.
13. 1 Kings 17:1.
14. "Greatest Convocation In Church's History Has Just Closed" *The Latter Day Messenger of Mt. Sinai Holy Church of America, Inc.*; given to the author by Elder Minerva Bell, Historian, Mount Sinai Holy Church of America.
15. Trulear, "Reshaping Black Pastoral Theology," 22–23.
16. Trulear, "Reshaping Black Pastoral Theology," 22.
17. Ezekiel 37:3.
18. Matthew 7:13–14. In the King James Version, the phrase is, "strait gate."
19. This transcribed sermon is included in Bettye Collier-Thomas, *Daughters of Thunder: Black Women Preachers and Their Sermons, 1850–1979* (San Francisco: Jossey-Bass, 1998), 201.
20. Trulear, "Reshaping Black Pastoral Theology," 27.
21. "Let every person be subject to the governing authorities; for there is no authority except from God, and those authorities that exist have been instituted by God."
22. Cited in Dean Trulear, "Ida B. Robinson: The Mother as Symbolic Presence," in *Portraits of a Generation: Early Pentecostal Leaders*, eds. James R. Goff and Grant Wacker (Fayetteville: University of Arkansas, 2002), 317.
23. Trulear, "Reshaping Black Pastoral Theology," 24.
24. The Word of God is Jesus Christ. See John 1:1, 14.
25. Trulear, "Reshaping Black Pastoral Theology," 30.
26. Luke 24:5. Trulear, "Reshaping Black Pastoral Theology," 31.
27. Galatians 3:28.
28. Acts 2:17.
29. *The Latter Day Messenger of Mt. Sinai Holy Church of America, Inc.* (1934), 3; given to the author by Elder Minerva Bell, Historian, Mount Sinai Holy Church of America.
30. Trulear, "Reshaping Black Pastoral Theology," 23–24.

Faith-healing evangelist, radio and television evangelist, author of *I Believe in Miracles* and *Nothing is Impossible with God*

Courtesy of the Flower Pentecostal Heritage Center, photo by Doug Grandstaff Photography.

CHAPTER 17

KATHRYN KUHLMAN (1907–1976)

athryn Johanna Kuhlman was the third of four children born to Joseph and Emma Kuhlman of Concordia, Missouri. Her father was raised in a Baptist family, but as an adult, he did not attend church because he considered that preachers were mercenaries.[1] Kathryn was devoted to her father, and in return he showered her with love and affection. Her mother, who taught Sunday School and an afternoon meeting for youth at the Methodist church, was a strict disciplinarian. She frequently exercised this trait on Kathryn whose inquisitive nature and love of practical jokes got her into trouble. Once when she was visiting her grandfather's farm, he showed her his watermelon patch and explained that watermelons were red on the inside despite their green veneer. When her grandfather returned to the house, Kathryn, then nine years old, cut open more than one hundred watermelons just to be sure. Her mother was not amused.[2] In 1921, at the age of fourteen, Kathryn was converted during a two-week evangelistic meeting in the Methodist church. A year later, she transferred to the Baptist church, where she was baptized by immersion.

On Her Conversion

Recently I returned to that little Methodist church in Concordia, Missouri, where I was converted. I was in Kansas City holding services in the opera house. I took members of my staff along with me, and we drove over to Concordia.

"Oh, you must see where I first accepted Jesus," I told them. I tell you the truth, I was so shocked when I found out how small that little Methodist church had gotten through the years. There was a time when it looked so big to me, it looked almost like a cathedral. Then I realized that perhaps it doesn't seat any more than 75 or 100 people. I walked into the little vestibule. There was the same rope that rang the bell—the first bell, the second bell, you know, announcing the time of the services. It was the same bell they always tolled when someone died in town. One ringing meant a child had died, two rings meant a middle-aged person had passed away. When an elderly person died, they rang it three times. This would cause everyone to rush to the telephone and ask the operator, "Who died?" That's Concordia, Missouri.

That afternoon I walked into the church. The same pews were still there, the same railing, the same pulpit. Nothing had really changed in that little church. But, oh, how I had changed.

I thought back to that Sunday morning so many years before. Standing there, holding the Methodist hymnal in my hands, I was standing next to mama. Everybody in mama's family was Methodist. Grandpa Walkenhorst always attended that church and sat in the same pew until the day before he died. He lived and died believing sincerely that only Methodists would make it to heaven. Since that time I've often thought what a shock it must have been for Grandpa Walkenhorst—if he got to heaven himself—to find out there were Baptists, Presbyterians, Lutherans, and Catholics in heaven! I'm not quite sure whether he could have adjusted to all that.

Anyway, that Sunday morning was my first introduction to the Holy Spirit. I knew nothing about the third person of the Trinity, but He came with great conviction upon me. And standing there, holding that Methodist hymnal in my hands, I began to shake with great conviction. I was only fourteen years old—so I did the only thing I knew to do. I stepped out from where I was standing and went to the front pew, sat down in the corner, and wept. Not out of sorrow, but because of the great feeling that came upon me. Something had happened to me.

One cannot really describe spiritual experiences, because they *are* spiritual. There are no words in the human vocabulary to describe spiritual things. But I knew, in that exact moment, I had been born again. I never doubted my new birth experience from that moment until this very hour. I knew something had happened to me. I knew my sins had been forgiven. I knew my sins were covered with the blood. In that moment, Jesus Christ became very real to my heart.[3]

The summer after her sophomore year in high school, Kathryn joined her older sister and brother-in-law, Myrtle and Everett Parrott, who were itinerant evangelists, for their summer tent meeting season in the Pacific Northwest. Kathryn had intended to do evangelistic work only as a summer stint, but it turned into a five-year apprenticeship. While she was working with the Parrotts, Kathryn experienced her own call to preach.

On Her Call to Preach

My call to the ministry was just as definite as my conversion. You can say anything you want about me, as a woman, having no right to stand in the pulpit and preach the gospel. Yet even if everybody in the world told me that, it would have no effect on me whatsoever. Why? Because my call to the ministry was just as definite as my conversion. And it's just like that.

I preached my very first sermon in Idaho. I preached to those farmers. Name any little town in Idaho, and you'll discover that one time, years ago, Kathryn Kuhlman came through trying to evangelize it. I would find a little country church that was closed because they couldn't afford a preacher.

I would go to the deacons, or the board, or the members and ask to preach. I remember going to the head of the board of a Baptist church and saying, "Your church is closed anyway. You haven't anything to lose, and maybe a little to gain." And he let me open the church for meetings. Twin Falls, Emmett, Payette, Boise—those were the days when I got my early spiritual training.

All I knew how to preach was salvation, the new-birth experience. No one can give any more than what one has experienced himself. All I knew was what I had experienced in that little Methodist church in Concordia. The very first sermon I preached was Zacchaeus up a tree.[4] And God knows if anybody was up a tree, I certainly was when I preached that sermon. I remember well that after the sixth sermon I honestly felt I had exhausted the Bible. I'm telling you the truth. I felt there was nothing more to preach about. Six sermons! I had preached on Zacchaeus, I had preached on heaven, I had preached on hell, I had preached on the love of God—you know—and what more was there to preach about? But years have come and years have gone, and I have found out that you can never exhaust the deep truths in God's Word.

I know so well what the Apostle Paul meant when he declared that he was called of God to preach. Why He called me, I do not know. I haven't the slightest idea why I was chosen to preach the gospel. There are millions who could do a better job, I am sure. Millions better equipped than I. The only reason I can give you is the fact that I knew I had nothing, and I never forgot from whence I came. When you have nothing, and you admit you have nothing, then it's so easy to look up and say, "Lord Jesus, if you can take nothing, use it. Take my hands, take my voice, take my mind, take my body, take my love—it's all I have. If you can use it, I give it to you." And He has taken my nothing and used it to His glory. . . .

One day I will have preached my last sermon, I will have prayed my last prayer, and I will stand in His glorious presence. Oh, I have thought of this many, many times. I have often wondered what would be my first words to Him, the One whom I have loved so long yet have never seen. What will I say when I stand in His glorious presence? Somehow I know the first words I shall say when I look in His wonderful face.

"Dear Jesus, I tried. I didn't do a perfect job, because I was human and made mistakes. There were failures. I am sorry. But I tried."

But—He knows that already.[5]

Kathryn never returned to live in Concordia, nor did she graduate from high school. She took courses from Simpson Bible Institute in Seattle as well as from Aimee Semple McPherson's LIFE Bible College in Los Angeles,[6] but she was never graduated from either institution. Kathryn boasted instead that her education came from the Holy Spirit. "I got my schooling at the feet of the greatest teacher in the world. It wasn't in some great university or theological seminary. It was in the school of prayer under the teaching of the Holy Spirit."[7]

In 1928, Kathryn and pianist Helen Gulliford formed an evangelistic partnership that would last ten years, known as "God's Girls." Kathryn preached, and Helen provided the music. Their first five years together were spent evangelizing in the state of Idaho. They ventured into Colorado in 1933. A two-week evangelistic meeting in Denver lasted five years and resulted in the organization of a church, the Denver Revival Tabernacle, as well as a radio ministry. Also in Denver, she was ordained by a nondenominational ministerial organization, The Evangelical Church Alliance.

Visiting evangelists were frequently invited to conduct services at the Tabernacle. One evangelist who came to preach was Burroughs A. Waltrip. He and Kathryn became attracted to each other, and eventually he left his wife and two children, secured a divorce, and married Kathryn. Their marriage, considered scandalous by Kathryn's closest friends, admirers, and the Tabernacle's members, ended her ministry in Denver. For nearly a decade, little is known about their life together. In the end, Kathryn's agonizing conviction was that she had to end the marriage and begin her evangelistic work again.

> I had to make a choice. Would I serve the man I loved, or the God I loved. I knew I could not serve God and live with Mister. [She called him "Mister" from the very first time she met him.] No one will ever know the pain of dying like I know it, for I loved him more than I loved life itself. And for a time, I loved him even more than God. I finally told him I had to leave. God had never released me from that original call.[8]

She began again in Franklin, Pennsylvania, when she was invited to hold a two-week evangelistic meeting in the Gospel Tabernacle, where years earlier Billy Sunday[9] had held meetings. Her intended two-week stay extended to four years. During these years, she also began "Heart-to-Heart," one of the most popular religious radio programs of the twentieth century. In her folksy, conversational style, she asked her audience this question in her opening line, "Hello there, and have you been waiting for me?" The demand for her radio program persisted for six years after her death, and the Kathryn Kuhlman Foundation responded by re-broadcasting her taped radio programs.

On Her Evangelistic Method: Faith Healing

Also in Franklin, there was the first report of a healing during one of her services. This report by a woman healed of a tumor was followed by more reports of healings. Kathryn moved to Pittsburgh and regularly held healing services in Carnegie Hall from 1948 until 1967, when the city reconfigured the large auditorium into smaller rooms.[10] She then moved her services, at the pastor's invitation, to the sanctuary of The First Presbyterian Church in downtown Pittsburgh. Denominations were not sacrosanct for her, and her services were quite ecumenical. "Every Friday for years I have conducted a miracle service in the First Presbyterian Church here in Pittsburgh, Pennsylvania. . . . The services begin around

9:30 A.M. and continue to about 1:30 P.M. . . . They come—Roman Catholic, Greek Orthodox, Lutheran, every denomination, people from around the world—gathering in the sanctuary of the First Presbyterian Church. Everybody forgets their denominational ties. We worship together on the common ground of Calvary."[11]

When asked about her healing services, Kathryn declared repeatedly that there was an integral connection between spiritual and physical healing, and she always maintained that spiritual healing was primary, as this excerpt clarified.

For years I have made it a practice to disassociate myself from anything written about me or said about me. If I listened to my critics—or my fans—I would quickly be destroyed. I have never considered myself to be the best known woman preacher in the world. In fact, I never think of myself in the terms of "preacher." That's the reason I never use the word "Reverend." I really do not consider myself a woman preacher. Believe me. I'm just somebody who loves souls. I love people. I want to help them. It's just that simple.

Helping people is the most rewarding thing in the whole world. You do not have to be a Kathryn Kuhlman to help people. The goal of every Christian, every born-again man and woman,[12] should be helping people. God's children are born to serve. That's what Jesus did. Jesus lived to serve. And if you are a born-again man or woman, you, too, will feel your responsibility in serving and helping people. It's the most rewarding thing in the world.

Last Christmas among the cards and gifts I received there was a little card with a great big Santa Claus on it. It came from a twelve-year-old girl. The doctors had said that perhaps she would not be living by Christmas. They had wanted to amputate her leg because of cancer. But she sent me this card, and in the card she had written these words: "I am living to see this Christmas. I still have two good legs, because God answered prayer, and you helped." I cannot begin to tell you the tears I shed over that Christmas card. It was the greatest gift I received. Some people put angels on the top of their Christmas trees. Others beautiful ornaments. But I had the most beautiful gift of all, for I put that little girl's card at the very top of my tree.

Rewarding? There's no way to buy what I felt.

When I walk out on the stage at the great miracle services, I realize that sitting there in the audience are men and women who have made great sacrifices to be there. For many of them it is their last hope. The doctors have given up. Medical science says no hope. But I see beyond physical healing. I know that spiritual healing is far greater than the physical. So even though I believe in miracles, I know that far more important is the call for a spiritual healing—for it may be their last chance.

The physical healing is so very secondary, believe me. You can well afford to live and die with a sick body, not having been healed physically. But when those last moments come and the Holy Spirit is speaking at the close of a service, I always remember the spiritual healing is far greater than the greatest physical healing. It's wonderful to see a body healed from cancer. It's glorious to see a man or woman come out of a wheelchair, and see that wheelchair pushed down the aisle—empty. But there is something that's far greater—that new birth experience. I stand there in those last moments of a great service and give an altar call[13] and realize there may be those who are receiving their last call from God, spiritually. And the destiny of that soul is at stake. That, my friends, is the most awesome feeling. That is when the great responsibility is really felt. And when the lights have been turned out in the great auditorium, my only concern is whether I gave every ounce of strength I had, whether I could have done a better job than what I did—not performing miracles, for I am no miracle worker, but in calling men and women to Jesus Christ.

Oh, sure, there is a responsibility when it comes to those who come for physical healing. And I'm just human enough to say the responsibility is so great that sometimes I wish I had never been called to this type of ministry. Sometimes that responsibility is almost overwhelming. It isn't hard work. I can stand on a platform, the stage of some auditorium, for four and a half hours and never feel the weariness because I am completely yielded to the Holy Spirit. But the burden of the responsibility drains the physical body.

I know better than anyone else that Kathryn Kuhlman has no healing virtue. I'm not a faith healer, please understand that. I have no healing power. I have never healed anyone. Know that. I'm absolutely dependent on the power of the Holy Spirit, on the power of God. I have stood before sick people and cried, wishing I could give them the strength from my own body. But without the Holy Spirit I have nothing to give. Nothing.

I remember something that my papa, who worked so very hard, said to me when I was a little girl. I remember him as he extended his open hands, and he said, "You know, baby, you can have anything in the world you want if you'll work hard enough with your hands."

That made a very great impression on me, because my papa was a hard worker. I've learned to work, and to work very hard. But papa didn't quite understand the work of the Holy Spirit. I've stood before people thinking if it was only hard work that was needed, I'd work the flesh off my bones. When I see a daddy standing there with a little child who has cancer, or perhaps a deformity, and I see those great big tears rolling down the cheeks of that big strong man, I would gladly give my life if that child could live. But I have no power. Hard work won't impart healing. And in those moments, I know better than anyone else how dependent I am on the power of God.

It's just like that.

People ask, "Is this not a thrilling experience? Being chosen by God for such a responsibility?" No, not thrilling, but awesome. Sometimes so awesome I wish I had never been called.

But with the responsibility come the rewards—like that child's card at Christmas. And even though I'll probably burn myself out and die in the ministry, I'll die happy—and satisfied. For the great God who called me has given me, also, a glimpse of His glory.[14]

On Women

When asked in an interview—What do you think of women's lib?—
Kathryn responded, "You want to know something? Women's lib won't like
to hear what I have to say. I'd give anything if I could just be a good housewife, a good cook."[15] Her desire to be a more traditional woman was at
odds with her determined commitment to her evangelistic work. These
conflicting desires seemed to evoke an internal tug-of-war, as this excerpt
indicated. Nevertheless, she attested to God's call to women in ministry,
just as she was called.

I sometimes wonder what it would have been like had I been a man. I really
don't know. For I am very much a woman.

A lot of people seem to think that being a woman in the ministry means
I have two strikes against me. I've never felt that way. I just lift my chin a little
higher and act like I don't hear the insults. I didn't ask for this ministry. God
knows I'd much rather be doing something else. But He put me in the
ministry and those who don't like having a woman preach should complain
to God—not me. It's just like that.

I'll tell you something very confidentially—the true conviction of my
heart. I do not believe I was God's first choice in this ministry, in the ministry
He has chosen for these last days. It's my firm conviction. You'll never argue
me out of this conviction, never. I'm not quite sure whether I was God's
second choice, or even His third choice. Because I really believe the job I am
doing is a man's job. I work hard. Few people know how hard I really work—
sixteen, seventeen hours a day. I can outwork five men put together, and
I'll challenge you on this. Only those who know me best know how little
sleep I get, the hours I put into the ministry. Those who attend our services
know I am on the stage, behind the pulpit, three and a half to four and a half
hours. I never sit down.

I believe God's first choice for this ministry was a man. His second choice,
too. But no man was willing to pay the price. I was just naïve enough to say,
"Take nothing, and use it." And He has been doing that ever since.

That is why I say to you, I know the power of the Holy Spirit is real. You
can't give without receiving. After all those hours, I can still leave the stage
as strong as when I walked on. I have given myself completely to the Holy
Spirit. I have given my body as an empty vessel to be used by the Holy Spirit,
but as I give, I receive. Even more than I give.

One day in Los Angeles a representative of women's lib called to ask if I
would appear on a television program for women's lib. I laughed. "You won't
want to hear what I have to say!"

You see, I'd give anything if I could just be a good housewife, a good cook.
Oh, I'd like to be a good cook. I'd like to have about twelve children.
Sometimes I feel like the mother of the world now. I've got so many spiritual
children I don't know what to do. I worry about them. I mother them. I love
them. I care for them. It would be so nice to have a man bring in the

paycheck. I would just love to have a man boss me. It might not last long, but for a little while it would be just great!

So when it comes to women's lib, I'm still as old-fashioned as the Word of God. I still think that the husband should be the head of the family. I know how it was at our house. Papa was always the head of the family, and if papa said it, it was just as though God had said it. We never had any women's lib at our house, but we had a mighty happy family. Papa did the work, and mama ran papa without papa knowing it. It was a beautiful situation.

A woman's place is where God puts her. For the housewife and mother, it is with her husband and children. For me it is in this ministry. This is my place, because God put me here.

In I Timothy 2:11–12, Paul says, "Let the woman learn in silence with all subjection." It looks like Paul didn't believe in women's lib either. Verse 12: "But I suffer not a woman to teach, nor to usurp authority over the man, but to be in silence."

Let me give you something very simply. I am quite certain that if it was contrary to the will of God to let women preach, Paul certainly would have reprimanded Philip, in whose home he visited. Philip, you remember, had four daughters who were preachers (Acts 21:9). Now that's a houseful of preachers, I'll tell you! Paul visited Philip and all four daughters were there. They wouldn't have missed seeing Paul for anything in the world. But I cannot find a single Scripture that says that Paul forbade these four daughters to preach. Peter quotes Joel in Acts 2:17, saying in the closing hours of this dispensation, not only will your sons prophesy and preach, but your daughters shall also prophesy and preach. Powerful words.

So what do we do about Paul's command for women to keep silent in the church?[16] Look at the situation. In the synagogues of that day, women would sit in the balcony. This is still done in parts of the world today, such as India, where the women are on one side and the men on the other. The women would talk so loudly from their places in the balcony that the rest of the people could not hear the speaker. Women are just the same today as they were then. I can just hear John's wife calling down and saying, "John, do you remember? Did I turn the stove off?" Or maybe they were doing a little voting and Elizabeth would call down and say, "Abe, say no, say no, you know I don't like him, don't put him in office." They talked so loudly no one else could hear. They just couldn't keep their mouths shut. So Paul said, "Let the women be quiet." That did not mean that women were inferior. The Bible teaches that men and women each have their proper places. Each has God-given responsibilities. The man, for example, is the head of the woman. That doesn't mean he is a tyrant, that he goes around with a big stick. Thank God there is a difference between men and women. But that does not mean that women are somehow lesser—just different. Some of the greatest leaders in Hebrew history were women. I admire Golda Meir[17] very much. She's a strong personality, a strong leader. What Golda wants, Golda gets. I admire Deborah, a judge of early Israel. I admire Queen Esther. I admire Sarah. I admire Mary, the mother of Jesus. All strong women.

Down through the centuries, in every society, there have been some things men have naturally done and other things that women have done. But it was Christianity that freed the woman from her subservient role. I have never understood how any woman could reject Christ, for it was Christ who gave dignity to women. Christians may have problems with women in ministry—but Christ never did. He elevated us. He set us free. I am glad I am a woman.[18]

In the late 1960s, Kathryn branched out into television broadcasting with her popular, long-running television series, "I Believe in Miracles." During the thirty-minute program, she gave a short inspirational talk, and then she interviewed someone who had been healed at one of her services. Her book, by the same title as her television program, sold over one million copies.

Kathryn died on February 20, 1976 at the age of sixty-nine due to health complications, which were compounded by exhaustion. On her tombstone was inscribed her oft-repeated claim, "I believe in miracles because I believe in God."

Notes

1. Wayne E. Warner, *Kathryn Kuhlman: The Woman Behind the Miracles* (Ann Arbor: Servant Publications, 1993), 40.
2. Jamie Buckingham, *Daughter of Destiny: Kathryn Kuhlman... Her Story* (Plainfield, NJ: Logos International, 1976), 16.
3. Kathryn Kuhlman with Jamie Buckingham, *A Glimpse Into Glory* (Plainfield, NJ: Logos International, 1979), 9–11.
4. Luke 19:1–10.
5. Kuhlman, *A Glimpse Into Glory*, 11–13.
6. Warner, *Kathryn Kuhlman*, 32–36. For more on Aimee Semple McPherson, see chapter 15.
7. Buckingham, *Daughter*, 48; cited in Warner, *Kathryn Kuhlman*, 34.
8. Buckingham, *Daughter*, 88.
9. See chapter 13.
10. Warner, *Kathryn Kuhlman*, 166.
11. Kuhlman, *A Glimpse Into Glory*, 22. For more on Calvary, see n. 10, chapter 10.
12. John 3:7.
13. See n. 14, chapter 5.
14. Kuhlman, *A Glimpse Into Glory*, 1–5.
15. Kuhlman, *A Glimpse Into Glory*, 31.
16. 1 Corinthians 14:33b–35.
17. Golda Meir (1898–1978) was Israel's Prime Minister from 1969–1974. Previously she was appointed to various positions within the Israeli government, such as Ambassador to the Soviet Union, Foreign Minister, and Minister of Labor.
18. Kuhlman, *A Glimpse Into Glory*, 30–34.

Child evangelist, editor of *Petals from the Rose of Sharon*, author of *Why I Am a Preacher*

Courtesy of the Flower Pentecostal Heritage Center.

CHAPTER 18

ULDINE UTLEY (1912–1995)

Uldine Mabelle Utley was born in rural Oklahoma to Hattie Ellen Bray and Azle Herbert Utley. Her family eventually settled in Fresno, California, where her father worked on a raisin farm. Uldine dreamed of becoming a Hollywood star, so she enrolled in a local drama club at the age of nine and was cast in the leading role for a production. When Uldine and her grandfather drove to town to pick up her script, they found the door locked. Despite her protests, on the way home her grandfather stopped at an evangelistic meeting preached by Aimee Semple McPherson.[1] Uldine, who was nine years old, was converted at this meeting.

On Her Conversion

Being in California—where Hollywood was!—helped me greatly in deciding what I intended to do as soon as ever I could. All the day I wanted to dance and play "theatre" or the like, for what was there to hinder me? 'Way back in Colorado, even before seeing the beautiful theatres of California, or hearing about movie actresses, had I not sung and danced for my own entertainment (no one else could have possibly been entertained, I am sure!)? My ambition was, of course, indefinite except in my own mind, for I could not expect much encouragement from Mother and Daddy when their daughter wanted to be a dancer on the stage or a star on the screen—it didn't matter much to the daughter which. . . .

Daddy and Mother saw my increased interest in things of that sort and failed to be enthusiastic, but I don't suppose that they could think of a way to keep me from being interested, since so many friends encouraged me and said that some day I would do what I wanted to do then. Mother didn't want me to be rebellious (I know that was her reason) so she allowed me to join a school dramatic club and I knew I would have "just a lot of fun." I went, I guess, about three times, not more.

Then Something Happened!

I hadn't known, of course, that it would happen, but it did, and oh, I've been so glad ever since.

I was converted! . . .

But let me tell you the details:

You will recall the Junior Dramatic Club I told you about a moment ago, which Mother let me join? Did I tell you that the director gave me the leading role in the play they were to introduce at the first of the season in one of the Fresno theatres? Well, he did, to my astonishment, although I had been there but three times. So you can imagine I was very excited. It was to be such a big event, and I was to do what I wanted to do so long! The story I was to play in was explained to me partially, although I was to receive my part on the next afternoon of rehearsal, which was Saturday. . . .

You see, it was Saturday, the day I was to get my part to practise; the director had said so, adding that he was counting on me, which, of course, made me all the more anxious to do my best. . . . Grandpa took me to the clubrooms and turned the doorknob to go in. It would not open. He turned harder, shook it. It was closed and locked. I kicked it, "I must get in," I cried. Grandpa reasoned, "If the door is locked this is not the day to practise . . . there would be lots of children here." "Yet this *was* the day," I frowned.

"But we can't help it now," concluded Grandpa, philosophically, "and I am going to a revival meeting in the Civic Auditorium. You might as well come with me." I protested, declaring that I didn't care anything about church, anyway, and that Sunday School once a week was too often as it was, and that nine-year-old girls couldn't possibly understand a sermon, or care to, either, for that matter. But, of course, we went.

Grandpa sat on one side of the building, and I on the other, in order to get seats at all, for the place was filled. The afternoon sermon was about David and Goliath.[2] The evangelist said that each one of us ought to have as much faith in God as the little shepherd boy had, regardless of the power of Goliath (who represented the devil's power and threatenings). Also, that if we would give our lives to Jesus to be His followers we would have worthwhile influence in the world, and no matter how little we were, or young, or unlearned, or how many obstacles were in our way, we would know victory as David knew it when he said to Goliath, "You come to me with your spear and with your shield, but I am come in the name of the Lord of hosts, the God of the armies of Israel, whom thou hast defied."[3]

The Holy Spirit seemed to burn each word into my heart. Had I said that a nine-year-old girl could not be interested in what a preacher had to say? Then I had been wrong. I listened to every word that was spoken, feeling as I might have felt had I lived in Galilee two thousand years ago when the Peasant-Prophet, Jesus, drew little children to His side and laid His hand upon their heads and blessed them.[4] I know that Jesus really did lay His hand upon me then. How else can I explain to you the reason that I sat there with tears in my eyes as I heard the sermon?

"There is nothing to cry about like this, and in public, too," I thought, desperately trying to wipe away the tears.

My heart was touched by the power of the Holy Spirit and I wept for the same reason that thousands before me have wept when they came face to face with such a Saviour as Jesus. I felt keenly my need of Christ. This was not of my own reasoning, naturally, for I had never thought about it before. It was the blessed Spirit of God wooing me unto the only One who could make my life what it really ought to be.

I raised my hand for prayer—not very high, I admit—and then put it right back down again. But I found myself not only standing but out in the aisle facing the altar, being drawn to it as definitely as though the nail-pierced hand of Jesus were drawing me. The aisle was a very, very long one—it seemed to me, at least three blocks long! To make it harder, a woman sitting on the last seat of the row, right next to the aisle, turned to the man next to her, and nudging him with her elbow, said, "There goes a little girl. I wonder if she knows what she's doing."

I walked faster after that, and fell on my knees at the altar, weeping aloud and *really praying.* . . .

That afternoon at the altar, I did not say any prayer that Mother had taught me. There is a difference, you know, in saying prayers and praying prayers. Some learn some lovely bit of poetry, some beautiful thought and repeat to their God—the God of the Universe—as though He had never heard it before. Oh, listener, prayer means more than that! I found it out when I was nine years old and knelt at a wooden altar-bench and really prayed. I talked to the Lord. I told Him how sorry I was for the many things I had done wrong which seemed to be not only many but very wrong when I came to tell Jesus about them. I told Him many things, especially that I wanted all my life to be His disciple and always to please Him.

And, He really heard me when I prayed for pardon. He saved me out of all my sins—including those I would have committed in the future had He not saved me, then! He put a joy in my heart I had never known before. The joy from which service begins! . . . I believed that Jesus was the Saviour of the world, I prayed that His precious blood might flow over my heart and take all my sins away—and I believed that He did what I asked Him to do. . . .

I felt so different when I stood up again by the altar. I knew that I *was* different than before. A woman stepped up to me, and bending over, looked into my face and said kindly, "Little girl, what are *you* going to do for Jesus?" I thought for a minute, and then said, "I'm only a little girl, I know, but I *am* going to be a little David and fight old Goliath." . . .

Like old, dead leaves dropping off to make room for new green ones, my ambition for worldly fame just "dropped off." I wakened up to the fact one day when Mother and I, walking down the street, were overtaken by the Director of the Dramatic Club, who urged Mother to bring me back again.

"Uldine," Mother asked, "what do you want to do about it?"

"I'm afraid I don't want to do anything about it," I answered.

"You're not coming back?" asked the Director. "Just because you were converted at that *revival* meeting?" Then he said some harsh things about evangelists, adding an exaggerated statement about "this foolishness, taking a girl away from such big possibilities," and then left us abruptly.

But I hadn't found out why the door to the Clubroom was locked; afterward, however, I found out it was because the announcement about the change of address for the place of rehearsal had been lost in the mail and had not reached me. So the door was shut! And another door—into salvation and Christian service—was opened. I walked in through that open door and was saved. And I praise the Lord because I've been able, this far, to stay on the inside of that door!

The school children thought I was joking when I brought my New Testament to school and preferred reading it during recess to entertaining them with my dancing. Soon they were laughing at me, having great sport by calling after me: "Preacher girl! There goes the preacher girl!" Just the same, I won my first soul for Christ on the school playground and, soon after, a Bible-study class was organized to which almost all the boys and girls of our class in fifth grade attended.[5]

Uldine began to speak about her conversion on Sunday mornings at her church and on Sunday afternoons at an evangelistic tabernacle in Fresno. After hearing her, a couple invited her to preach in Sanger, a neighboring town. She made a favorable impression, so she continued to preach there for several weekends. Before leaving Sanger, the congregation presented her with two gifts: a handmade, white, pulpit dress and a new Bible from the Montgomery Ward catalogue. After these weekends in Sanger, Uldine experienced a call to preach at the age of eleven.

On Her Call to Preach

A Definite Call

One afternoon I was praying as usual, and also, as usual, praying longer than I had at first intended. With me, praying had grown to be not a religious form to carry out, or a duty to be remembered daily, but fellowship with my Great Teacher, in Whose presence I had rather be than in the presence of presidents or kings. Yet, strange to say, as I prayed I forgot the things I particularly wanted to ask the Lord for, for myself, and offered my petition for others. The day of which I want now to speak was like others before it. I was pleading with tears that men and women might be saved; those multitudes whose upreaching hands I had constantly seen. At last I ventured to ask despondently, "I don't suppose I can, but do you think I could help win them, Lord?" I was half afraid, yet half-impatient for His reply.

But when it came, it was so far removed from what I expected it to be, that I was dumbfounded! Can you imagine what it was? It was nothing less than the commission Jesus gave to His disciples of old: yet I heard His voice differently than did the disciples, for these words came to me from the Bible: "As ye go, preach, saying, The kingdom of heaven is at hand. Heal the sick, cleanse the lepers, raise the dead, cast out devils; freely ye have received, freely give."[6] Through almost blinding tears I could read the words plainly and the more I looked the more stupendous they appeared to become, until they seemed to be imprinted upon my heart there to abide forever.

I dried my tears, and stood up trembling.

"I must not tell anyone," I said to myself. "None would believe me . . . and I mustn't believe it either."

But I did—almost. Do you understand me at all? *I was afraid to believe the Lord had called me to preach.* A call to preach the Gospel? Surely there was a mistake somewhere! It was too good to be true, and certainly too great to be true. How could I ever be meant to do anything so important in the world as to "carry the good tidings of great joy" unto all the people?[7]

"I *would* if I *could*, certainly," I reasoned. "Jesus knows I would do anything that was possible for me to do. That's what I asked Him to give me, a work I could do, and I can't do this. Not in a million years!" . . .

Day after day I increased in certainty, while praying; that is to say, that while upon my knees I *knew* the Lord had meant that I should receive that Scripture just as I had read it—that it *did* mean for me to preach the Gospel. But when I arose from my knees and began to reason it out in my own mind—how often we make that mistake after praying—I would increase in fear. All that I would like to do for the Lord was impossible. I simply couldn't do as He has asked me to. In the first place, I was only in the sixth school-grade. A lot I knew to tell people—I in the sixth grade! . . . Only in the sixth school-grade—how could I preach? And where could I go to preach? Who would listen to me after I got there? If they would listen, what would I say? Would I not be too afraid to speak? If I should face a great audience wouldn't I be too awed to speak? When if I were really to "GO" as that Scripture had said—travel from place to place—how could I? Mother and Daddy wouldn't go with me, of that I was sure; they were too interested in their home, and Daddy would never think of quitting his work, and I couldn't go all by myself. So what was I to do?

I thought out these things in my mind, over and over again. Thoughts like these are very disturbing, you know, and to say I was miserable would not exaggerate my state of mind in the least. I walked in a sort of daze. The Lord had called me to carry His message to the people and I couldn't do it. Yet, finally it took just about five minutes to settle it . . . and, as you may imagine— it was the Lord who settled it after all.

It happened on a Wednesday night. A woman was taking me to the church prayer-meeting and as it turned out we were the only passengers on the street-car. I was weary with my reasoning; then, suddenly, I thought that the Lord did not intend me to be struggling with this problem. How utterly fool-ish I had been to raise any objection! Did not the Lord know what He was doing, if He called a child to preach His Gospel? And if He created this great world, He ought to be able to enable a little girl to deliver His message if she were willing to do it. The whole question seemed suddenly simplified—every wrinkle ironed out, every problem solved.

I bowed my head in the street-car, and with my Bible in hand, prayed: "I accept Thy commission, Lord," I said, "Lord, I believe. But I do ask Thee to give me a confirmation of that commission Thou didst give me before, so that when I tell people of it, they may never say, 'It was by chance.' Lord Jesus, give me a Scripture that is definitely for me—that no one may doubt and that I may be strengthened when I am tried."

This is exactly the way I prayed. I had read Matt. 18:16.[8] The Lord had given me one Scripture. Now, as confirmation, I asked for a second. I asked the Lord to do it and believed He would. And, praise His name, He *did*!

Today, it seems to me the same as it did then—that the very hand of God must have opened my Bible to the page and the chapter that I saw when finishing my prayer. I looked down upon my Bible which I had, as a matter of habit, brought with me. These were the words I saw, and upon hearing them you will readily see why all my fears were swept away in a moment, and why, from that time to this, I have never doubted that God enables you to do what He asks you to—provided you are willing to do it. Here are the words: "Then said I, Ah, Lord, God! behold I cannot speak: for I am a child; for thou shalt go to all that I shall send thee, and whatsoever I command thee thou shalt speak. Be not afraid of their faces: for I am with thee to deliver thee, saith the Lord. Then the Lord put forth his hand, and touched my mouth. And the Lord said unto me, Behold, I have put my words in thy mouth."[9]

These words thrill me still, even as they did when I first saw them! I never knew before that the Bible could be so *personal*, so *individual*. That which had been spoken to an Old Testament prophet hundreds of years before my time so fitted my case, that, for a moment, it seemed hard for me to believe I was reading them out of so ancient and world-wide a book as the Bible.

That night I told the people at church about the Scripture. They looked at one another, and then at me in only half-concealed amazement, and some of them opened their Bibles. It seems strange to tell it, now, but when it was all happening it seemed a very natural thing: invitations began coming in from other churches asking me to speak for them. Realizing that I was going to school through the week, pastors and church-boards would inquire if I could not speak for them on Sundays and it was not long before I was going through the entire valley speaking Friday night, Saturday morning, afternoon and night, and Sunday morning, afternoon and night. This meant, sometimes, seven services each week-end, or at least, four or five.[10]

Uldine's evangelistic meetings became larger and more frequent. Soon she was unable to attend school regularly because the meetings extended beyond the weekends, so a tutor was hired to help her with her studies as she traveled. Her schedule was frantic. In one year alone, she held evangelistic meetings in more than fifteen cities in the United States and Canada, including St. Petersburg and Jacksonville in Florida; Savannah, Georgia; Florence, South Carolina; Lumberton, North Carolina; Baltimore, Maryland; Pittsburgh, Pennsylvania; Fayetteville, West Virginia; Erie, Pennsylvania; New York City; Astoria, Long Island, New York; Winnipeg, Manitoba and Saskatoon, Saskatchewan in Canada; Chicago and Joliet, Illinois. Not surprisingly, she described that year as "densely crowded—almost overexpanded with ceaseless activity."[11] The size of her meetings were quite large for a time. In the winter of 1925,

Uldine preached twice daily for five weeks in Indianapolis, and for the Sunday services alone, an estimated 15,000 people came to hear her.

Uldine's parents and younger sister, Ovella, traveled with her, and her parents handled every aspect of Uldine's ministry:

> Accepting invitations for revival campaigns; discussing with laymen and clergymen the essential preparations of a meeting; getting out advertising; overseeing the details connected with evangelistic work. Indeed, it must have been a tremendous responsibility. But he [her father] was cheerful about it all, and Mother was just as cheerful in her work. My pulpit uniforms were always spotless, and whether I wanted to study or pray there was always Mother's insistent voice when mealtime came: "Uldine, you must have hot food—and get out in the air, too, for some exercise."[12]

On Her Evangelistic Method: Publishing a Magazine

When she had been preaching for about a year, at the age of twelve, Uldine began publishing a monthly magazine to keep in contact with those who had attended her meetings. *Petals from the Rose of Sharon*, later entitled, *The Vision*, contained one or two of her sermons, testimonies from people converted at her meetings, and reports about her upcoming meetings.[13] The magazine was dedicated "To Those We Leave Behind."[14]

How the Magazine Started

The converts of every meeting we held were so anxious to "keep up" with us, as they expressed it, that they were always asking for sermons and reports of meetings, and for our future address by letter. Of course, this was impossible unless the same letter was sent to them all. And even this could not be done, unless each could share in the cost of such a procedure. Then, there were the stenographically reported messages, too; the people of cities already visited were wanting the messages delivered in future campaigns.

During the Eugene revival, one of the converts, a man of about fifty, solemnly informed me, as he straightened out a one dollar bill from the others, that he wanted to be the first name on the subscription-list, if I ever decided to publish a magazine.

"But you'd better keep it, sir," I said. "I have never thought of a magazine."

Yet from that time on the thought persisted and although it seemed a great responsibility to assume, I grew very anxious to do it. But Daddy didn't see how, at the age of twelve, I could be expected to see to the publishing of a fourteen-page magazine every month. But I knew he felt the same way about my preaching at the age of eleven. So I kept on gathering material, and knew that Daddy would look after the business side of the matter if I could only keep up the editorial side.

"Well, Uldine," Daddy said, unexpectedly, one morning, "if you still want to try out editing a magazine, I guess we have enough money to print the first number."

Oh, I was so excited! That very morning I had gotten up early and had been hard at work editing the material I already had on hand and completing several new articles. By that time my wrist was really quite "achy," and at that very moment, on my bedroom desk, was material for the first number, all completed!

So, when we got to Savannah, Georgia, Daddy took the typewritten pages to a firm of printers. The secretary, of course, had typed what I had written, and the first issue of *Petals from the Rose of Sharon* came off the press. The title of the magazine was suggested, of course, by my Vision of the Rose. Feeling that Jesus, the blessed Rose of Sharon,[15] gives to us continually His words and messages for our every need, I regarded them as "Petals"—daily unfoldings of grace and power and peace and joy—hence the name adopted for our little magazine, now discontinued.

Every month, then, revival messages, stenographically reported, and articles by myself were printed and sent to first hundreds and then thousands of friends all over the United States and foreign countries, with a prayer that they might prove to be real "petals from the Rose of Sharon," a breath of fragrance and beauty for every soul that needed the Lord.

Thus it was, that the dollar-bill which Mr. Goodenough gave me back in Oregon, engendered the thought of a magazine that finally became a reality. It has increased from fourteen pages to sixteen, from sixteen to eighteen, and having been translated into several foreign languages by missionaries who have used it in their work, it has become, so many have assured me, a source of blessing to the peoples of many lands.[16]

On Women

In 1925, Uldine met the Rev. Dr. John Roach Straton, pastor of Calvary Baptist Church in New York City and a leader in the Fundamentalist movement.[17] His nickname was "the Fundamentalist pope."[18] Straton became Uldine's most prominent advocate, which prompted rigorous criticism from other Fundamentalist leaders. One critic declared, "Dr. Straton has made a good fight against modernism in the past but in his endorsement of the girl evangelist he denies the authority of the Scriptures, discredits Paul, and in doing so deals a heavy blow against Genesis for which he has fought against the liberals."[19] To defend himself and Uldine's preaching, Straton penned an essay titled, "Does the Bible Forbid Women to Preach and Pray in Public?" He argued that the Bible must be interpreted as a whole, so that it is in harmony with itself. Because there exists evidence in the Bible that women preached the gospel, therefore, the few texts which might seem to contradict this evidence, must be interpreted in a way that maintains the Bible's internal consistency.

> What, then, does the Word of God teach concerning the relationship of women to the Gospel testimony? Years of faithful study on my part have convinced me absolutely that, seen in the large and taken as a whole, the teaching of Scripture is clear that woman has her rightful place both in the ministry of prayer and in the proclamation of the saving truths of the Gospel. Who can really give the whole Bible,—which we Baptists claim as our sole rule of faith and practice—careful and prayerful study without

seeing this truth, and without being driven to the conclusion that one or two texts, which may seem upon the surface to be contrary to the general teaching of Scripture, *must be interpreted in harmony with the whole*, in accordance with the accepted principles of sound Bible exegesis?[20]

Straton's essay concluded with this statement about Uldine. ". . . in my judgment, she is today the most extraordinary person in America. She is the Joan of Arc of the modern religious world."[21]

Straton had more to say about women preaching than Uldine did. The few references she made to her gender and age are excerpted below.

Understand, I never thought of preaching; such a thought had not once entered my mind. Who ever heard of a girl preaching? I had not, that was certain, and I'm sure it would have seemed even foolish, to me, to think of a little girl doing it. Why, only great, big men, who knew lots and lots of things and had studied years and years to learn them, could ever be able to please the Lord by their preaching. But wasn't it wonderful that the Lord had given me that little time at Sanger in which to testify for Him? Anybody could testify for the Lord, even if only great big men could preach! . . .[22]

Do you think I have told you why I am a preacher? I hope so, for I want you to understand why. Not because Daddy and Mother had such an ambition for me; not because there were "preachers in the family"; not because I was compelled to be a preacher for any reason but one—the love of Christ and by my love for His will and pleasure. That's why I am a preacher. That's also why I was preaching at the age of eleven instead of beginning ten years later. That, also, is why I am a preacher although I'm a girl, and some people think I'm not supposed to be preaching. That's why I was a preacher who hadn't even finished grammar school, and why I am having to keep right on studying my school-lessons, and preaching at the same time.

I am compelled to preach because of the love of Christ. He called me to preach, and I cannot fail to do what He asks. I delight too much in His will; I want His favor in my life, too much. I put up no big profession; I agree with anybody who says it is foolish for a girl to preach. I honestly believe that, and I also believe what Paul says, "It pleased God by the foolishness of preaching to save them that believe."[23] Listen, a moment. This Scripture says God saves men by the "foolishness of preaching." Then preaching is foolish, and if a girl preaching the Gospel is more foolish than a man preaching it, why should any objection be made, if souls can be saved through the method of peaching [sic], which is more foolish?

You smile over that thought and I smile over it too, but one thing I do not smile over and that is this: God says, He will take a worm to thresh a mountain and things that are not to confound the things that are (Isa. 41:15). He says, in Isaiah 29:14, that "The wisdom of their wise men shall perish."

I make no boast—there is nothing of which I *can* boast—"I glory not, save in the cross of Christ."[24] I fully realize that, naturally, I do not belong on this platform, today, or before you thousands of people, as a preacher. I am not worthy of so high an honor, but although I cannot understand it He not only called me here but in the language of the Scripture, "Hither hath the Lord brought me."[25] Praise be to His Name![26]

As she grew out of childhood, Uldine's popularity began to wane, and then her beloved supporter, John Roach Straton, died in 1929. She joined a Methodist congregation in Chicago and was given a Methodist preacher's license. A Methodist bishop endorsed her book, *Why I Am a Preacher*, published in 1931. At the age of twenty-three, she was ordained by the Methodists, an event noteworthy enough to be written up in *Time* magazine's religion page. The article on her ordination was accompanied by a picture of Uldine in a bathing suit. It also included several comments about her physical appearance: "Last week in Chicago the Methodist female ministry received its youngest and best looking member thus far" and "Not above displaying her attractions in a bathing suit . . . "[27] Her marriage to Wilbur Eugene Langkrop also reached *Time*'s religion page.[28] This was the last news about Uldine. Shortly after her marriage, she succumbed to a "complete mental collapse." Utley's husband had the marriage annulled and eventually remarried. Uldine lived her remaining fifty-seven years in mental institutions. ". . . her whereabouts [were] kept a closely guarded secret by the few who knew them. She died alone in a San Bernardino County facility in October 1995."[29]

Rendezvous with Life
By Uldine Utley

I have a rendezvous with life,
A midst some uncompleted task,
Or when with tightened grasp
I wage (start) new wars with sin.

I might even have begun a work
With thought of what Its end would mean,
And then have the life beyond come between
My present one and all my dreams.

God gives only life—by this I know
That, that which calls me far away
From this present and industrious day
Is appointed by Him. Therefore, I have no fear.

From [*sic*] my rendezvous is not with death
Whatever else I might wish first to do
Before departing for the other life and new
This I know, my rendezvous is made with God.

The uncompleted task shall to another fall,
And whether in the day or darkened night,
I'll go to God where all is light.
This is my rendezvous with life.[30]

Notes

1. For more on Aimee Semple McPherson, see chapter 15.
2. 1 Samuel 17:1–54.
3. 1 Samuel 17:45.
4. Matthew 19:13–15; Mark 10:13–16; Luke 18:15–17.
5. Uldine Utley, *Why I Am a Preacher: A Plain Answer to an Oft-Repeated Question* (New York: Fleming H. Revell, 1931), 17–28.
6. Matthew 10:7.
7. Luke 2:10.
8. "But if you are not listened to, take one or two others along with you, so that every word may be confirmed by the evidence of two or three witnesses."
9. Jeremiah 1:6–9.
10. Utley, *Why I Am a Preacher*, 50–57.
11. Utley, *Why I Am a Preacher*, 88.
12. Utley, *Why I Am a Preacher*, 64.
13. Aimee Semple McPherson launched a similar type of publication shortly after she began holding evangelistic meetings. Edith Blumhofer describes Uldine as Aimee's "best-known would-be clone." Edith L. Blumhofer, "Child Evangelist Uldine Utley," in *The Contentious Triangle: Church, State, and University*, eds. Rodney Petersen and Calvin Peter (Kirksville, MO: Thomas Jefferson University, 1999), 308.
14. Uldine Utley, "Dedication," *Petals from the Rose of Sharon*, vol. 1, no. 1, 3. I am grateful to Kristen Kobes Dumez for copies of Uldine's magazine.
15. Song of Solomon 2:1.
16. Utley, *Why I Am a Preacher*, 69–72.
17. See n. 10, chapter 13.
18. Janette Hassey, *No Time for Silence: Evangelical Women in Public Ministry Around the Turn of the Century* (Grand Rapids, MI: Academic Books, 1986), 2.
19. Straton quotes the critic in his essay, "Does the Bible Forbid Women to Preach and Pray in Public?"; cited in Hassey, *No Time for Silence*, 189.
20. Straton, "Does the Bible Forbid Women to Preach," 190. Italics added.
21. Straton, "Does the Bible Forbid Women to Preach," 210.
22. Utley, *Why I Am a Preacher*, 49.
23. 1 Corinthians 1:21.
24. Galatians 6:14.
25. Genesis 45:8.
26. Utley, *Why I Am a Preacher*, 77–78.
27. "Reverend Miss" *Time* (December 30, 1935): 19. I am grateful to Lee Canipe for this reference.
28. "Terror's Troth" *Time* (January 10, 1938): 49.
29. Blumhofer, "Child Evangelist Uldine Utley," 315. Reflecting upon Uldine's brief years as a prodigious, child evangelist, Blumhofer poignantly summarized her life in these words, "Adulthood ended her career, and changed circumstances abruptly hid her from public view, so for those she touched in the 1920s, she remained the perennial innocent. Sadly, Utley's youthful innocence and the hopeful gospel her hearers applauded failed to assure her own well-being. Emotionally drained by the time she reached adulthood, Utley in the end became a tragic victim of her own success." Blumhofer, "Child Evangelist Uldine Utley," 317.
30. I am grateful to Kristin Kobes Dumez for a copy of this poem.

Glossary of Biblical Figures[*]

AARON. Brother of *Moses* and *Miriam* and progenitor of the priesthood. He was Moses' aide in the events of the Exodus (Exodus 4:27–5:9). When Moses was on Mount Sinai receiving the tablets of stone, the so-called Ten Commandments, from God, Aaron allowed the people to fashion a golden calf as a god to worship (Exodus 32:1–35). According to Numbers 18:1–20, and various other biblical texts, his descendants were given the responsibility for certain aspects of the Jewish priesthood.

ANNA. An elderly woman who was present during the dedication of Jesus in the Temple. She spoke to *Mary* and Joseph about Jesus' connection with the redemption of Jerusalem (Luke 2:22–38).

BARAK. Leader of the Israelite militia under the command of *Deborah*, a strong and cunning judge. Together they defeated the more powerful Canaanite forces (Judges 4:1–5:31).

DANIEL. Devout Israelite who lived in Babylon during the exile. According to the book that bears his name, he was skillful at interpreting dreams and omens, such as handwriting on the wall (Daniel 1–6). Although he was thrown into a den of lions as punishment for disobeying a command to worship the king of Babylon, he remained unharmed and rose to extraordinary heights in the halls of foreign power (Daniel 6:1–28).

DAVID. King of Israel from approximately 1010 to 970 B.C.E. He solidified a unified state with its capital in Jerusalem. As a young man, he killed the Philistine giant, Goliath. (1 Samuel 17:1–54), receiving as his reward marriage to the king's daughter. Many psalms are attributed to David (e.g. Psalm 3, 5, 52, 141).

DEBORAH. An Israelite prophet and judge. She and *Barak* led the Israelite forces to victory against the more advanced Canaanite military forces of *Sisera* (Judges 4:1–5:31).

DIVES. A name that has become attached to a rich man in one of Jesus' parables, even though in the biblical account he is not named. At his gate every day lies a poor man named *Lazarus*, who is covered with sores. In the story, both men die. *Lazarus* goes to heaven where he is comforted; the rich man goes to hell where he is tormented (Luke 16:19–31). Dives is derived from a Latin word for "wealth."

---

* These descriptions are based upon the biblical narratives. I have made no attempt to assess their historical veracity because the women in this volume would, for the most part, have assumed that they are historically accurate.

DORCAS. Christian woman in Joppa whose Aramaic name was Tabitha. Known for acts of charity and kindness, she became ill and died, but *Peter* brought her back to life (Acts 9:36–42).

ELIJAH. An Israelite prophet during the reign of King Ahab during the ninth century B.C.E. He was known both for miracles and for his intransigent opposition to King Ahab, who gave official status to foreign gods, such as Baal. In a climactic confrontation, Elijah set up a contest with the prophets of Baal in which his was the only god capable of miraculously lighting wood on an altar with fire (1 Kings 17:1–21:29).

ESTHER. Jewish wife of the Persian king, Ahasuerus. She delivered Israel from extinction by courageously appearing before the king to request that he revoke an edict of annihilation against her people. Together, she and her uncle, Mordecai, plotted the overthrow of their nemesis, Haman (Esther 7:1–8:18). The Jewish festival of Purim celebrates this event (Esther 9:20–32).

EVE. The first woman, the mother of all human beings (Genesis 3:20). After being tempted by a serpent (which in later lore came to be identified with *Satan*) in the Garden of Eden, she and Adam, the first man, ate from the fruit that God had forbidden them to eat. Eve and Adam were then banished from the Garden (Genesis 3:1–24). She subsequently bore sons and daughters, including, most notably, Cain, Abel, and Seth.

EZEKIEL. A priest and prophet of the Israelites during the crisis of the first destruction of the Jewish temple in approximately 586 B.C.E. He was known for extraordinary visions, including the valley of dry bones (Ezekiel 37:1–14), for serving as a watchman (Ezekiel 33:1–9), and for his words of warning to the people (Ezekiel 6:1–14). His prescient visions of a divine throne capable of moving in all directions at once (Ezekiel 1–3) and of the departure of God's glory from the temple (Ezekiel 8–10) would prepare Israel for a life of exile by dissociating God's presence from the singular locale of the temple in Jerusalem.

HANNAH. Mother of *Samuel*, the key transitional figure between the period of judges in Israel and the united monarchy. When she was barren, Hannah promised that, if she bore a son, she would dedicate him to God, which she did when *Samuel* was about three years old (1 Samuel 1:1–28). Her song of praise to God, which celebrated the end of her barrenness, probably provides the exemplar for the song of *Mary*, Jesus' mother, known as the Magnificat (1 Samuel 2:1–10; Luke 1:46–55).

HULDAH. A prophet in Jerusalem during the late seventh century B.C.E. She prophesied the death of king Josiah prior to Jerusalem's destruction. Her prophecy helped to initiate many religious reforms (2 Kings 22:14–23:3; 2 Chronicles 34:22–33).

JONATHAN. Son of Saul, the first king of Israel. He and *David* had a deep friendship, and he was instrumental in helping *David* to escape from Saul's jealous attempt to kill him (1 Samuel 18:1–4; 19:1–7; 20:1–42).

JOSEPH. Jacob's favorite son, the youngest of twelve brothers who were the ancestors of the twelve tribes of Israel, and protagonist of one of the richest narratives in the Bible. To show his affection for his youngest son, Joseph's father made him a long-sleeved—or many-colored—robe. After relating to them a dream in which they would bow down to him, his brothers sold Joseph into slavery, after which he was transported to Egypt (Genesis 37:12–36). Because of his skill at interpreting dreams, he eventually became powerful in Egypt, second only to the Pharaoh (Genesis 41). He was reunited with his family when a severe famine compelled them to come to Egypt to buy food; Joseph himself orchestrated the move of his family to Egypt (Genesis 42–47).

JULIA. A woman to whom *Paul* sends his greeting. She may have established a church within her home (Romans 16:15).

LAZARUS. A poor man in one of Jesus' parables who is covered with sores and spends his days lying at a rich man's gate. The rich man has no name, but he has sometimes been called *Dives*, which comes from a Latin word for "wealth." In the parable, both men die. Lazarus goes to heaven, where he is comforted; the rich man goes to hell, where he is tormented (Luke 16:19–31).

MARY. Mother of Jesus and wife of Joseph, though her pregnancy is attributed to the overshadowing of the Holy Spirit rather than sexual intercourse with Joseph (Matthew 1:18–25; Luke 1:26–56). She traveled with Joseph to Bethlehem for a Roman census and gave birth to Jesus there (Matthew 1:18–25; Luke 1:26–56; 2:1–38). Her celebratory song upon hearing that she was pregnant, known as the Magnificat (Luke 1:46–55), was similar to one sung by *Hannah*. The Gospel of John records that she was present at Jesus' crucifixion (John 19:25–27), and she was one of the group gathered for prayer in Jerusalem after Jesus' death and resurrection (Acts 1:14).

MARY MAGDALENE. A follower of Jesus, traditionally believed to have had a sordid past. She witnessed Jesus' empty tomb and met the risen Jesus. In response, she proclaimed the news to the disciples (Matthew 27:55–56, 61; Mark 15:40–41, 47; John 20:1–18).

MIRIAM. A prophet and sister of *Aaron* and *Moses*. When *Moses* was rescued as a baby from the Nile by Pharoah's daughter, Miriam courageously offered their mother as a wet nurse (Exodus 2:4–8). She led a song of triumph after the Israelites escaped through the Red Sea from the Egyptians (Exodus 15:20–21).

MOSES. Brother of *Miriam* and *Aaron*, the first leader of Israel, who led the Israelites out of Egypt, and the recipient of the Ten Words or Commandments. He is arguably the central figure in the Hebrew scriptures—prophet, judge, and lawgiver, and traditional author of the Torah (Genesis through Deuteronomy).

NAOMI. A Jewish woman during the period of the judges living in Moab. After her husband and two sons died, she returned to Bethlehem with *Ruth*, one of her daughters-in-law. She encouraged a kinsman named Boaz to marry *Ruth*, and their son, Obed, was in the lineage of King *David* (Ruth 4:18–22) and of Jesus (Matthew 1:1–6).

NARCISSUS. Mentioned by *Paul* in a list of greetings. She was known as having a "family" that included Christians (Romans 16:11).

PAUL. A Roman citizen and member of the Pharisees, an influential Jewish group renowned for their own interpretations of the Torah, the first five books of the Hebrew Bible. Paul, originally named Saul, encountered the risen Jesus while on a mission to destroy early Christians (Acts 9:1–19). As a result, he became the leading missionary of the early church and is responsible for many letters included in the New Testament.

PERSIS. A woman mentioned by *Paul* as a "hard worker in the Lord" (Romans 16:12).

PETER. A disciple of Jesus along with his brother, Andrew. He was known as the "rock" on which Jesus' church would be built (Matthew 16:16–19), even though he denied knowing Jesus while Jesus was on trial (Matthew 26:69–75; Mark 14:66–72; Luke 22:55–62; John 18:25–27). He became one of the central figures of the church, and he delivered a powerful public speech which led to the baptism of 3,000 people during the Jewish feast of Pentecost, when the Holy Spirit descended for the first time upon early Christian believers in tongues of fire (Acts 2:1–42). It was a vision of Peter's that proved instrumental in opening the church to those who were not Jewish in background (Acts 10–11). The letters of 1 and 2 Peter in the New Testament are ascribed to him.

PHILIP. An evangelist who carried the gospel to Samaria (Acts 8:4–40). He had four unmarried daughters who had the gift of prophecy (Acts 21:8–9).

PHOEBE. A leader of the church in Cenchreae, near Corinth. *Paul* referred to her as a sister and deacon to whom many in her domain of influence were indebted (Romans 16:1–2).

PILATE. Controversial fifth governor of the Roman province of Judea during the time of John the Baptist and Jesus (26–36 C.E.). He played a crucial role during the trial and crucifixion of Jesus (Matthew 27:1–2, 11–26; Mark 15:1–15; Luke 23:1–25; John 18:28–19:16).

REBEKAH. Mother of twin sons, Jacob and Esau, and wife of Isaac. She is perhaps remembered best for conspiring with Jacob to dupe Isaac into giving Esau's birthright, which was his by right as the oldest son, to Jacob (Genesis 27:1–40).

RUTH. A widowed Moabite woman who left her country to travel with her mother-in-law, *Naomi*, to Bethlehem. After a period of gleaning in the fields, she married Boaz, a kinsman of *Naomi*, and they bore a son, Obed, grandfather of King *David* (Ruth 4:18–22) and an ancestor of Jesus (Matthew 1:1–6).

SAMUEL. A key transitional figure between the period of judges and the United Monarchy, Samuel resolutely resisted Israel's desire for a king, for he regarded this as nothing more than assimilation to the monarchies of other nations. Nonetheless, Samuel, who is presented in the biblical tradition as prophet, priest, judge, and leader of Israel, anointed Saul, then *David*, as kings. His mother, *Hannah*, dedicated him to God's service before he was born (1 Samuel 9:1–10:16; 16:1–3).

SARAH. Mother of Isaac, wife of Abraham. When she was well past childbearing age, she bore Isaac (Genesis 21:1–7), through whom God's promise of "a great nation" was carried on (Genesis 12:1–3).

SATAN. In later books of the Hebrew Bible, Satan is portrayed as an adversary of God and humans (Job 1–2; 1 Chronicles 21:1; Zechariah 3:1–2). The English word is related to the Hebrew word meaning "adversary." In the New Testament, Satan is "the devil," and he appears frequently, particularly in the Gospels, as Jesus' adversary (Matthew 4:1–11; Mark 1:12–13; Luke 4:1–13) and the ruler of this world (John 12:31). Elsewhere, as in Revelation 20:1–10, his defeat is depicted vividly, though he is consistently perceived as an aggressive enemy of truth and believers.

Although Satan plays no role in Genesis 3, in later literature, such as John Milton's *Paradise Lost*, the tempter in Eden came to be seen less as a serpent and more as Satan.

SISERA. Leader of enemy Canaanite military forces, including 900 chariots, which were defeated by the Israelites, led by *Deborah* and *Barak*. Sisera himself was killed by Jael, a Kenite woman and ally of *Deborah*, who drove a peg vigorously through his head into the ground (Judges 4:1–22).

TRYPHAENA. A woman who receives good wishes from *Paul*, along with Tryphosa. Both were active within the church at Rome (Romans 16:12).

ZACCHEUS. Wealthy tax collector who climbed a tree to get a better look at Jesus. When Jesus told him that he would be eating in Zaccheus' house, he announced that he would give half of his possessions to the poor and repay any dishonesty fourfold. Jesus responded to this promise by calling Zaccheus a son of Abraham (Luke 19:1–10).

GLOSSARY OF CHURCHES AND DENOMINATIONS

AFRICAN METHODIST EPISCOPAL. In response to racism in the *Methodist* church, Richard Allen, a former slave and *Methodist* minister, led African Americans to begin their own church, "Mother Bethel" Church, in 1794. Allen's congregation later joined with other African American churches to form The African Methodist Episcopal Church in 1816 in Philadelphia, and Allen was consecrated as the first bishop.

ASSEMBLY OF GOD. A Pentecostal denomination that traces its roots to the Azusa Street Mission revival in Los Angeles in the early 1900's. In 1914, there was a "general council" held in Hot Springs, Arkansas, which led to the founding of the denomination. One of their central tenets is that baptism in the Holy Spirit will be evidenced by speaking in tongues.

CHRISTIAN CONNECTION. From its beginning in 1803, its membership grew quickly in the first decades of the nineteenth century. Women in this denomination were encouraged to exhort, preach, participate in funerals, and vote on church matters.

CHURCH OF GOD (WINEBRENNER). Founded by Philip Winebrenner (1797–1860), a minister in the German Reformed Church, whose evangelistic preaching catalyzed the formation of a new denomination, The Church of God. His followers were called Winebrennerians. Foot washing is one of their sacraments.

CHURCH OF THE NAZARENE. Founded in 1908 with the merger of The Association of Pentecostal Churches of America, The Church of the Nazarene, and The Holiness Church of Christ (formerly The New Testament Church of Christ). They trace their roots to John Wesley and the *Methodist* church. A central tenet of the denomination is the experience of sanctification. From the outset, women were welcomed into all levels of participation and governance in the denomination, including the ordained ministry.

CONGREGATIONAL. Began in the late sixteenth century in England and came to America shortly after. Central to their church polity is the autonomy of each congregation, thus the name Congregational, rather than the authority of bishops or a clergy council. Congregationalists founded Harvard College in 1636. Jonathan Edwards (1703–1758) was a Congregational minister and a leading figure in the First Great Awakening. In the twentieth century, Congregationalists joined with several other denominations to form The United Church of Christ.

DISCIPLES OF CHRIST (THE DISCIPLES, OR THE CHRISTIAN CHURCH). Emerged in the 1830s, under the leadership of Alexander Campbell and Barton Stone, from a mixture of camp meeting evangelism and American frontier religion. It is deemed a "restoration movement" because its primary purpose was to restore the Christian Church to its earliest, first-century roots before creeds and clerical titles. Its early motto was, "Where the Scriptures speak, we speak. Where the Scriptures are silent, we are silent."

FREEWILL BAPTIST. Springing originally from Baptist settlers in North Carolina, the largest group of Freewill Baptists was organized on June 30, 1780 by Benjamin Randall in New Durham, New Hampshire. In 1803, this same church listed three women as public preachers and exhorters. Freewill Baptists believe that salvation is possible for all people as opposed to the Calvinist belief that salvation is only for God's elect.

INTERNATIONAL CHURCH OF THE FOURSQUARE GOSPEL. Founded by evangelist, Aimee Semple McPherson. For more information on this denomination, see chapter 15.

LUTHERAN. In 1517, Martin Luther (1483–1546) posted his infamous 95 Theses, a document which questionned the *Roman Catholic* practice of granting indulgences for the forgiveness of sins, on the church door in Wittenberg, Germany. He was excommunicated from The *Roman Catholic* Church, and his teachings on justification by faith and the universal priesthood of believers became central tenets of the Protestant Reformation. Luther's followers became known as Lutherans.

METHODIST. Began as an eighteenth-century renewal movement within The Church of England, led by Charles and John Wesley. Methodists emphasize humanity's free will along with God's grace which enables the Christian believer to progress in holiness, or sanctification. Francis Asbury and Thomas Coke established Methodism in America beginning in the late eighteenth century.

MOUNT SINAI HOLY CHURCH OF AMERICA. Founded by evangelist, Ida Robinson. For more information on this denomination, see chapter 16.

ORTHODOX CHURCH. One of the three main branches of Christianity along with *Roman Catholicism* and Protestantism. Like *Catholics*, the Orthodox also claim direct lineage from Jesus and the apostles. In 1054, the bishops of Constantinople (Orthodox) and Rome (*Catholic*) mutually excommunicated each other. A central divergence between these two churches relates to their understanding of the Trinity. Orthodox services are replete with liturgy and symbolism.

PILLAR OF FIRE. Founded by evangelist, Alma White. For more information on this denomination, see chapter 10.

PLYMOUTH BRETHREN. Began in the 1820s to 1830s in Great Britain under the leadership of John Nelson Darby (1800–1882), who had a strong interest in interpreting biblical prophecies related to the timing of Jesus' return to earth. Darby divided history into dispensations, or time periods, which correspond to God's plan for the ages. The Plymouth Brethren hold strict views against women's public participation in worship services.

PRESBYTERIAN. Emerged between 1534–1560 during the Protestant Reformation in France and Switzerland. John Calvin (1509–1564) was the central theologian of Reformed theology, which emphasizes God's sovereignty over everything, including who will ultimately be saved. Presbyterian comes from the Greek word, *presbuteros*, or elder, and it describes their church government, which is centered in a council of elders.

QUAKER (RELIGIOUS SOCIETY OF FRIENDS, OR FRIENDS). Began in the seventeenth century in England's Lake District by George Fox, who believed in the inner light, or "that of God in everyone." With a great focus inward, Quakers believe God speaks to both men and women; therefore, men and women are equal in the family, church, and society. From the beginning, Quakers have recorded women as ministers. Quakers have been at the forefront of every reform movement in the United States, including the abolition of slavery, women's rights, pacifism, prison reform, and humane treatment of the mentally ill.

ROMAN CATHOLIC CHURCH. Traces its beginning to Jesus appointing Peter as guardian of the keys of heaven and earth and chief of the apostles (Matthew 16:18–19), thus making him the first Pope. Papal authority is supreme in all matters of faith and discipline. Like the *Orthodox*, Catholic services are highly liturgical.

UNITARIAN. Originally within *Congregationalism* in the American context, they formed their own denomination in the early nineteenth century. Their basic tenet is that there is only one God; therefore, Jesus is not divine, so he should be followed, not worshipped. In 1961, the Unitarian and *Universalist* churches in the United States and Canada joined together to form The Unitarian Universalist Association of Congregations in North America.

UNITED BRETHREN. Formed in the early eighteenth century by a group of German ministers. They emphasized the gathering together of small groups of Christian believers who formed what they called, "the little church within the church." They referred to themselves as a "united brethren." Later called The Evangelical United Brethren, this body merged with The *Methodist* Episcopal Church in 1968 to form The United *Methodist* Church.

UNITED HOLY CHURCH. An African American, holiness, Pentecostal denomination founded in May 1886, in North Carolina. Two central tenets of their doctrine are sanctification and speaking in tongues.

UNIVERSALIST. The first Universalist congregation was organized in London by James Relly (1722–1778) in 1750, and the movement began in the United States in 1790. They affirm that everyone will be restored to harmony with God, regardless of their religious belief or lack thereof. They supported various nineteenth and twentieth century reform movements, including the abolition of slavery, prison reform, pacifism, and free public education. In 1961, the *Unitarian* and Universalist churches in the United States and Canada joined together to form The Unitarian Universalist Association of Congregations in North America.

WESLEYAN METHODIST. Named in honor of John Wesley, they separated in 1843 from the *Methodist* church over issues of church government and slavery. They worked with the underground railroad, helping escaped slaves to freedom. Orange Scott, Lucius Matlack, and Luther Lee were founding leaders of the denomination. Wheaton College in Illinois was chartered by the Wesleyan Methodists in 1848 but passed to the *Congregationalists* for financial reasons. In 1968, The Wesleyan Methodist Church merged with The Pilgrim Holiness Church to form the Wesleyan Church.

SELECT BIBLIOGRAPHY OF SECONDARY SOURCES

Andrews, William L. *Sisters of the Spirit: Three Black Women's Autobiographies of the Nineteenth Century*. Bloomington: Indiana University, 1986.

Barbour, Hugh. "Quaker Prophetesses and Mothers in Israel." In *Seeking the Light: Essays in Quaker History in Honor of Edwin B. Bronner*, eds. J. Frost and J. Moore, 41–60. Wallingford, PA: Pendle Hill, 1986.

Barfoot, Charles H. and Gerald T. Sheppard. "Prophetic vs. Priestly Religion: The Changing Role of Women Clergy in Pentecostal Churches." *Review of Religious Research* 22 (September 1980): 2–17.

Bassard, Kathryn Clay. *Spiritual Interrogations: Culture, Gender, and Community in Early African American Women's Writing*. Princeton, NJ: Princeton University, 1999.

Bednarowski, Mary. "Outside the Mainstream: Women's Religion and Women Religious Leaders in 19c America." *Journal of the American Academy of Religion* 48 (June 1980): 207–31.

Bendroth, Margaret Lamberts. *Fundamentalism and Gender, 1875 to the Present*. New Haven, CT: Yale University, 1993.

——. "The Search for 'Women's Role' in American Evangelicalism, 1930–1980." In *Evangelicalism and Modern America*, ed. George Marsden, 122–34. Grand Rapids, MI: Eerdmans, 1984.

Billington, Louis. "Female Laborers in the Church: Women Preachers in the Northeastern United States, 1790–1840." *Journal of American Studies* (Great Britain) 19 (1985): 369–94.

Blumhofer, Edith L. "A Confused Legacy: Reflections on Evangelical Attitudes Toward Ministering Women in the Past Century." *Fides et Historia* 22 (Winter–Spring 1990): 49–61.

Brasher, Brenda E. *Godly Women: Fundamentalism and Female Power*. New Brunswick, NJ: Rutgers University, 1998.

Braude, Ann. *Radical Spirits: Spiritualism and Women's Rights in Nineteenth-Century America*. Boston: Beacon, 1989.

——. "Women's History IS American Religious History." In *Retelling U.S. Religious History*, ed. Thomas A. Tweed, 87–107. Berkeley: University of California, 1997.

Brekus, Catherine A. *Strangers and Pilgrims: Female Preaching in America, 1740–1845*. Chapel Hill: University of North Carolina, 1998.

——. "Studying Women and Religion: Problems and Possibilities." *Criterion* 32 (Autumn 1993): 24–28.

Brereton, Virginia. *From Sin to Salvation: Stories of Women's Conversions, 1800 to the Present*. Bloomington: Indiana University, 1991.

Carpenter, Delores Causion. "Black Women in Religious Institutions: A Historical Summary from Slavery to the 1960s." *Journal of Religious Thought* 46, no. 2 (Winter/Spring 1989–1990): 7–27.

Chavez, Mark. *Ordaining Women: Culture and Conflict in Religious Organizations.* Cambridge, MA: Harvard University, 1997.

Chilcote, Paul Wesley. *John Wesley and the Women Preachers of Early Methodism.* ATLA Monograph Series, No. 25. Metuchen, NJ: Scarecrow, 1991.

Collier-Thomas, Bettye. *Daughters of Thunder: Black Women Preachers and Their Sermons, 1850–1979.* San Francisco: Jossey-Bass, 1998.

Cott, Nancy. "Young Women in the Second Great Awakening." *Feminist Studies* 3 (Fall 1975): 15–29.

Davidson, Phebe. *Religious Impulse in Selected Autobiographies of American Women (c. 1630–1983): Uses of the Spirit.* Lewiston, NY: Mellen, 1993.

DeBerg, Betty. *Ungodly Women: Gender and the First Wave of American Fundamentalism.* Minneapolis: Fortress, 1990.

Douglas, Ann. *The Feminization of American Culture.* New York: Knopf, 1977.

Douglass-Chin, Richard J. *Preacher Woman Sings the Blues: The Autobiographies of Nineteenth-Century African American Evangelists.* Columbia: University of Missouri, 2001.

Epstein, Barbara Leslie. *The Politics of Domesticity: Women, Evangelism, and Temperance in Nineteenth-Century America.* Middletown: Wesleyan University, 1981.

Fox-Genovese, Elizabeth. "Religion and Women in America: An Introduction." In *World Religions in America*, ed. Jacob Neusner, 223–32. Louisville, KY: Westminster John Knox, 1994.

———. "Two Steps Forward, One Step Back: New Questions and Old Models in the Religious History of American Women." *Journal of the American Academy of Religion* 55 (1987): 211–33.

Godbey, William B. *Woman Preacher.* Louisville, KY: Pentecostal Publishing, 1891.

Goff, James R. and Grant Wacker, eds. *Portraits of a Generation: Early Pentecostal Leaders.* Fayetteville: University of Arkansas, 2002.

Goode, Gloria Davis. "Preachers of the Word and Singers of the Gospel: The Ministry of Women Among Nineteenth-Century African-Americans." Ph.D. Dissertation, University of Pennsylvania, 1990.

Grammer, Elizabeth Elkin. *Some Wild Visions: Autobiographies by Female Itinerant Evangelists in Nineteenth-Century America.* New York: Oxford University, 2003.

Griffith, R. Marie. *God's Daughters: Evangelical Women and the Power of Submission.* Berkeley: University of California, 1997.

Hackett, David G. "Gender and Religion in American Culture, 1870–1930." *Religion and American Culture* 5 (Summer 1994): 127–57.

Hamilton, Michael S. "Women, Public Ministry, and American Fundamentalism." *Religion and American Culture* 3 (Summer 1993): 171–96.

Hardesty, Nancy A. *Women Called to Witness: Evangelical Feminism in the Nineteenth Century.* Nashville, TN: Abingdon, 1984.

———. *Your Daughters Shall Prophesy: Revivalism and Feminism in the Age of Finney.* Brooklyn, NY: Carlson, 1991.

Hassey, Janette. *No Time for Silence: Evangelical Women in Public Ministry Around the Turn of the Century.* Grand Rapids, MI: Academic Books, 1986.

Hatch, Nathan. *The Democratization of American Christianity.* New Haven: Yale University, 1989.

Haywood, Chanta. *Prophesying Daughters: Black Women Preachers and the Word, 1823–1913.* Columbia: University of Missouri, 2003.

Hewitt, Nancy. *Women's Activism and Social Change: Rochester, New York, 1722–1872.* Ithaca, NY: Cornell University, 1984.

Higginbotham, Evelyn Brooks. *Righteous Discontent: The Women's Movement in the Black Baptist Church, 1880–1920.* Cambridge, MA: Harvard University, 1993.

Houchins, Sue, ed. *Spiritual Narratives.* New York: Oxford University, 1988.

Humez, Jean. " 'My Spirit Eye': Some Functions of Spiritual and Visionary Experiences in the Lives of Five Black Women Preachers, 1810–1880," In *Women and the Structure of Society*, eds. Barbara Harris and JoAnn McNamara, 129–43. Durham, NC: Duke University, 1984.

Hunter, Fannie McDowell, ed. *Women Preachers.* Dallas: Berachah Printing, 1905.

James, Janet Wilson, ed. *Women in American Religion.* Philadelphia: University of Pennsylvania, 1980.

Jelinek, Estelle C., ed. *Women's Autobiography: Essays in Criticism.* Bloomington: Indiana University, 1980.

Juster, Susan. " 'In a Different Voice': Male and Female Narratives of Religious Conversion in Post-Revolutionary America." *American Quarterly* 41 (March 1989): 34–62.

Keller, Rosemary Skinner, ed. *Spirituality and Social Responsibility: Vocational Vision of Women in The United Methodist Tradition.* Nashville, TN: Abingdon, 1993.

——. "Women and the Nature of Ministry in the United Methodist Tradition." *Methodist History* 22 (January 1984): 99–114.

Keller, Rosemary Skinner and Rosemary Radford Ruether, eds. *In Our Own Voices: Four Centuries of American Women's Religious Writing.* Louisville, KY: Westminster John Knox, 1995.

——. *Women and Religion in America.* 3 vols. San Francisco: Harper & Row, 1981–86.

Keller, Rosemary Skinner, Ann Braude, Maureen Ursenbach Beecher, and Elizabeth Fox-Genovese. "Forum: Female Experience in American Religion." *Religion and American Culture* 5 (Winter 1995): 1–12.

Lawless, Elaine J. *Handmaidens of the Lord: Pentecostal Women Preachers and Traditional Religion.* Philadelphia: University of Pennsylvania, 1988.

Lindley, Susan Hill. *"You Have Stept Out of Your Place": A History of Women and Religion in America.* Louisville, KY: Westminster John Knox, 1996.

Loewenberg, Bert James and Ruth Bogin, eds. *Black Women in Nineteenth-Century American Life: Their Words, Their Thoughts, Their Feelings.* University Park: Pennsylvania State University, 1976.

Noll, Mark. *America's God: From Jonathan Edwards to Abraham Lincoln.* New York: Oxford University, 2002.

Noll, William. "Women as Clergy and Laity in the 19c Methodist Protestant Church." *Methodist History* 15 (January 1977): 107–21.

Overton, Betty. "Black Women Preachers: A Literary View." *The Southern Quarterly* 23 (Spring 1985): 157–66.

Peterson, Carla L. *"Doers of the Word": African-American Speakers and Writers in the North.* New York: Oxford University, 1995.

Porterfield, Amanda. *Feminine Spirituality in America: From Sarah Edwards to Martha Graham.* Philadelphia, PA: Temple University, 1980.

Robert, Dana. *American Women in Mission: A Social History of Their Thought and Practice.* Macon, GA: Mercer University, 1996.

Roebuck, David. "Pentecostal Women in Ministry: A Review of Selected Documents." *Perspectives in Religious Studies* 16 (Spring 1989): 29–44.

Ryan, Mary P. *Cradle of the Middle Class: The Family in Oneida County, New York, 1790–1865.* Cambridge: Cambridge University, 1981.

Schmidt, Jean Miller. "Denominational History When Gender is the Focus: Women in American Methodism." In *Reimagining Denominationalism*, eds. Robert Bruce Mullin and Russell A. Richey, 203–21. New York: Oxford University, 1994.

———. *Grace Sufficient: A History of Women in American Methodism, 1760–1968.* Nashville, TN: Abingdon, 1997.

Smith, Timothy. *Revivalism and Social Reform.* Nashville, TN: Abingdon, 1957.

Stanley, Susie C. *Holy Boldness: Women Preachers' Autobiographies and the Sanctified Self.* Knoxville: University of Tennessee, 2002.

Sweet, Leonard I. *The Minister's Wife: Her Role in Nineteenth-Century American Evangelicalism.* Philadelphia: Temple University, 1983.

Taves, Ann. *Fits, Trances, & Visions: Experiencing Religion and Explaining Experience from Wesley to James.* Princeton, NJ: Princeton University, 1999.

———. "Women and Gender in American Religion(s)." *Religious Studies Review* 18 (October 1992): 263–70.

Thomas, Hilah, Rosemary Skinner Keller and Louise L. Queen, eds. *Women in New Worlds: Historical Perspectives on the Wesleyan Tradition.* 2 vols. Nashville, TN: Abingdon, 1982.

Tucker, Cynthia Grant. *Prophetic Sisterhood: Liberal Women Ministers of the Frontier, 1880–1930.* Boston: Beacon, 1990.

Wacker, Grant. *Heaven Below: Early Pentecostals and American Culture.* Cambridge, MA: Harvard University, 2001.

Weisenfeld, Judith and Richard Newman, eds. *This Far By Faith: Readings in African-American Women's Religious Biography.* Columbia: University of South Carolina, 1996.

Wessinger, Catherine, ed. *Religious Institutions and Women's Leadership: New Roles Inside the Mainstream.* Columbia: University of South Carolina, 1996.

Zink-Sawyer, Beverly. *From Preachers To Suffragists: Woman's Rights and Religious Conviction in the Lives of Three Nineteenth-Century American Clergywomen.* Louisville, KY: Westminster John Knox, 2003.

Subject Index

Index of Scripture References